CANADA'S CHANGING FAMILIES:
IMPLICATIONS FOR INDIVIDUALS AND SOCIETY

Edited by Kevin McQuillan and Zenaida R. Ravanera

In recent years Canadian families have undergone dramatic change, as evidenced by high rates of separation and divorce, declining fertility, greater popularity of alternative family arrangements such as cohabitation, and increasing involvement of women in paid labour. In addition, changes in the domestic and global economies and in the larger society have brought new pressures to bear on families. For instance, major shifts in labour market conditions, such as the greatly expanded number of jobs with non-traditional hours, have forced families to alter their routines and the division of responsibilities within the household. At the same time governments, striving to maintain or increase competitiveness in the economy, have moved to control spending, restrain taxes, and reduce deficits. The result has been new demands on the family to provide or supplement services that might otherwise be supplied by the state. *Canada's Changing Families* explores the impact of these and other developments on family life.

The volume is divided into three parts. Part 1 examines the dimensions of family change related to childbearing, work patterns, and delayed transitions to adulthood. Part 2 focuses specifically on children and how investments in the young have been affected by family transformation. Part 3 examines family solidarity in Canada and the many ways through which individuals integrate into society. The contributors to the volume are demographers and sociologists who make use of a variety of methodologies and draw on the most current data available for the study of family life and family change in Canada. Together their work clarifies our knowledge of the ongoing transformation of family life, explores the consequences of these changes for individuals and communities, and raises some of the critical policy issues posed by these trends.

KEVIN MCQUILLAN is a demographer and a professor in the Department of Sociology at the University of Western Ontario.

ZENAIDA R. RAVANERA is a research associate in the Population Studies Centre at the University of Western Ontario.

Canada's Changing Families

Implications for Individuals and Society

EDITED BY KEVIN MCQUILLAN AND
ZENAIDA R. RAVANERA

UNIVERSITY OF TORONTO PRESS
Toronto Buffalo London

ISBN-13: 978-0-8020-8966-3 (cloth)
ISBN-10: 0-8020-8966-6 (cloth)
ISBN-13: 978-0-8020-8640-2 (paper)
ISBN-10: 0-8020-8640-3 (paper)

∞

Printed on acid-free paper

Library and Archives Canada Cataloguing in Publication

Canada's changing families : implications for individuals and society /
  edited by Kevin McQuillan and Zenaida Ravanera.

ISBN-13: 978-0-8020-8966-3 (bound)
ISBN-10: 0-8020-8966-6 (bound)
ISBN-13: 978-0-8020-8640-2 (pbk.)
ISBN-10: 0-8020-8640-3 (pbk.)

1. Family – Canada.   I. McQuillan, Kevin   II. Ravanera, Zenaida R.

HQ560.C344 2006   306.85'0971   C2005-905866-8

The editors and contributors thank the Social Science and Humanities
Research Council of Canada for the grant to the Family Transformation and
Social Cohesion project that supported the research for this book.

University of Toronto Press acknowledges the financial assistance to its
publishing program of the Canada Council for the Arts and the Ontario
Arts Council.

University of Toronto Press acknowledges the financial support for its
publishing activities of the Government of Canada through the Book
Publishing Industry Development Program (BPIDP).

Contents

Contributors

Roderic Beaujot
Department of Sociology
University of Western Ontario

Don Kerr
Department of Sociology
King's University College
University of Western Ontario

Evelyne Lapierre-Adamcyk
Centre interuniversitaire
    d'études démographique
Département de démographie
Université de Montréal

Céline Le Bourdais
Département de sociologie
Université McGill

Karen Mac Con
Employment Services
Human Resources
City of Toronto

Nicole Marcil-Gratton
Centre interuniversitaire
    d'études démographique
Département de démographie
Université de Montréal

Kevin McQuillan
Department of Sociology
University of Western Ontario

Nancy Meilleur
Commission scolaire de Mon-
    tréal
Bureau de la planification institu-
    tionnelle et de la vérification
    interne

Ali Muhammad
Department of Sociology
Brock University

Claudine Provencher
Ministère de l'Éducation, Québec
Direction de la recherche, des
    statistiques et des indicateurs

Benoît Rapoport
Maison des Sciences
   Economiques
Université Paris

Fernando Rajulton
Department of Sociology
University of Western Ontario

Zenaida R. Ravanera
Population Studies Centre
University of Western Ontario

CANADA'S CHANGING FAMILIES

1 Introduction

ZENAIDA R. RAVANERA AND KEVIN MCQUILLAN

Canada, like other advanced industrial societies, has witnessed profound changes to its economic and social institutions in recent years. The globalization of the economy, the changing nature of work, rapid technological growth, and the increasing diversity of the population have reshaped many facets of social life. On the whole, these developments have produced positive results. Rising incomes and rising life expectancy support such a conclusion. At the same time, social scientists have expressed concern about other trends that have accompanied these improvements. Growing income inequality, declining civic engagement, and persistent high levels of child poverty have led some to worry that an increasing emphasis on productivity, efficiency, and mobility may undermine the social institutions that have held societies together and marginalize or exclude those who cannot compete in the new international marketplace. In these analyses, which have considered the consequences of economic and social changes for individuals and communities, rather little attention has been paid to the crucial mediating role of the family. Yet, as Esping-Andersen (2001) has written, the family, along with the market and the state, remains one leg of the triad of key institutions in the modern welfare state. Moreover, the family plays a critical role in the formation of the social capital enjoyed by its members (Coleman 1990).

Two trends that touch the family are of particular importance and have attracted the interest of the researchers whose work is presented in this volume. One is that families themselves have been undergoing dramatic change. The major dimensions of family change are well known and have been the topic of often fierce public debate. They include such trends as rising rates of separation and divorce, the greater popularity of alternative family arrangements such as cohabitation, declining fertility, and the increasing involvement of family members in paid labour. The other is that changes occurring in the economy and the larger society have brought new pressures to bear on families. Changes in the labour market, for example, have greatly expanded the number of jobs with non-traditional hours, forcing families to alter their routines and the division of responsibilities within the household. Governments, concerned to maintain or increase the competitive position of their economies, have moved to control spending, restrain taxes, and reduce deficits. The result, in many cases, has been new demands on the family to provide or supplement services that might otherwise be provided by the state. How have these developments altered family life? What consequences do these changes have for the adults and children who live in these families? Has the changing nature of family life made families more or less able to deal with the demands they face from their members and the larger society? These are some of the questions addressed in the chapters that follow.

The volume consists of three parts. Part 1 examines the dimensions of family change related to childbearing, work patterns, and delayed transitions to adulthood. Part 2 focuses specifically on children and asks how investments in the young have been affected by family transformation. Part 3 examines family solidarity in Canada and the many ways through which individuals integrate into society.

The contributors are demographers and sociologists who make use of a variety of methodologies and draw on the most current data sets available for the study of family life and family change. Their work clarifies our knowledge of the ongoing transformation of family life, explores the consequences of these changes for individuals and communities, and raises some of the critical policy issues posed by these trends.

Changes in Families: Childbearing, Work Patterns, and Life Course Transitions

A family, while occupying a separate private sphere, is also fully integrated into society's economic and political systems, and thus, what are often seen as 'private decisions' are shaped by economic and social influences. This is particularly so in the case of childbearing, the decisions about which are made by couples, but which reflect prevailing social and economic pressures. The decisions made by Canadian couples have produced a pattern of below replacement-level fertility, which is contributing to population aging, and which will soon result in a negative rate of natural increase. Roderic Beaujot and Ali Muhammad in Chapter 2 examine some of the factors that lie behind the movement to lower fertility and the shift to childbearing at older ages. They point to values and ideals that support childbearing, while also identifying a variety of constraints which lead couples to have fewer children. Among these constraints are the changed nature of relationships, particularly in the allocation of tasks between partners, and the desire of many women to be integrated into the labour market before having children. Below-replacement fertility results from the pressure of a variety of social and economic forces on couples, but it also has important consequences for Canadian society as a whole. As the authors note, persistent low fertility 'can undermine the solvency of intergenerational arrangements, particularly regarding pensions and health care.' It is true that all advanced industrial societies now experience low rates of fertility, but Beaujot and Muhammad note that there remains significant variation among these nations. Drawing on the experience of other countries, they point to factors that might lead to a fertility rate closer to the replacement level such as policies that support families and gender equality, acceptance of births within cohabiting unions, degendering of caring activities, and flexibility of work schedules.

Work is another aspect of family life that reflects the interplay of personal aspirations and social forces. Involvement in paid labour not only provides the income families need, it offers men and women a route to greater involvement in society. As is well known, rising rates of labour force participation among women mean that, for two-parent families, the dual-earner model is now the norm. Yet, as several of the contributions in this collection make clear, dealing with the demands of work and family life is an increasingly complex challenge for many Canadian families. Two incomes for the family mean greater material and financial resources that can be invested in children. Ravanera, Rajulton, and Burch (2003) have shown, for example, that children of mothers who were employed when they were growing up are more likely to stay in school longer and to complete higher levels of education. But employment of both father and mother constrains family life in important ways. Indeed, the constraints have grown as some workers contend with long hours of work or juggle complex schedules brought out by the increasing use of non-traditional work schedules. Evelyne Lapierre-Adamcyk, Nicole Marcil-Gratton, and Céline Le Bourdais in Chapter 3 examine the strategies that families employ to balance their family and work roles. They show the variety of approaches families use in their efforts to generate sufficient income for the family while meeting the demands of childcare. While work schedules are often imposed by employers, many parents nevertheless themselves arrange their lives to maximize the time available to care for their children. This may involve decisions about both the amount of time parents will spend at work and the schedule for their time at work. These strategies are not without cost, however. Young mothers, in particular, are likely to work part-time or to withdraw from the labour force altogether to care for their children. While this approach helps solve the time crunch in busy families, it may also result in long-term loss of income and occupational mobility for these women. The authors underline the need for supportive employment practices and labour laws that would make easier the task of meeting the demands of both family and work.

Work schedules and their impact on time spent with children are also the focus of Chapter 4 where Benoît Rapoport and Céline Le Bourdais examine the distinction between *family time*, which involves shared activities that include parents and children, and *parental time*, which involves one parent supervising or caring for the children. It is family time that is increasingly eclipsed by the growth of non-standard work schedules. Many families appear to arrange their work schedules to allow one parent to remain with children as much as possible. This has the positive effect of increasing the involvement of many fathers in childcare activities. But it also means there is less time for the family to be together and engage in social and leisure activities that include all family members. The problem of coordinating work and family life is even more acute in one-parent families, and Rapoport and Le Bourdais find that such families have very little time available for family social activities. Although the effect of non-standard work hours varies by family structure and by sex, in general, the result is increased strain on family life. This leads Rapoport and Le Bourdais to warn about the negative impact, particularly on children, of the labour market trend towards '24/7' service – service every hour of every day of the week – that requires parents to take on non-standard work schedules in the evenings, late nights, and weekends.

The challenge of balancing family and work demands is one factor that young Canadians must consider when making decisions about career and family. The tension between the two has undoubtedly contributed to the increase in the average age at which young people now make the transition to adulthood. But, as Roderic Beaujot notes in

Chapter 5, there are other economic and sociocultural factors that lead to later ages in leaving the parental home, in forming unions either through cohabitation or marriage, and in becoming parents. These include, above all, the increasing need for educational credentials, but also the difficulty of finding permanent, well-paid employment and affordable housing. Beaujot examines the transitions to completion of education and entry into the labour force and their connections to early family life events. He then explores the implications of the delay in transitions not only for the youth themselves, as they move through life, but for those at other stages of the life course as well. He concludes that, for the most part, delays in transition to adulthood have had positive effects for young adults and their children. When marriage and childbearing are delayed so that young adults can increase their human capital, they become more productive (and better paid) workers and more successful parents. Waiting longer to form a union and have children tends to lead to lower fertility, however, and ultimately population aging. Beaujot argues for a shift in the balance between the demands of work and family and for more help for young persons to allow them to make a successful transition into family formation.

Family Transformation and Investment in Children

Some of the changes that have occurred in family life, such as fewer siblings and more mature and highly educated parents have been beneficial for children, as demonstrated by Beaujot in Chapter 4. But there have been other changes that appear to be detrimental for children: in particular, the increasing fragility of marriages and other forms of partnership has led to increases in the proportion of lone-parent families and in step- and blended families. While some studies remind us of the resilience of children in the face of family breakdown (see, e.g., Haddad 1998), the consensus in the literature is that the growing instability in unions has had adverse effects on children.

Reviewing what is now a very large literature, and drawing on insights from Coleman (1988), Don Kerr in Chapter 6 discusses the impact of family structure as it relates to transfers in financial, human, and social capital to children. He shows that the overall level of child poverty in Canada has not changed much between 1980 and 2000. While arguing for more refined analysis with longitudinal data to disentangle social causation and social selection effects, Kerr nevertheless concludes, on the basis of his own analyses and those of others, that 'children living in lone-parent families and stepfamilies are not only experiencing higher levels of income poverty, but also, on average, they appear to have greater behavioural and psychological difficulties.' Karen Mac Con, whose study is reported in Chapter 7, focuses on the emotional health of adolescents. She comes to a similar conclusion: that is, that children from non-intact and less cohesive families, as well as from families with low socioeconomic status are more likely to experience high levels of emotional disorder.

The effects of dissolution of parental relationships extend into young adulthood. Claudine Provencher, Céline Le Bourdais, and Nicole Marcil-Gratton, in Chapter 8 show that children's family experiences in their early years influence their own behaviour in matters of family formation and dissolution. In general, children raised in non-intact families have higher chances of forming a conjugal union at a young age although this effect differs for men and women and depends on how old the children were when the parents separated. The unions thus formed are more likely to involve cohabitation rather than marriage, and typically begin before these young people complete higher education. They are also at greater risk of bearing a child outside of a union and of facing a breakup of their own marriage or common law relationship.

These findings point to a critical issue for Canadian society: How can the community make up for the underinvestment in children that results from family breakup? This subject is addressed in Chapter 9 by Nancy Meilleur and Evelyne Lapierre-Adamcyk with particular emphasis on the issue of child care. When separation occurs, the most common consequence is a decline in income that often causes the lone-parent family to live for some period of time in poverty. Meilleur and Lapierre-Adamcyk argue that the best way out for these families is for the lone mothers to find paid employment. There are barriers to their entering the labour force, however, not the least of which are the presence of young children in need of care and, for many lone mothers, limited skills that would allow for successful integration in the labour market. Meilleur and Lapierre-Adamcyk's comparative study of the work patterns of single mothers in Alberta, Quebec, and Ontario shows that the participation rates of lone mothers vary significantly among the provinces. While economic conditions in the three provinces obviously play an important role, their results also suggest that social assistance programs and childcare services have much to do with the different levels of employment of lone mothers. In particular, a combination of factors – greater availability of reasonably priced daycare centres, lower levels of social assistance benefits, and a younger age requirement for children to qualify for social assistance – contributes to the higher participation rates of lone mothers in Alberta.

A commitment to early childhood education is one important route to offsetting some of the negative consequences associated with family dissolution, especially for children in lone-parent families. Other policy-related factors merit serious study as well. For example, policies that would ensure that absent parents meet their child support obligations, and related measures such as advance maintenance payments and a guaranteed annual income for children are high priority issues (Beaujot and Ravanera 2001). It would also help if policy considerations on the care and custody of children are based on a gender-symmetrical model, which features a more equal sharing of paid parental leaves and, if divorce does happen, joint custody as a default condition (Beaujot and Ravanera, 2001). The ways through which post-divorce agreements are reached also matter. Marcil-Gratton, Le Bourdais, and Lapierre-Adamcyk (2000) have found that when parents reach a private agreement, non-custodial fathers see their children more often than when agreement is established judicially. Private agreements between parents imply co-parenting, which has the potential to promote investment in children from both the resident and non-resident parent.

Family Solidarity and Societal Integration

The changes experienced by the family during the second half of the twentieth century have led some to believe that the family is now an inadequate institution, unable to provide enduring support for the well-being of its members (Popenoe, 1993 et al.). However, in Chapter 10 Fernando Rajulton and Zenaida R. Ravanera show that familial support remains strong. Their analytical approach focuses on family solidarity using the dimensions of affinity, opportunity structure, and functional exchange. They find that 90% of Canadians contribute to family solidarity in at least one of three ways: by providing to or receiving services from other family members; living proximate in residence to family; or giving and receiving emotional support to family members. They point to several factors as key determinants of family cohesion with living arrangement, particularly presence of children, and life course stage among the most important. Interestingly, income and education have little or no effect when it comes to fostering family solidarity.

Changes in families have affected as well the ways through which individuals adhere to society. As Zenaida R. Ravanera and Fernando Rajulton demonstrate in Chapter 11, the general pattern of integration over the life course is modified by individual, family, and community characteristics. Men and the highly educated, for example, are more likely to be integrated through economic inclusion, whereas those with children, the Canadian-born, and residents of rural areas feel a stronger sense of belonging to communities. There might well be a shift in the manner of integration among the younger cohorts in the future but, as Ravanera and Rajulton find, gender continues to play an important role. They argue that further improvement in the economic inclusion of women depends on greater sharing of caring responsibilities (for children and the elderly) by men, the state, and/or the market. And, while the elderly of the future will be healthier and more highly educated, there may be a need for conscious effort on the part of the employers, the government, and the voluntary sector to help bring about greater economic inclusion of elderly persons and their participation through volunteering.

The present collection of studies pays attention to the role of the family, an institution that has been buffeted by broader economic and social changes yet still contributes in a very important way to both individual development and functioning of society. While many roles formerly performed by families have been transferred to more specialized institutions, the family continues to play a critical task in building human and social capital for children, providing social and emotional support for its members, and effectively and efficiently supplying aid to members in need. Perhaps the broadest conclusion one can draw from this collection of studies is that all of society benefits when families work well. Thus, it is in our collective interest to find ways to support families in achieving their goals.

REFERENCES

Beaujot, R., and Z.R. Ravanera. 2001. 'An Interpretation of Family Change, With Implications for Social Cohesion.' Paper presented at the conference 'Have the Factors of Social Inclusiveness Changed?' organized by the Centre de recherche inter-universitaire sur les transformations et les regulations economiques et sociales (CRITERES) and the Policy Research Secretariat, Montreal, PSC Discussion Paper 01-1, 22 Feb.

Coleman, J. 1988. 'Social Capital in the Creation of Human Capital.' *American Journal of Sociology* 94: S95–S120.

Coleman, J.S. 1990. *Foundations of Social Theory.* Cambridge, MA: Belknap Press of Harvard University Press.

Esping-Andersen, G. 2001. *Social Foundations of Postindustrial Economies.* Oxford: Oxford University Press.

Haddad, Tony. 1998. 'Custody Arrangements and the Development of Emotional and Behavioural Problems by Children.' Paper presented at the conference investing in Children, Ottawa, 27–9 Oct.

Jenson, J. 1998. *Mapping Social Cohesion: The State of Canadian Research.* Ottawa: Canadian Policy Research Network, Study No. F-03.

Marcil-Gratton, Nicole, Céline Le Bourdais, and Evelyne Lapierre-Adamcyk. 2000. 'The Implications of Parents' Conjugal Histories for Children.' *Isuma: Canadian Journal of Policy Research* 1(2): 32–40.

Popenoe, D., N.D. Glen, J. Stacey, P.A. Cowan. 1993. 'American Family Decline, 1960–1990: A Review and Appraisal.' *Journal of Marriage and the Family,* 55(3): 527–55.

Putnam, R. 1995. 'Bowling Alone: America's Declining Social Capital.' *Journal of Democracy* 6(1): 165–78.

Putnam, R. 2000. *Bowling Alone: The Collapse and Revival of American Community.* New York: Simon and Schuster.

Ravanera, Z.R., F. Rajulton, and T.K. Burch. 2003. 'Early Life Transitions of Canadian Youth: Effects of Family Transformation and Community Characteristics.' *Canadian Studies in Population* 30(2): 327–54.

PART ONE

Changes in Families: Childbearing, Work Patterns, and Life Course Transitions

2 Transformed Families and the Basis for Childbearing

RODERIC BEAUJOT AND ALI MUHAMMAD

One of the most significant family changes is in terms of numbers of children. Given the importance of childbearing to individuals, to the demographic reproduction of society, and to the relative size of age groups, much attention is placed on observing and interpreting the trends.

Childbearing can be viewed in terms of the desires that people have, and the constraints under which they operate. There is debate in the literature with regard to the relative importance of economic and cultural questions in influencing fertility change. Caldwell (1997) develops a 'unifying theory' based both on the changed socioeconomic circumstances of people's lives, and changing ideas and norms on appropriate family behaviour. Axinn and Yabiku (2001) propose that cultural considerations operate in terms of desires to have children, while economic considerations are more relevant to the constraints on childbearing.

In theorizing about low fertility, McDonald (2002) proposes that there is considerable desire for children, as seen through childbearing intentions, but the risks and uncertainties of a globalizing world make people hesitate to have children. A globalizing world probably produces more risks that are partly handled through stronger investment in one's own human capital, leaving less time for reproduction. There is also a heightened awareness of risk, along with sustained efforts to manage and control it (Hall 2002). People may feel that their relationships are insufficiently secure to have children, they may feel insecure in the labour market, or they may feel a lack of support from the broader society, in terms of childcare and other services for families.

Relationships, childbearing, and work can thus be theorized in terms of life strategies for optimizing lifetime welfare. At the individual level, having or not having children may be a means of self-fulfilment (Van de Kaa 1987; 2001) or of reducing uncertainty (Friedman et al. 1994). That is, children can be seen as enduring interpersonal links, particularly when other relationships are less stable. At the social level, childbearing may be a means of increasing social capital (Schoen et al. 1997) and social mobility (Ariès 1980) or a means of creating family relations and achieving a life that is more family-centred. A birth in an insecure relationship may also be a strategy to strengthen the relationship, and having a child may be a means of dealing with labour market failure (Ni Bhrolchain 1993).

Conversely, having children may present obstacles to self-actualization, to the dyadic relationship within a couple, and to integration in market and non-family sectors of society. For instance, Folbre (1983) and McDonald (2000) theorize that as women gained status in families they had fewer children, which in turn promoted women's status in non-familial institutions. In looking at childbearing within given occupations, Ranson (1998) observes considerable differences across occupations in the potential to have a child without loss of work status. In other cases, having children may not be a function of weighing the costs and benefits, but of a series of life events and circumstances (Currie 1988).

After reviewing the fertility trend, this chapter will consider the values and costs of children, the desire for children, and the constraints on childbearing. The focus is placed on integration in relationships and in the labour market as part of the basis for childbearing. In the discussion, we suggest that sharing the costs of children can lead people to envisage children as a 'common project' that creates stronger relationships between parents, and in communities and societies.

The Fertility Trend

The past twenty years have shown considerable stability in both period and cohort fertility. After passing below 2.0 in 1972, the total fertility rate has been between 1.65 and 1.51 for the period 1981 to 2001. The cohort born in 1948 was the last to have completed fertility above 2.0, and the cohorts born in 1950 to 1970 have had or are projected to have rates between 1.95 and 1.69 (Bélanger 2003: 37). Compared with the rapid changes observed for generations born before 1950, there has been a slow change in a downward direction across more recent cohorts. While fertility has declined over time, the timing of childbearing has changed more substantially, from a mean age at first birth of 24.4 in 1976 to 27.1 in 2001 (2003: 35).

Numbers of Children

The most common family size is now two children, with three children being the next most prevalent. The next categories are women having one or no children, which each amount to about 15% of the total. Based on the 2001 General Social Survey, the proportion of women with no children at age 39 increased from 11.1% in the 1941–5 birth cohort, to 16.3% in the 1956–60 cohort (Beaujot and Efrani 2004). Among those with one child, the progression to a second child declined only from 85.5% to 81.5% over these cohorts. However, the progression is much lower to third parity, at 52.2% in the 1941–45 cohort and 38.8% in the 1956–60 cohort. Nonetheless, by age 39, 26.5% of women in the 1956–60 cohort had at least three children.

The fertility decline over cohorts has mostly involved lower proportions of third or higher order births and a greater concentration at the level of two births (Péron, Lapierre-Adamcyk, and Morissette 1987). Consequently, three-quarters of children are in families of size two or three children. The proportion of women with one child has increased slightly, but it has remained under 15% that is, very similar to the proportion who have no children.

The concept of the 'second demographic transition' is the most relevant context for interpreting the trends of the past forty years. The first transition, from about 1870 to 1945, brought smaller families, especially because of changes in the economic costs and benefits of children, along with a cultural environment that made it more appropriate to control family size. The second transition, since the mid-1960s, has been linked to an increased flexibility in marital relationships (Lesthaeghe 1995; Beaujot 2000: 85-96).

The most obvious indicators of this increased flexibility are seen in the means of entry and exit from relationships. Divorce as a means of exit was first envisioned as a solution to extreme problems in a marriage, and the presence of children was often an important reason not to divorce (Keyfitz 1994: 7). The norms have since changed to the point that people consider a good divorce to be better than a bad marriage (Lesthaeghe and Surkyn 1988). According to current trends of divorce by duration of marriage, 35.5% of marriages will end in divorce (Bélanger 2003: 30). Cohabitation as a means of entry into relationships was originally a period of living together before marriage, but it has come to be the most common route of entry into relationships, and a prevalent living arrangement for people who have previously been married. Just as cohabitation has transformed premarital relationships, it has transformed postmarital relationships and marital relationships themselves. The proportion of births occurring to women who were not married, most of whom are cohabiting, increased from 9% in 1971 to 38% in 2001.

The contrasts between the first and second demographic transitions suggest important differences in the relevance of children to social cohesion (Lesthaeghe and Neels 2002). The first transition is associated with the economic development that brought higher standards of living and aspirations for increased consumption. The cultural side of this transition included the social legitimacy of deliberate control over births, but it also included a uniform family model based on 'prudent marriage' and 'responsible parenthood.' The second transition is linked with secularization and the growing importance placed on individual autonomy. Thus, one family model based on intact marriages gave way to a diversity of family types corresponding to the interest in autonomy and postmaterial aspirations. Lesthaeghe and Neels (2002) further propose that the first demographic transition saw increased social cohesion. Structural conditions permitted greater integration into a common economic market, and cultural features included strong identification with a homogeneous family type characterized by intact marriages with children. In contrast, the greater importance of individual autonomy during the second demographic transition is linked to a weakening of the role of families in social cohesion. Childbearing is largely seen now as a means of individual gratification (Ariès 1980; Giddens 1991). It will therefore be important to observe how childbearing can be seen in terms of social values and of benefits and costs to individual adults.

Timing of Childbearing

The second demographic transition includes a shift in the timing of family events towards later ages. The patterns over cohorts are rather uniform (Beaujot 2000: 97). For the birth cohorts 1916–20 to 1941–5 there was a general downward trend in the age at leaving home, first marriage, first birth, last birth, and of the children leaving home. Conversely, subsequent cohorts have experienced an upward trend. We

Figure 2.1 Fertility rate (per 1,000) by age group, Canada, 1972–2000.

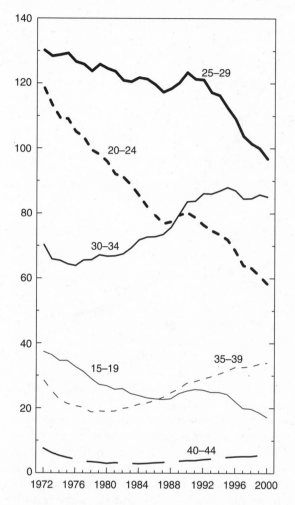

Source: Bélanger (2003: 34).

can now speak of delays not only in home leaving, forming relationships, and childbearing, but also in leaving school and starting consistent employment (Beaujot 2004; and Chapter 5, this volume).

   These delays are visible in age-specific fertility rates (figure 2.1). Fertility has especially declined at age 20–24, but also at age 15–19 and 25–

Figure 2.2 Age-specific fertility rates (per 1,000), selected birth cohorts of
mothers, Canada, 1946–1975.

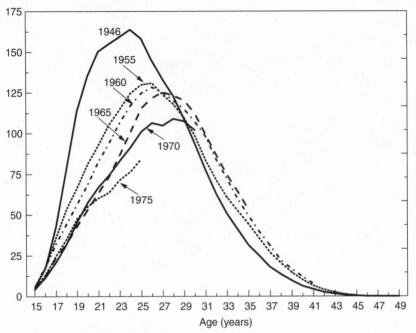

Source: Bélanger (2003: 34).

29. Consequently, the proportion of births occurring to women aged 30
and over increased from 19.6% in 1976 to 46.9% in 2001.

Lesthaeghe and Moors (2000) show that, in a number of countries,
the same cohorts that saw delays at younger ages showed recuperation
at older ages. Canada here follows the pattern of Northern Europe,
along with United Kingdom, France, United States, Australia, and
Japan: that is, the cohorts that reached 15–19 after 1960 show declines
from cohort to cohort in fertility at age 20–29, and the same cohorts
show increases at age 30–44 (figure 2.2). The cumulation of fertility
over ages shows that cohorts born between 1947 and 1965 have experienced delay and partial recuperation (Beaujot and Bélanger 2001). As
seen in figure 2.2, the 1970 and 1975 cohorts show particularly strong
reductions in fertility before age 30. It is too early to know the extent to
which the sharp decline of birth rates at age 25–29 since the early 1990s
will be compensated with higher rates after age 30.

Delays reflect the needs of both men and women to put off entry into relationships, and especially childbearing, until they are better able to handle the trade-offs between investing in themselves and investing in reproduction (Kaplan 1997). There are important differentials associated with earlier and later childbearing. Based on census data, Lochhead (2000) finds that delayed childbearing is more pronounced among women who have university education, and that there are increasing income differentials to the disadvantage of younger first-time mothers, even in two-parent families. Using data from the United States, Martin (2000) finds that delayed childbearers, who tend to have more education, are increasingly likely to raise their children in intact marriages, while early childbearers are more likely to raise children outside of marriage.

From the point of view of children, Bianchi (2000) speaks of a possible bifurcation of models, with one group taking advantage of parental investment from both mothers and fathers, and the other where fathers are absent and mothers do not have adequate time and resources to invest in children. Children born to mature parents are more likely to have the advantages of a mother with more human capital, along with the presence of a father in a two-income family, which contrasts with the greater likelihood of lone parenthood for those who bear children early.

Value and Costs of Children

If having children is a means of individual gratification, it is important to observe how childbearing entails benefits and costs for men and women. As we have seen, the second demographic transition includes a weakening of the norms against divorce, premarital sex, cohabitation, and voluntary childlessness. That is, there is a greater focus on individual rights along with less regulation of the private lives of individuals by the larger community (Thornton 2001).

In particular, the values of the modern family include choices in childbearing, including the choice not to have children. However, there are also ideals that support childbearing, including the very pleasures associated with interacting with children and the long-term relationships that children represent. At the same time, children may be obstacles to self-actualization, and childbearing is not an intrinsic element of 'pure relationships' (Hall 2003). On the other hand, the benefits of children as a means of self-expression and social embeddedness may outweigh the negatives (Van de Kaa 2001).

The benefits and costs that are associated with children can best be appreciated through open-ended questions that ask about the advantages and disadvantages associated with various life-course decisions. We undertook such a survey in the region surrounding London, Ontario, in the year 2000, and the summary presented here is based on 124 respondents aged 18 and over in the selected households (see Beaujot and Efrani 2004). The purpose of the survey was to obtain people's basic orientation to various family questions. Respondents were asked a series of open-ended questions regarding relationships, children, and the division of work.

People's orientations on the benefits and cost of children were sought by asking 'why do people have children?' and 'What are the advantages and disadvantages of having children?' Some respondents simply saw it as natural to have children, and others were more likely to see it as a choice. The benefits were described in terms of reproducing oneself, the joys of children, and the special relationships with children. The costs were first described in financial terms, but then also in terms of both the time and energy that parents have to give of themselves and the state of being tied down. While respondents could often say more about the disadvantages of having children, the vast majority felt that the advantages outweighed the disadvantages.

Two children was often stated as the ideal number, but many gave a range, especially two-to-three, or two-to-four. In defending these numbers, people again spoke first of financial questions, but on further reflection they often said that if you wait for the finances you may never have children. When asked if they would have had more children if they had twice the income, most said not and that this was not the right way to make the decision. The reasons for not having fewer than two children were rather uniformly described in terms of it not being good to be an only child. Without siblings, a child would lack the opportunity to experience close interpersonal relationships with someone of his or her own age, which was seen as an important life skill. It seemed that there was more prejudice against having one child than against having no children. When asked what couples should do if they disagreed on the number of children to have, most had some difficulty really dealing with the question; some said it should be the one who would mostly look after them who should decide, but ultimately most said that couples should not have children that they do not both want. This corresponds to conclusions on the basis of the 1987–88 to

1992–94 National Survey of Families and Households in the United States (Thomson 1997). The likelihood of having a child was least if both partners did not want a child, but couples who disagreed had lower than average births, and if they disagreed, each partner's intentions were shifted towards not having a child.

While there has been a weakening of the normative consensus that marriage and childbearing are integral parts of the adult role, most women and men nevertheless want children. Children are often valued for the special relationships that they represent, and as long-term links with other people. The costs are seen in terms of time and energy, given other interests and priorities that people have in life. Present norms also imply that people should not have children if they are not in secure relationships, and not secure in the labour market. There are high standards regarding what parents want to provide for their children. Children should also be desired by both partners, and thus the balance of benefits and costs needs to be positive for both in order to plan a pregnancy at a given time.

The Desire for Children

Many women and men clearly balance the value of having children against other priorities in life, but for most there is a strong desire for children. In our small sample of 124 respondents, only five indicated no children and four indicated one child either as their family size on completion of childbearing or as the expected family size. Although our sample may have underrepresented persons who had low desires for children, most of these nine respondents did not manifest negative attitudes towards having children, and they saw important advantages to having children (Beaujot and Efrani 2004). It appeared to be life circumstance that brought these respondents to want no children or only one child: lack of partners, fecundity/pregnancy problems, or the presence of stepchildren.

We cannot claim that this small number of respondents is representative, but larger surveys indicate that at the beginning of adult life, only a small proportion of people do not intend to have children (table 2.1). The question on expected family size was asked in the 2001 General Social Survey (Statistics Canada 2003). There were separate questions on children born to you (for women) or fathered (for men), adopted children, and stepchildren. Respondents who were able to have children were then asked 'the number of children you intend to have.' In calculating total expected family size we have included adopted children, but

TABLE 2.1 Expected Births, and Average Expected Family Size, by Age and Sex, Canada, 2001

Sex	Age (years)	No child	One child	Two children	Three children	Four+ children	Missing data	Average[a]
Male	15–19	6.3	5.9	51.9	18.8	3.4	13.7	2.12
	20–24	6.1	7.8	45.1	19.8	6.2	15.0	2.24
	25–29	6.0	8.3	47.3	17.6	6.6	14.1	2.16
	30–34	8.7	8.2	42.3	18.6	7.3	14.8	2.12
	35–39	12.4	12.7	40.0	16.5	6.5	11.9	1.94
	40–44	15.7	13.1	39.4	17.6	5.6	8.6	1.86
	45–49	15.3	15.2	39.0	16.5	7.6	6.5	1.90
	50–54	18.2	13.7	36.7	20.5	9.7	1.2	1.94
	55–59	13.2	14.1	38.3	23.4	10.4	0.7	2.08
	≥60	15.2	9.0	25.4	22.3	27.5	0.7	2.70
	Total	12.1	10.7	39.1	19.2	10.7	8.2	2.16
Female	15–19	6.9	6.8	50.5	20.4	6.7	8.7	2.18
	20–24	7.2	4.3	46.8	24.5	8.0	9.2	2.27
	25–29	6.5	7.4	46.1	20.3	7.8	12.0	2.20
	30–34	5.7	11.6	43.4	16.8	7.7	14.7	2.15
	35–39	8.8	14.9	43.3	19.0	6.4	7.6	2.01
	40–44	12.7	16.9	42.5	17.1	7.3	3.4	1.91
	45–49	11.7	17.5	42.3	18.6	8.3	1.5	1.97
	50–54	13.7	14.1	42.7	20.1	9.5	0.0	2.03
	55–59	11.2	12.4	37.6	22.5	16.2	0.0	2.29
	≥60	11.7	10.2	23.6	20.5	33.7	0.5	2.97
	Total	9.9	11.7	39.5	19.9	13.8	5.1	2.29

Source: Tabulation based on Statistics Canada, (2001). GSS 2001.
Note: Results are weighted; sample size is 24,310 including 1,540 cases of missing data on expected family size. Adopted children are included, but not stepchildren.
[a] Excludes those with missing data.

not stepchildren. In the whole 2001 GSS sample, 8.2% of men and 5.1% of women did not declare an expected family size. The proportion expecting no children is only 6% to 7% of men and women age 15–19, and rises to 12% to 14% for women age 40–54 and to 12% to 18% for men age 35–54. In each of the age-sex groups under age 60, two children constitutes the largest proportion of expected family sizes, and the second most common expected family size is three children. Thus, the average expected family size, ignoring those who have missing data, declines from 2.1 or 2.2 at age 15–19, to 1.9 at age 40–49.

At age 20–29 only some 6% to 7% of 2001 GSS respondents indicate that they intend to have no children. The lack of realism about some of these expectations can be seen in the 25% of men and 30% of women who intend to have three or more children. Over time, the expected family size has a tendency to decline. For instance, women age 25–29 in 1984 intended to have an average of 2.17 births, but this was reduced to 2.03 when they were 36–41 in 1995 (Dupuis 1998: 5), and to 1.93 when they were 41–46 in 2001.

There is not a large variation in these average expected births within various subpopulations. For instance, the average is 1.5 births or more in each of the categories of Table 2.2, except for never-married persons age 40 and over. Expected births are slightly higher for persons who were themselves born in places other than North America and Europe, and for persons who do not have completed secondary education. Research based on the 1995 GSS indicates that education operates differently for men and women, with men who have more education expecting more children, while an inverse relation applies to women age 30–39 (Dupuis 1998: 4). As would be expected, the average number of intended births is higher for respondents who have already had one or two children. The averages are slightly lower for those who had a first child when age 30 or more, but even they expect an average of more than two children.

The 2001 GSS results are not very different from those of other countries. There is a debate in the literature about the extent to which one should trust these indicators of expected family size. Massimo Livi Bacci (2001) proposes that they mostly measure the predominant family size norm of two children. Nonetheless, longitudinal research suggests that intentions regarding future fertility and the degree of certainty expressed by the respondent and spouse are strong predictors of the likelihood of having a birth within the next five years (Schoen et al. 1999). Still, expected family size is a rather abstract notion for persons who are not in relationships, and significant proportions do not answer the question. These missing data obviously inflate the population averages on expected family size.

Constraints on Childbearing

Analysis of attitudes towards having children and on expected family size suggest that there is a cultural orientation in favour of childbearing. We now need to investigate why this orientation does not translate into

TABLE 2.2 Average Number of Expected Births, by Various Characteristics of Respondents, Age 20–59, 2001

	Cases	20–29	30–39	40–49	50–59
Sex					
Male	7,006	2.2	2.0	1.9	2.0
Female	8,835	2.2	2.1	1.9	2.1
Union status					
Single	2,727	2.2	1.5	0.6	0.3
First union	8,147	2.3	2.2	2.1	2.2
Second (and subsequent) unions	2,320	2.1	2.1	1.8	2.1
Post-union	2,647	2.2	1.8	1.6	1.9
Age at first birth (years)					
<25	4,910	2.5	2.4	2.3	2.6
25–29	3,332	2.4	2.3	2.2	2.2
≥30	2,408	–	2.1	2.0	2.2
Interval between first and second birth (months)					
<30	3,467	2.8	2.5	2.5	2.7
30–52	2,646	2.9	2.4	2.4	2.5
≥53	1,489	2.3	2.4	2.3	2.4
Education completed					
Post-secondary	8,154	2.2	2.0	1.9	2.0
Secondary	5,130	2.2	2.0	1.9	2.0
Not completed secondary	2,490	2.2	2.3	2.0	2.3
Work status throughout the career					
Men					
Worked FT	5,258	2.2	2.1	1.9	2.0
Worked FT and/ or PT	1,030	2.4	1.8	1.7	1.9
Never worked	417	2.1	1.9	1.9	1.6
Women					
Worked FT	4,696	2.2	2.0	1.8	2.0
Worked FT and/ or PT	2,895	2.3	2.2	2.1	2.3
Never worked	902	2.2	2.4	2.3	2.5

TABLE 2.2 (Concluded)

	Cases	20–29	30–39	40–49	50–59
Work History					
Men					
Never worked	417	2.1	1.9	1.9	1.6
Work interruption >1 year	641	2.1	2.0	1.7	2.0
No work interruption or <1 year	4,989	2.2	2.0	1.9	2.0
Women					
Never worked	902	2.2	2.4	2.3	2.5
Work interruption >1 year	1,217	2.4	2.0	1.8	2.0
No work interruption or <1 year	4,848	2.1	2.0	1.9	2.1
Siblings (*n*)					
0	612	2.0	1.8	1.5	1.8
1	3,148	2.1	1.9	1.8	1.9
≥2	12,032	2.3	2.1	1.9	2.1
Birthplace					
Canada	13,128	2.2	2.0	1.9	2.0
Europe or North America	1,134	2.3	2.2	1.9	2.1
Other	1,499	2.2	2.3	2.2	2.4
Religious attendance					
Weekly	2,565	2.5	2.4	2.4	2.3
Other	10,064	2.3	2.0	1.9	2.1
Not applicable	3,212	2.0	1.9	1.7	1.8
Would stay married for the sake of children					
Yes	3,650	2.4	2.2	2.2	2.3
No	4,185	2.3	2.1	1.9	2.1
Don't know	1,518	2.2	2.1	2.0	2.2
Not applicable	6,488	2.2	1.8	1.5	1.7
Total (cases) average	15,841	(3,187) 2.2	(4,484) 2.0	(4,409) 1.9	(3,761) 2.0

Source: Tabulations based on the GSS 2001.

Note: In work history, those who are currently interrupted are counted with work interruptions of one year or more. FT = full-time; PT = part-time.

a fertility rate that is closer to replacement levels. As already visible in the discussion of the desire for children, there are several ways in which initial desires may be frustrated. Young respondents who are asked about their intentions are probably envisioning a life where various things will work out for them, in terms of relationships, labour market integration, and the division of paid and unpaid work. Lapierre-Adamcyk and Lussier (2003) observe that aspirations are adjusted in the face of constraints, including the precariousness of unions, difficulties in the labour market, costs of children, and competing aspirations for economic well-being. In his theory on low fertility, McDonald (2002) proposes that globalization creates risks, which can be averted through human capital investment and delays in childbearing. The societies with particularly low fertility have less progression beyond the first birth. He proposes that this is not the result of differential values, because desired family size is higher than actual childbearing. Instead, it reflects constraints, represented especially by opportunity costs for women. These opportunity costs rise with women's income but they can decrease with institutional arrangements that provide for better integration of parents in the labour market, like paid leave, part-time work with good benefits, and subsidized childcare (McDonald 2002).

Integration in Relationships

Although union formation is occurring at later ages, and more likely to occur through cohabitation, there is a strong preference for living in unions. Over the cohorts of women born between 1926–35 and 1956–65, at least 94% had at least one union (Le Bourdais, Neill, and Turcotte 2000: 14). From figures as high as 95% over the lifetime for the male cohort born in 1938, the proportion married by age 40 declined to 60.5% for men and 70.8 per cent for women in the 1965 cohort (Dumas and Bélanger 1997). The cohabitation experience is found to delay entry into marriage, partly because it prolongs the period of information gathering on the appropriateness of a marital choice, and it reduces the interaction with other potential partners (Wu 1999; 2000). At the same time, one-fifth of cohabitations can be seen as substitutes to marriage in the sense that a first birth occurred before a marriage. Two out of five are stable in the sense that they last for at least three years (Dumas and Bélanger 1997: 150). Nonetheless, cohabitation increases the overall instability of relationships (Marcil-Gratton 1993; Marcil-Gratton and Le Bourdais 1999).

Although there is some substitution of cohabitation for marriage, there remains a significant increase in the numbers of people who are not living in relationships. For instance, at age 25–29 the proportion who were neither married nor currently cohabiting increased from 32.0% to 53.3% for men and from 20.0% to 38.9% for women between 1981 and 2001 (Beaujot and Kerr 2004: 220).

McDaniel (1989) proposes that the relationship between marital status and childbearing is no longer simple, and needs to be reconceptualized. Nonetheless, persons who are married or intend to marry expect more children. At age 20–29, but especially at age 40–49, expected births are lowest for those who have never married, and those who used to be married but are not currently in union.

Other evidence in table 2.2 show that integration in relationships has a positive influence on childbearing. In particular, expected births are higher for people who attend religious services more frequently, for those who have more siblings, and for those who would stay married for the sake of children. Conversely, fertility is low when religious attendance is 'not applicable,' which mostly represents persons who do not indicate a religious affiliation. For each age group, the number of children ever born is higher in married than in cohabiting relationships (Beaujot 1995: 50; Dumas and Bélanger 1997: 159). The formerly married also have more children than do those in cohabiting unions, and the lowest fertility is found among people who have never married (Dumas and Bélanger 1997: 156). Remarried persons are more likely to consider having a third child than formerly married persons who are in a new common-law union (Wu and Wang 1998).

Our 2000 qualitative survey (discussed earlier) asked things like What do you think it means to be married? How might that differ from living together? What are reasons for forming a union? What are the advantages of having a partner compared with being single? and what are the advantages of being single? Largely the advantages of being married or in an enduring relationship were described in terms of companionship and having someone with whom to share life, while the perceived advantage of being single was the freedom to make decisions without taking someone else into account. While some saw these as trade-offs, the vast majority of our respondents felt that there were more advantages to being in a relationship generally, and for most of them this included marriage. A secure relationship was largely seen as an essential basis for childbearing. The ideal age for beginning this relationship was seen to be in the mid-20s, with questions of maturity and financial security being more important than age.

Thus, marital status and childbearing remain related. The lower prevalence of marriage and the greater prevalence of cohabitation have

tended to reduce fertility. Later entry into unions and greater prevalence of union dissolution can also result in lower fertility.

Integration in the Labour Market

The relevance of integration in the labour market to childbearing
depends on family models for the division of paid and unpaid work.
When paid work and family work were each full-time jobs necessary
to family well-being, there was a predominance of the complementary-
roles approach to the division of work (Becker 1981). However, with
less unpaid work to be done in the home, the breadwinner model is
clearly giving way to the dual-earner strategy for family and work
(Beaujot 2000). Starting from a strong norm in the middle of the twentieth century that mothers of young children should be full-time housewives, Rindfuss et al. (1996) propose that behavioural changes have
led to attitudinal changes that have undermined this norm and have
helped to stabilize fertility. But the dual-earner model is not without
stress, and women have carried the main burden in terms of the
accommodations between production and reproduction (Kempeneers
1992). Having fewer children becomes one of the ways to handle this
stress.

Lower fertility is often related to higher female labour force participation. Yet, in the time series data, the inverse relationship between
women's labour force participation and fertility was limited to the
period of about 1960 to 1975 (Beaujot 2000: 259). In the 1950s women's
education and labour force participation were rising, as was fertility.
Since the mid-1970s labour force participation has continued to rise,
but fertility is much more stable. Here again, the relationships are not
simple.

At the individual level, the relevance of labour market integration is
different for men and women. Men with more education and more
consistent labour force participation have more children. For instance,
at age 30–39, men who have always worked full-time expect 2.1 children compared with 1.8 expected by those who have sometimes
worked part-time (table 2.2). At age 40–49, men expecting the fewest
children are those who have had work interruptions. Based on data
from Germany, Tolke and Diewald (2003) find that men who have a
more difficult start to their working lives, or insecurities during their
working lives as measured by unemployment, part-time work, or self-
employment, are less likely to enter relationships and less likely to

become fathers. Conversely, men who have had greater success and security in their careers are more likely to have children. In particular, development of a successful career increases the propensity to then have children.

For women in Canada, there are probably two coexisting models. Some women are delaying having children until they are integrated in the labour market, while other women with poor integration in the labour market have children. Women who had worked without interruptions had the lowest number of expected births. At age 30–59, women who have never worked have the highest expected births, followed by women who have sometimes worked part-time (Table 2.2). Other analyses find that the likelihood of a second or third birth is lower for those who were employed in the previous interval (Bélanger and Dumas 1998; Bélanger 2000). There are differences across occupational groups. Based on a study of recent university graduates, Ranson (1998) finds that the likelihood of having a child after starting to work is higher in professions like teaching, where there are more job guarantees for people who take leaves. In other occupations like engineering or business, women are often insecure and so put off having children until they have established their careers.

There is also evidence from Sweden that once the conflict in women's roles is reduced, a positive relation can emerge between women's employment and childbearing (United Nations 2000: 16). For instance, Olah (2003) finds that in Sweden the likelihood of having a second birth is higher for more educated women, while the educational gradient is flat in Hungary, suggesting that policy measures have been able to reduce fertility costs for more educated women in both countries.

Integration in Labour Market and in Relationships

Integration in the labour market is also relevant to the likelihood of being in a stable relationship. In earlier cohorts, men who were more integrated in the labour market were more likely to marry, while the opposite held for women. However, for cohorts born since 1960, both men and women who have never entered the labour market are much less likely to marry or cohabit than are those who have worked without interruption (Mongeau et al. 2001). That is, for these younger cohorts of women and men, those with more education and greater capacity for economic integration in the labour market have a higher likelihood of entering relationships. Work interruptions particularly reduce men's likelihood of entering relationships. Turcotte and Goldscheider (1998) conclude that union formation increasingly requires the earning power of both partners. Results for marital dissolution remain different for women and men. The probability of separation is typically higher for women who have a longer period of employment (Le Bourdais, Neill, and Vachon 2000). For men, higher education and higher earnings reduce the risk of separation (Goldscheider and Waite 1991: 104–6).

Alternate models for the division of paid and unpaid work are related to the relationship between labour market integration and fertility. In Sweden, where there are more policies facilitating the combination of employment and parenting, couples who share family work more equally are more likely to have a second child (Olah 2003). It has been argued that gender-equal structures in the public and private spheres may enable society to avoid particularly low fertility, as long as there also remains a strong desire to have children (Matthews 1999; McDonald 1997). Nonetheless, for some couples, childlessness might be the easiest route to establish gender equality. One might expect that couples with no children or fewer children would be more likely to have a more symmetrical division of paid and unpaid work. However, Canadian results based on time-use data show that the double burden is actually more common where there are no children in the household (Beaujot and Ravanera 2003).

It would thus appear that both integration in the labour market and integration in relationships are relevant to the opportunities and constraints for childbearing. For most, accommodations both at work and at home largely make it possible to achieve family and work goals in ways that include children. In other cases, difficulties in labour market integration, in establishing relationships, or in meshing of family and work, are probably responsible for an inability to achieve life goals in childbearing. These constraints also encourage older ages at childbearing, with more mature mothers being more able to negotiate a better sharing of the costs of children with their spouses and workplaces.

It is useful to briefly consider the effect of children on other relationships. For instance, childbearing itself can be seen as a means of establishing enduring relationships. Children represent a form of enduring relationship, which may be particularly important when other relationships are less stable. In 'Why Do Americans Want Children,' Schoen et al. (1997: 350) observe that people are more likely to intend to have another child when they attach importance to the social relationships created by children. These authors conclude that 'childbearing is purposive behaviour that creates and reinforces the most important and most enduring social bonds.' Others speak of children providing a 'deep connection to the continuity of life' (Rutledge 1998: D2). Children are a possible means to enhance social integration, not only in terms of family ties but also at the community level. They can provide contact with others in the neighbourhood, at school, and in the community. That is, for both men and women, becoming a parent is associated with increases in social integration (Nomaguchi and Milkie 2003). For instance, parents of adult children are more likely to provide support when their own children become parents.

Determinants of Childbearing

The desire for children and the associated constraints can be further analysed in terms of the determinants of first, second, and third births. We are here adding the 2001 General Social Survey, to update an analysis performed by Bélanger of the 1995 GSS (Bélanger and Dumas 1998; Bélanger and Oikawa 1999; Bélanger 2000). Event-history analysis is used to estimate the relationship between certain characteristics and the likelihood of having a birth of a given order. The likelihood of a first birth takes advantage of the experience of all women since age 15, while the probability of a second birth is based on the experience of women who had a first birth, and the third birth probabilities start with women who have had two children. Thus, the analyses for second and third births are based on an increasingly selective sample. Table 2.3 presents both the 'univariate' estimates for the categories of a given variable and the 'multivariate' estimates or net effects after the other variables in the model have been controlled. The results are shown as risk ratios, compared with the value of 1.0 for the reference category. Both union status and work status are here introduced as time-variant characteristics, with other measures based on the history of the respondent or taken at the time of the survey. It is also important to appreciate that all women respondents to the 2001 General Social Survey have been included in this analysis. Thus, the cohort measure for women born before 1945 would be dominated by those who were less involved in the labour force and had less education. Also, few women in the cohort born after 1975 would have had a second birth by the time of the survey, making this group rather unique.

Previous fertility history plays a significant role in second and third births. Younger ages at first birth are related to higher probabilities of

TABLE 2.3 Relative Risks of First, Second, and Third Birth by Various Characteristics of Women, Canada, 2001

	1st Birth		2nd Birth		3rd Birth	
	Univariate	Multivariate	Univariate	Multivariate	Univariate	Multivariate
Birth cohorts						
Before 1945	1.00	1.00	1.00	1.00	1.00	1.00
1945–54	0.95	0.92*	0.82*	0.72*	0.50*	0.57*
1955–64	0.76*	0.70*	0.79*	0.71*	0.46*	0.63*
1965–74	0.71*	0.73*	0.81*	0.68*	0.72*	0.77*
After 1975	0.65*	0.78*	0.67*	0.57*	1.06	0.97
Age at first birth (years)						
<25	–	–	1.73*	1.59*	1.33*	2.89*
25–29	–	–	1.57*	1.44*	0.85*	1.73*
≥30	–	–	1.00	1.00	1.00	1.00
Interval between first and second birth (months)						
<30	–	–	–	–	2.00*	1.95*
30–53	–	–	–	–	1.12*	1.17*
≥53	–	–	–	–	1.00	1.00
Union status						
Never married	0.75*	0.83*	0.94*	0.96*	0.99	1.00
First union	1.00	1.00	1.00	1.00	1.00	1.00
Second (and subsequent) unions	0.87*	1.03	0.78*	0.87*	1.12*	1.12*
Post-union	0.67*	0.80*	0.76*	0.87*	1.06*	1.02
Work status						
Working	0.70*	0.62*	0.80*	0.77*	0.76*	0.77*
Not working	1.00	1.00	1.00	1.00	1.00	1.00
Education						
No secondary diploma	1.88*	1.74*	1.08*	0.93*	1.63*	1.15*
Secondary diploma	1.34*	1.32*	0.99	0.92*	1.06	0.94*
Post-secondary	1.00	1.00	1.00	1.00	1.00	1.00
Siblings (n)						
0	0.84*	0.93*	0.83*	0.89*	0.76*	0.79*
1 or 2	0.80*	0.92*	0.89*	0.94*	0.80*	0.89*
≥3	1.00	1.00	1.00	1.00	1.00	1.00

TABLE 2.3 (Concluded)

	1st Birth		2nd Birth		3rd Birth	
	Univariate	Multivariate	Univariate	Multivariate	Univariate	Multivariate
Sex of first child						
Male	–	–	1.01	1.02	–	–
Female	–	–	1.00	1.00	–	–
Sex of first two children						
Both male	–	–	–	–	1.20*	1.20*
Both female	–	–	–	–	1.28*	1.31*
One male and one female	–	–	–	–	1.00	1.00
Religious practice						
Weekly	1.00	1.00	1.00	1.00	1.00	1.00
Others	0.97	1.02	0.84*	0.87*	0.70*	0.80*
Not applicable	0.72*	0.84*	0.74*	0.82*	0.69*	0.70*
Place of birth						
Canada	1.00	1.00	1.00	1.00	1.00	1.00
Europe and North America	1.05	1.01	0.85*	0.86*	0.94	0.86*
Other	0.85*	0.94*	0.83*	0.85*	0.82*	0.89*
Would stay married for the sake of children						
Yes	1.00	1.00	1.00	1.00	1.00	1.00
No	0.96	1.09*	0.93*	0.91*	0.72*	0.81*
Don't know	0.86*	0.90*	1.06	1.04	0.95	1.00
Not applicable	0.61*	0.70*	0.72*	0.65*	1.11*	0.95
Total	13,646		9,489		7,459	

Source: GSS 2001.

Note: Results are not weighted. Union status and work status are treated as time-varying covariates. The Cox regression procedure was used on the basis of structured data. For the multivariate analysis, among cases shown for the univariate analysis, the cases available for analysis are 92.2% for the first birth, 90.0% for the second birth, and 84.0% for the third birth; the censored cases were 21.2% for first birth, 18.5% for second, and 45.8% for third birth.

*p = .01.

second and third births. Shorter intervals between first and second birth increase the probability of a third birth, while having children of both sexes reduces the likelihood of a third child. After controls, the sex of the first child has no effect on the probability of a second child, but the likelihood of a third child is highest if the two previous children were of the same sex, particularly if they were both girls.

The effect of previous family history extends to the respondent's experience of her own childhood. That is, the respondent's number of siblings has a systematic effect on the likelihood of a given birth, with lower likelihood associated with fewer siblings. This effect is strongest in the case of the third birth, where the probability is reduced when the respondent herself has fewer than three siblings.

We have here combined marriage and cohabitations as unions, distinguishing women who are in a first union, a second or subsequent union, those are single (and never married) and those no longer in a union. Birth probabilities are higher for women in union. After controlling for other factors, first births are highest for women in a first union, followed by women who are in a second union, post-union, and single. For the second birth, the probabilities are also highest in first unions, while for the third birth, probabilities are highest in second or subsequent unions.

Turning to socioeconomic characteristics, education especially has an effect on the likelihood of a first birth, with higher probabilities of first births for women with lower levels of education. In the multivariate results, the opposite effect occurs for second births. Among women who have had a first birth, those with more education are now more likely to have a second birth. Third births are highest for women with no secondary diploma, and lowest for those with a secondary diploma but no postsecondary education. Measured as a time-variant covariate, being employed reduces the likelihood of given birth, with this effect being particularly strong for the first birth.

The last three variables in Table 2.3 concern cultural characteristics and values. There are systematic effects related to religious practice, with lower probabilities of given births among women who do not attend religious services on a weekly basis, especially if the religious practice is defined as 'not applicable' because no religious affiliation at all was given. The strongest effect of religious practice is for the third birth. There are also differences according to respondents' place of birth. After controls for other variables, women born in Canada have higher probabilities of second and third births. For first births, the important difference is that probabilities are lowest for women born outside of Canada, North America, or Europe.

The last question refers to values associated with marital dissolution. The question was, 'If you had young children (less than 15 years of age) and your marriage/common law union was in trouble and the differences with your spouse could not be resolved, would you still remain in your relationship for the sake of your child(ren)?' The question was only asked of persons who were married or cohabiting, so others are coded here as 'not applicable.' Those who answered that they would stay married had a higher likelihood of a second and especially a third birth. There are higher probabilities for the first birth among women who say they would not stay married, and lower probabilities for those who did not know if they would stay married. The 'not applicable' on this measure, that is, persons not in relationships at the time of the survey, had much lower probabilities of a first or second birth.

First Births

The likelihood of having a first birth, over the exposure time to the 2001 survey, is especially lower for women not in relationships, with more education, working, with few siblings, and not affiliated with a religion. It would appear that the lack of integration in relationships reduces the likelihood of a first birth, but first births are also reduced by greater integration in the labour force, by lack of religious affiliation, and by fewer siblings in the family of origin.

Second Births

While first births are equally likely in first unions as in second and subsequent unions, second births are more common in first unions. In contrast to first births, second births are most common for women who have postsecondary education. Women with higher education may be the ones most able to have a second birth, among women who have had a first birth. In another table (not shown), we found that the likelihood of second birth is also higher for women without work interruptions. The progression from first to second parity is high, and to some extent, those who have a first child simply go on to have a second. For instance, data from the United States suggest that certain values differentiate between women who have or do not have a first child, but neither women's nor men's values affected the likelihood of a second child (Thomson 2001). Judging from the 'not applicable' category on 'would stay married for the sake of children,' it is particularly women who are not in relationships who are less likely to have a second child.

That is, for those who had a first birth, the likelihood of a second would appear to be positively related both to integration in relationships and to integration in the labour market. On other dimensions of integration, second births are also higher for women who are more religious and for women born in Canada. On the basis of analyses from Sweden, the likelihood of a second child is enhanced by men's greater participation in unpaid family work (Olah 2003).

Third Births

Among women who have had a second birth, the likelihood of a third is lower for cohorts born after 1945, for those who were older at the birth of their first child, who had long birth intervals between the first two children, and when the previous children were of both genders. The probability of a third child was higher for women who were less integrated in the labour force, as measured by education and work status, but more integrated through religious practice and having more siblings.

Discussion

While there are clearly a number of priorities in life, for many Canadians children represent an irreplaceable value. Caldwell and Schindlmayr (2003) summarize that children provide a unique and different kind of fulfilment, they build up a network of relations, and they provide someone who will be there in old age. High standards for the care of children imply that large families are viewed as inconsistent with good parenting, given that each child is unique and deserves a substantial investment of parental time and energy (Morgan 2003). There is a common view that having one child is not the best for a child, especially in terms of forming close family relationships with others of one's own age. At the same time, the culture appears to allow much openness about the intention not to have children, and there is a prevalent view that people who do not want children should not have children. Also, when spousal preferences diverge, the common view is that one should not have a child unless both desire the child, and the relationship is considered to be stable.

It therefore makes sense that, before they experience the constraints associated with relationships and work, young people expect on average to have more than two children. At the same time, there are high expectations for consumption, a clear interest in having two-income families, much awareness of risk in employment security, and a cultural context that makes it legitimate not to have children when the financial basis for childbearing is judged inadequate.

Given the participation of both genders in the paid labour force, education is important for children of both sexes, and there is a long period of investment in oneself before investing in reproduction, for both men and women (Kaplan 1997). These delays mean that some people are unable to achieve the childbearing that represented one of their desired life goals. The patterns that we have reviewed in this chapter are consistent with the hypothesis that lack of integration in relationships represents a constraint on achieving desired childbearing. Economic conditions also influence family, partnership, and childbearing behaviour in a variety of ways. Given the importance attached to having childbearing occur in a context of economic and partnership security, many experience difficulties in achieving anticipated childbearing in the narrowed window of the late 20s and early 30s.

There are significant norms against having children too soon in life, which largely means not before age 20, and often not until the mid-20s, or until one is emotionally mature and financially secure. It is also largely seen as unacceptable to have children in insecure relationships. That leaves a small time frame to have children, and the window of opportunity might become closed if during that time the setting is not right to have children. For some there may be biological limitations, while others who put off having children may come to give higher priority to other life goals. It is noteworthy that rates of first and third births are highest among women who have the least education, while births of all parities are lowest for women who are working. In effect, while life is never completely within nor completely outside of families, Axinn and Yabiku (2001) make the observation that, as non-family organizations have spread, many activities of daily life have been relocated outside of families, reducing the importance of children as a means of social integration.

Low Fertility

Canada is not alone in experiencing fertility significantly below replacement levels (United Nations 2000; 2003). There is also much unexplained variation across these countries. In its analysis of low fertility, a United Nations (2003) publication focused on partnership behaviour, that is, the extent of marriage, timing of marriage, and the impact of cohabitation. Lapierre-Adamcyk and Lussier (2003) further observe that there has been a redefinition of all aspects that relate to reproduction: gender roles, relations between men and women, conjugal engagements, kin systems, and the links between parents and children.

Besides questions of labour market and partnership security, it would appear that fertility is higher in countries that have stronger policies in support of families and gender equality, and where there is greater acceptance of alternate forms of family living. These societal-level questions can be interpreted in terms of features that enhance the integration of various kinds of families.

Fertility is particularly low in southern Europe and Japan, where social security is heavily based on families and where women are forced into a tradeoff between careers and children (McDonald 1997; Chesnais 1996). It was once thought that the only way to go back to higher fertility was to constrain women to be housewives once again. On the contrary, the modern societies where women's domestic roles are more traditional have particularly low fertility, largely because women are not interested in absorbing so much of the cost of children if they have opportunities for equality in the market economy, at school, and at work. In these circumstances, childlessness is the easiest route to equality. In contrast, modernizing the family will reduce women's share of the costs of having children.

It would appear that societies that constrain people in the direction of only one model are at higher risk of low fertility. This occurs in Japan, where there are strong constraints against births outside of marriage. This may also apply to Italy and Spain, where the model is for young people to live with their parents until they get married. In contrast, fertility is higher in societies that are more open to cohabitation and to births in cohabiting relationships, as in the Nordic countries and France. That is, there are some aspects of postmodern family conditions that may pose fewer risks of particularly low fertility.

Another element of flexibility, as indicated by the contrast between southern and northern Europe, is the opportunity for part-time work. When the alternatives are full-time work or no work, there may not be adequate economic basis for childbearing unless there is a strong income on the part of a breadwinner. But part-time work, when it comes with strong benefits as in the case of Nordic countries, provides flexibility in terms of accommodating children. It is better for women's economic independence than no work and it can facilitate the return to full-time work once the family situation changes and there is less need for time in child care (Sundstrom 1991). It is best, of course, if this part-time work is better shared by both genders.

The examples of Norway, Sweden, and France suggest that policies that support families make a difference. The specific type of policy seems to matter less than the supportiveness of a set of policies that give parents and prospective parents a sense that the society will carry some of the cost of having children (Rosen 2001). Conversely, the example of Eastern Europe suggest, that movements in the direction of less family friendly policy are particularly problematic in terms of low fertility. Downsizing creates a fear of not knowing how much the benefits will be further reduced.

Societies may be in less danger of particularly low fertility if there is state support for families and for gender equality, and if families of various types are accepted. That is, childbearing can be integral to postmodern family conditions, which include the acceptance of births in cohabiting relationships, the degendering of caring activities, and the flexibility of opportunities for both part-time and full-time work.

At the same time, the example of the United States indicates that fertility can be relatively high in the context of a relative absence of supportive policy (see Bélanger and Ouellet 2002). In the United States, it may be the high employment rates that give prospective parents a sense of economic security, as was the case in Canada during the years immediately after the Second World War.

Integration in Relationships, in the Labour Market, and in the Broader Society

In a context where births are planned, it appears that many things need to be in place for individuals to have children, in spite of the strong desires for children. When justifying a smaller number of children, some respondents note matters of relationship insecurity, and they do not want more children than they could care for on their own. In historical circumstances, the close proximity of grandmothers benefited numbers of surviving children (Lahdenpera et al. 2004). In today's world, having the right partner increases the likelihood of having children. Besides integration in relationships and in a broader supportive family, many people are looking for the kind of relationships that will better distribute the costs of having children, through the sharing of associated family work.

Integration in the labour market is important both as a high priority for individuals and as a means of absorbing the costs of children. The preference for two-income families means delays as both careers are being established, and sometimes it means lack of opportunities to have children. In other cases, prospective parents with secure jobs can take advantage of leave benefits. In the United States, it may be that the high employment rates permit temporary departures from the labour force, in the knowledge that there will be employment opportunities when one wants to return to work.

There are broader questions at stake, including the importance of family supportive policy and economic security, that can be interpreted as integration in community and society. Reflecting on the thinking of early philosophers, Cunningham (2000) proposes that social cohesion can be seen as alliances across areas of differentiation, such as gender, age, race, or social class, based on inclusion and equality. In important ways, family projects are such alliances, at least as defined in terms of sharing responsibility for earning a living and caring for each other.

Family projects mostly involve building cohesion across genders and generations, within and across households. The common project of children can go beyond kin, to communities and societies. The supportive nature of communities in terms of childcare and other child-friendly structures, and of societies in terms of provisions for families with children, not only absorb some of the costs of having children, but they ultimately enhance the very continuity of the society.

In contrast, low fertility can undermine the solvency of intergenerational arrangements, particularly regarding pensions and health care. Observing the 'decisive shift to an older age structure' in Europe and other advanced societies, Lutz et al. (2003) propose that this shift 'will challenge social security and health systems, may hinder productivity gains, and could affect global competitiveness and economic growth. It could also strain relations among generations, particularly between those who are on the contributing and receiving ends of public transfer programs.'

These authors go on to propose that childbearing should come to be seen as a 'social act' rather than a purely private decision, and thus reproduction should be supported by policies ranging from childcare and flexibility in work arrangements to subsidizing some of the direct costs of having children.

REFERENCES

Ariès, Philippe. 1980. 'Two Successive Motivations for the Declining Birth Rate in the West.' *Population and Development Review* 6(4): 645–50.

Axinn, William, and Scott Yabiku. 2001. 'Social Change, the Social Organization of Families, and Fertility Limitation.' *American Journal of Sociology* 106(5): 1219–61.

Beaujot, Roderic. 1995. 'Family Patterns at Mid–Life (Marriage, Parenting and Working).' In R. Beaujot, Ellen M. Gee, Fernando Rajulton, and Zenaida Ravanera (eds.), *Family over the Life Course*. Ottawa: Statistics Canada, cat. no. 91-543.

– 2000. *Earning and Caring in Canadian Families*. Peterborough, ON: Broadview.

– 2004. *Delayed Life Transitions: Trends and Implications*. Contemporary Family Trends Paper on The Modern Life Course. Ottawa: Vanier Institute of the Family.

Beaujot, Roderic, and Alain Bélanger. 2001. 'Perspective on Below Replacement Fertility in Canada: Trends, Desires, Accommodations.' Paper presented at the International Union for the Scientific Study of Population, Working Group on Low Fertility Meeting, Tokyo, 21–3 March. Available as: http://www.ssc.uwo.ca/sociology/popstudies/dp/dp01-6.pdf.

Beaujot, Roderic, and Amir Efrani. 2004. 'Attitudes that Differentiate Alternative Family Sizes.' Paper presented at the meetings of the Population Association of America, Boston, 1–3 April.

Beaujot, Roderic, and Don Kerr. 2004. *Population Change in Canada*. Toronto: Oxford University Press.

Beaujot, Roderic, and Zenaida Ravanera. 2003. 'Relative Participation of Men and Women in Paid and Unpaid Work: An Analysis of Variations by Individual, Family and Community Characteristics.' Paper presented at the meetings of the Canadian Sociology and Anthropology Association, Halifax, 31 May–5 June.

Becker, Gary. 1981. *A Treatise on the Family*. Cambridge, MA: Harvard University Press.

Bélanger, Alain. 2000. 'Reflections on the Evolution of Components of Demographic Growth in Canada in the Context of the Triennial Review of the Canada Pension Plan.' Paper presented at the Seminar on Demographic and Economic Perspectives of Canada, Years 2000 to 2050, Ottawa, 17 March.

– 2003. *Report on the Demographic Situation in Canada 2002*. Ottawa: Statistics Canada, cat. no. 91–209.

Bélanger, Alain, and Jean Dumas. 1998. *Report on the Demographic Situation in Canada 1997*. Ottawa: Statistics Canada, cat. no. 91-209.

Bélanger, Alain, and Cathy Oikawa. 1999. 'Who Has a Third Child?' *Canadian Social Trends* 53: 23–6.

Bélanger, Alain, and Geneviève Ouellet. 2002. AA Comparative Study of Recent Trends in Canadian and American Fertility, 1980–1999.' In A. Bélanger (eds.), *Report on the Demographic Situation in Canada 2001*, 107–36. Ottawa: Statistics Canada, cat. no. 91–209.

Bianchi, Suzanne. 2000. 'Maternal Employment and Time with Children: Dramatic Change or Surprising Continuity?' *Demography* 37(4): 401–14.

Caldwell, John C. 1997. 'The Global Fertility Transition: The Need for a Unifying Theory.' *Population and Development Review* 23(4): 803–12.

Caldwell, John, and Thomas Schindlmayr. 2003. 'Explanations of the Fertility Crisis in Modern Societies: A Search for Commonalities.' *Population Studies* 57(3): 241–64.

Chesnais, J. 1996. 'Fertility, Family and Social Policy in Contemporary Western Europe.' *Population and Development Review* 22(4): 729–39.

Cunningham, Frank. 2000. 'Social Cohesion: Philosophical Perspectives.' Presented at the Workshop on Globalization and Social Cohesion. Toronto, 27–8 Oct.

Currie, Dawn. 1988. 'Re-thinking What We Do and How We Do It: A Study of Reproductive Decisions.' *Canadian Review of Sociology and Anthropology* 25(2): 231–53.

Dumas, Jean, and Alain Bélanger. 1997. *Report on the Demographic Situation in Canada 1996*. Ottawa: Statistics Canada, cat. no. 91–209.

Dupuis, Dave. 1998. 'What Influences People's Plans to Have Children?' *Canadian Social Trends* 48: 2–5.

Folbre, Nancy. 1983. 'Of Patriarchy Born: The Political Economy of Fertility Decisions.' *Feminist Studies* 92(2): 261–84.

Friedman, Debra, Michael Hechter, and Satoshi Kanazawa. 1994. 'A Theory of the Value of Children.' *Demography* 31(3): 375–401.

Giddens, Anthony. 1991. *Modernity and Self-Identity: Self and Society in the Late Modern Age*. Cambridge: Polity Press.

Goldscheider, Frances, and Linda J. Waite. 1991. *New Families, No Families?* Berkeley: University of California Press.

Hall, David. 2002. 'Risk Society and the Second Demographic Transition.' *Canadian Studies in Population* 29(2): 173–93.

– 2003. 'The Pure Relationship and Below Replacement Fertility.' *Canadian Studies in Population* 30(1): 51–70.

Kaplan, Hillard. 1997. 'The Evolution of the Human Life Course.' In K. Wachter and C. Finch (eds.), *Between Zeus and the Salmon: The Biodemography of Longevity*, 175–21. Washington, DC: National Acadamy Press.

Kempeneers, Marianne. 1992. *Le Travail au féminin*. Montreal: Presses de l'Université de Montréal.

Keyfitz, Nathan. 1994. 'Preface.' *Cahiers Québécois de Démographie* 23(1): 3–10.

Lahdenpera, Mirkka, Virpi Lummaa, Samuli Helle, Marc Tremblay, and Andrew Russell. 2004. 'Fitness Benefits of Prolonged Post-reproductive Lifespan in Women.' *Nature* 428(6979): 178.

Lapierre-Adamcyk, Evelyne, and Marie-Hélène Lussier. 2003. 'De la forte fécondité à la fécondité désirée.' In V. Piché and C. Le Bourdais (eds.), *La démographie québécoise: Enjeux du XXie siècle*, 66–109. Montreal: Presses de l'Université de Montréal.

Le Bourdais, Céline, Ghyslaine Neill, and Nathalie Vachon. 2000. 'Family Disruption in Canada: Impact of Changing Patterns of Family Formation and of Female Employment.' *Canadian Studies in Population* 27(1): 85–105.

Le Bourdais, Céline, Ghyslaine Neill, and Pierre Turcotte. 2000. 'The Changing Face of Conjugal Relationships.' *Canadian Social Trends* 56: 14–17.

Lesthaeghe, Ron. 1995. 'The Second Demographic Transition in Western Countries: An Interpretation.' In K. Oppenheim Mason and A.–M. Jensen (eds.), *Gender and Family Change in Industrialized Countries*, 17–62. Oxford: Clarendon.

Lesthaeghe, Ron, and K. Neels. 2002. 'From the First to the Second Demographic Transition: An Interpretation of the Spatial Continuity of Demographic Innovation in France, Belgium and Switzerland.' *European Journal of Population* 18(4): 325–60.

Lesthaeghe, Ron, and Guy Moors. 2000. *Recent Trends in Fertility and Household Formation in the Industrialized World*. Interuniversity Papers in Demography, WP 2000–2. Brussels: Vrije Universteit Brussel.

Lesthaeghe, Ron, and Johan Surkyn. 1988. 'Cultural Dynamics and Economic Theories of Fertility Change.' *Population and Development Review* 14(1): 1–46.

Livi Bacci, Massimo. 2001. 'Desired Family Size and the Future Course of Fertility.' *Population and Development Review* 27 (suppl.): 282–9.

Lochhead, Clarence. 2000. 'The Trend toward Delayed First Childbirth: Health and Social Implications.' *ISUMA: Canadian Jorunal of Policy Research*. 1(2): 41–4.

Lutz, Wolfgang, Brian O'Neill, and Sergei Scherbov. 2003. 'Europe's Population at a Turning Point.' *Science* 299: 1991–2.

Marcil-Gratton, N. 1993. 'Growing Up with a Single Parent: A Transitional Experience? Some Demographic Measurements from the Children's Point of View.' In J. Hudson and Galaway (eds.), *Single Parent Families, Perspectives on Research and Policy*, 73–90. Toronto: Thompson.

Marcil-Gratton, N., and C. Le Bourdais. 1999. *Custody, Access and Child Sup-*

port: Findings from the National Longitudinal Survey of Children and Youth. Research Report Child Support Team CSR-1999-3E. Ottawa: Department of Justice.

Martin, S.P. 2000. 'Diverging Fertility among U.S. Women Who Delay Childbearing Past Age 30.' *Demography* 37(4): 523–33.

Matthews, Beverly. 1999. 'The Gender System and Fertility: An Exploration of the Hidden Links.' *Canadian Studies in Population* 26(1): 21–38.

McDaniel, Susan. 1989. 'Reconceptualizing the Nuptiality/Fertility Relationship in Canada in a New Age.' *Canadian Studies in Population* 16(2): 163–85.

McDonald, Peter. 1997. 'Gender Equity, Social Institutions and the Future of Fertility.' Working Papers in Demography, No. 69. Canberra: Australian National University.

– 2000. 'Gender Equity in Theories of Fertility.' *Population and Development Review* 26(3): 427–39.

– 2002. 'Low Fertility: Unifying the Theory and the Demography.' Paper presented at the meetings of the Population Association of America, Atlanta, 9–11 May.

Mongeau, Jael, Ghyslaine Neill, and Céline Le Bourdais. 2001. 'Effet de la précarité économique sur la formation d'une première union au Canada.' *Cahiers Québécois de démographie* 30(1): 3–28.

Morgan, Philip. 2003. 'Is Low Fertility a Twenty-First-Century Demographic Crisis?' *Demography* 40(4): 589–604.

Ni Bhrolchain, Maire. 1993. 'Women's and Men's Life Strategies in Developed Societies.' Paper presented, at the meetings of the International Union for the Scientific Study of Population, Montreal, 24 Aug. – 1 Sept.

Nomaguchi, K.M., and Milkie, M.A. 2003. 'Costs and Rewards of Children: The Effects of Becoming a Parent on Adults' Lives.' *Journal of Marriage and the Family* 65(2): 356–74.

Olah, Livia. 2003. 'Gendering Fertility: Second Births in Sweden and Hungary.' *Population Research and Policy Review* 22(2): 171–200.

Péron, Yves, E. Lapierre-Adamcyk, and Denis Morissette. 1987. 'Les répercussions des nouveaux comportements démographiques sur la vie familiale: la situation canadienne.' *International Review of Community Development* 18(58): 57–66.

Ranson, Gillian. 1998. 'Education, Work and Family Decision Making: Finding the Right Time to Have a Baby.' *Canadian Review of Sociology and Anthropology* 35(4): 517–33.

Rindfuss, Ronald, Karin Brewster, and Andrew Kovee. 1996. 'Women, Work and Children: Behavioral and Attitudinal Change in the United States.' *Population and Development Review* 22(3): 457–82.

Rosen, Marit. 2001. 'Fertility and Family Policy in Norway: Is There a Connection?' Paper presented at the meetings of the International Union for the Scientific Study of Population, Working Group on Low Fertility, Tokyo, March 21–23, 2001.

Rutledge, Margie. 1998. 'Motherhood and the Muse.' *Globe and Mail*, 7 Nov. 1998, D1-D2.

Schoen, Robert, N.M. Astone, Y.J. Kim, and C.A. Nathanson. 1999. 'Do Fertility Interactions Affect Fertility Behavior?' *Journal of Marriage and the Family* 61(3): 790–9.

Schoen, Robert, Young J. Kim, Constance A. Nathanson, Jason Fields, and Nan Marie Astone. 1997. 'Why Do Americans Want Children?' *Population and Development Review* 23(2): 333–58.

Statistics Canada. 2003. *General Social Survey of Canada, 2001. Cycle 15: Family History. Public Use Microdata File Documentation and User's Guide.* Cat. No. 12M0015GPE. Ottawa: Ministry of Industry.

Sundstrom, M. 1991. 'Part-Time Work in Sweden: Trends and Equity Effects.' *Journal of Economic Issues* 25(1): 167–78.

Thomson, Elizabeth. 1997. 'Couple Childbearing Desires, Intentions and Births.' *Demography* 34(3): 343–54.

– 2001. *Motherhood, Fatherhood, and Family Values*. Madison, WI: University of Wisconsin-Madison, National Survey of Families and Households Working Paper, no. 88.

Thornton, Arland. 2001. 'The Developmental Paradigm, Reading History Sideways, and Family Change.' *Demography* 38(4): 449–65.

Tolke, Angelika, and Martin Diewald. 2003. 'Insecurities in Employment and Occupational Careers and Their Impact on the Transition to Fatherhood in Western Germany.' *Demographic Research*. On-line journal available at: *http://www.demographic-research.org*.

Turcotte, Pierre, and Frances Goldscheider. 1998. 'Evolution of Factors Influencing First Union Formation in Canada.' *Canadian Studies in Population* 25(2): 145–73.

United Nations. 2000. *Below Replacement Fertility: Population Bulletin of the United Nations*, Special Issue, nos. 40/41.

– 2003. *Partnership and Reproductive Behaviour in Low-Fertility Countries*. New York: United Nations, ESA/P/WP. 177.

Van de Kaa, Dirk. 1987. 'Europe's Second Demographic Transition.' *Population Bulletin* 42(1): 1–58.

– 2001. 'Postmodern Fertility Preferences: From Changing Value Orientation to New Behavior.' *Population and Development Review* 27 (suppl.): 290–331.

Wu, Zheng. 1999. 'Premarital Cohabitation and the Timing of First Marriage.' *Canadian Review of Sociology and Anthropology* 36(1): 109–27.

– 2000. *Cohabitation: An Alternative Form of Family Living.* Toronto: Oxford University Press.

Wu, Zheng and Hui Wang, 1998. 'Third Birth Intentions and Uncertainty in Canada.' *Social Biology* 45(1/2): 96–112.

3 A Balancing Act: Parents' Work Arrangements and Family Time

EVELYNE LAPIERRE-ADAMCYK, NICOLE MARCIL-GRATTON, AND CÉLINE LE BOURDAIS

Since the middle of the twentieth century the Canadian family has evolved dramatically, in particular because of the impetus of the massive entry of women into the labour force. At the outset, labour force participation was usually reserved for single and childless women, but it gradually extended to mothers of school-aged children, and finally also to mothers of young children. As a result, families where both parents work outside the home have become commonplace. This new reality entails aspects that profoundly modify the framework in which the relationships between men and women are expressed and within which couples raise their children.

Furthermore, for more than fifteen years now, changes in the labour market have created a new employment dynamic that has repercussions on working conditions and that affects family life. Thus, we observe an increase in 'non-standard' work, that is, temporary employment, jobs where the work is done at home rather than the workplace, part-time jobs in contrast to full-time work, and jobs outside conventional working hours, such as in the evening, at night, or on the weekend (Beaujot 2000; Presser 1999). On the one hand, the labour market, given its productivity goals, lays down the rules for those who work. On the other hand, those who wish to work can also have access to forms of employment other than 'standard' work, which allow some to pursue objectives beyond simply earning a living.

Do these new realities have ramifications for family life? When both parents in a family are faced with the imperatives of the workplace to earn enough money to support their family decently is the quality of family life threatened by the complexity of the parents' work arrangements (Presser 1989)? This question is particularly relevant since the model of a stable family based on marriage has been shaken by the development of conjugal instability and by the increase in cohabitation and stepfamilies. The image of the stable family of yesteryear, which was not all that long ago, endures in the popular imagination as a positive element of children's and adults' well-being. Similarly, the family based on a complementary division of tasks between men and women, and which guaranteed constant supervision of the children, seems reassuring, even in a context where reality is largely disassociated from these models (Bielby and Bielby 1989).

This chapter focuses on the search for a balance between the time necessary for a fulfilling family life for parents and their offspring, work arrangements for the parents which meet their professional aspirations, and the need to provide a comfortable standard of living for the family. Some studies, including that by Benoît Rapoport and Céline Le Bourdais, reported in Chapter 4, employ the term *parental time*, which puts emphasis on the time that men and women, respectively, devote to the raising of their children. Here the perspective is slightly different and suggests a consideration of the time when all the family members can join in common activities. It is, thus, the concept of *family time* that interests us. Intuitively and logically, it is considered necessary and even desirable that the members of a family are able to spend time together for joint activities. The traditional model of the family where the father works outside the home and the mother takes charge of the children's upbringing and household tasks implied straight-away that the father would not be available for family life during his hours at work. Furthermore, once children reached school age, they also were unavailable for sharing activities with their family during five days in the week. This is still the case in the new models of the family that are emerging. However, in the new model, where the mother increasingly works outside the home, maternal time is reduced when her work schedule demands that another caregiver replace her in minding her young children. To avoid having recourse to one or another form of childcare services, the mother may opt for work where her hours will be complementary to those of the father who, in turn, could look after the children while she is at work. This type of solution would maximize the time when the children are in the presence of at least one of their parents, but would lessen the time when all members of the family are together. Mothers' employment, corresponding both to the wish of women to participate in the workforce and the economic necessity of maintaining a satisfactory standard of living, could be envisaged as part of a strategy that would permit the attainment of the desired balance between parental time, if not family time, and economic well-being (Bianchi, 2000; Marcil-Gratton and Le Bourdais 2000; Lapierre-Adamcyk et al. 2004).

Diversity and Complexity in Parents' Work Arrangements

Previous research based on the Canadian National Longitudinal Survey of Children and Youth (NLSCY), which includes data on the professional situation of both parents, has shed light on the diversity and complexity of patterns of employment (Marcil-Gratton and Le Bourdais 2000; Lapierre-Adamcyk et al., 2002). In short, these studies show that in 72% of Canadian two-parent families with children under 12 years of age both parents are employed; in 25% one parent is working, and in only 3% is neither parent in the labour force. In 45% of families both parents work full-time, that is, thirty hours or more a week each. Furthermore, 29% of families have at least one parent who is in the labour force part-time.

If the traditional model of father as sole breadwinner has lost its place under pressure of the increasing incidence of working mothers, father's full-time employment remains the norm. When the family resorts to part-time work, it is the father who works full-time in 87% of cases. Moreover, when only one parent works, it is the father working full-time in 89% of cases. Among all families with children under 12, 48% of mothers work full-time, as do 92% of fathers.

The diversity of work arrangements also raises the issue of regular shifts (in the daytime from Monday to Friday) versus atypical shifts (evenings, nights, or weekends). In only 24% of all two-parent families both parents work regular shifts; in contrast, in 16% both have atypical shifts, of which 43% are identical. In the latter case, one may suppose that the parents are available at the same time, which encourages family time; they must, however, entrust their offspring to others when they are at work. Finally, 32% of families have one parent with a conventional shift and another whose schedule is atypical (Lapierre-Adamcyk et al. 2002). A more detailed analysis reveals that 48% of fathers who work have atypical shifts, while among working mothers the proportion is 41%. Moreover, when one of the parents has a conventional working schedule and the other has an atypical one, 58% of the time it is the father who has the atypical employment schedule.

When only the father works, 50% have atypical schedules; when only the mother works, 46% have atypical schedules.

Thus, contrary to what emerges from an examination of the full-time or part-time presence of fathers or mothers in the workforce, which shows that the traditional model of the father who devotes himself to work outside the home and the mother who focuses on family life seems to endure in a 'diluted fashion,' the adoption of atypical schedules, as common among fathers as mothers, raises issues more likely to be related to the requirements of the labour force and the characteristics of parents' occupations.

This chapter explores how parents balance family time and work in studying three questions: Does the variety of work patterns allow for a satisfactory standard of living for families, given the constraints related to the labour market requirements? Do the work patterns correspond to a family strategy? Does the adoption of complex working arrangements create living conditions with negative consequences for the quality of family life?

Population Studied and Source of Data

The population studied corresponds to Canadian two-parent families with at least one child aged 0 to 11 years, inclusively. The case of single parents deserves particular attention and some policy aspects of that question are addressed in Chapter 9.

This analysis is based on the first cycle of the Canadian National Longitudinal Survey of Children and Youth (NLSCY) done by Statistics Canada and Human Resources Development Canada (Statistics Canada 1997). It is a survey of a representative sample of 22,831 Canadian children aged 0 to 11 years in 1994–5, including 18,562 children in 10,978 two-parent families. For the purposes of this analysis, the sample of children was weighted to represent families with children less than 12 years old. The survey contains information on the work arrangements of both parents in the course of the previous year, on the conjugal and parental history of both parents, and on household income, as well as giving some indications of the quality of family life.

Relationship between Employment Patterns and Family Income

Do certain work arrangements allow for a higher income level? More particularly, given the focus of this analysis, does the pattern of work that competes the most with family time allow for an enviable lifestyle? Could one say that the deterioration of family time occasioned by the recourse to atypical working hours is compensated for by the attainment of a middle-class or better standard of living? Difficult question! In addressing it, we will examine three aspects successively.

Employment and Variations in Family Income

Workforce participation is based on whether or not parents worked in the course of the year prior to the survey, and whether they generally worked full-time or part-time. The classification includes six categories: both parents working full-time (44.7%); the father working full-time, and the mother part-time (25.3%); the mother full-time and the father part-time (1.6%); the father full-time and the mother at home (22.0%); a residual category including non-working fathers with working mothers, as well as both parents part-time (3.6%); and, finally, neither parent working (2.8%).

Family income varies as a function of labour force participation. When both parents work full-time, their annual income on average is $65,600. When the mother or father works part-time, the family has a lower income: the difference is around 12%. On the other hand, when the mother withdraws completely from the labour force, the average income represents only 69% of that of families with both parents working full-time. The contrast is striking: families with only one income have fewer resources than others. Moreover, the relatively small categories where parents have a weak (3.6%) or inexistent labour force participation (2.8%) have, respectively, average incomes that represent 52% and 30% of families' income where both parents work full-time.

Although the level of income is an important element, it reveals only part of the picture. A high income may just suffice to guarantee a comfortable standard of living for a large family, while a lower income may prove ample for a small family. An indicator of family income adequacy, which takes into account both income and the needs of the family, while considering the number of people it includes, is a useful instrument to better assess the impact of parents' choices. The indicator suggested by Statistics Canada in the NLSCY database, termed *adequate income*, comprises five categories defined in the following fashion:

1 Families with very insufficient resources: annual income below
   $10,000 for three or four people; below $15,000 for five people or more

2 Families with insufficient resources: annual income between $10,000 and $19,999 for three or four people; between $15,000 and $29,999 for five people or more

3 Families with tight budgets: annual income between $20,000 and $39,999 for three or four people; between $30,000 and $59,999 for five people or more

4 Comfortable families: annual income between $40,000 and $79,999 for three or four people; between $60,000 and $79,999 for five people or more

5 Very comfortable families: annual income higher than $80,000 for three people or more

While this indicator is rather arbitrary, it seems a better instrument than income for comparing the well-being of families.

Figure 3.1 shows the distribution of families with children under 12 years of age, according to the parents' employment and the family income adequacy. Overall, we find 1% of families whose income is very insufficient, 9% who have insufficient income, 30% whose budget is tight, 42% who are comfortable, and 18% who are very comfortable. This distribution varies markedly as a function of labour force participation. To highlight these differences, the sum of disadvantaged categories ('tight budget,' 'insufficient resources,' and 'very insufficient resources') will be mainly used:

- Overall, these people represent about 40% of the sample, of whom a quarter have insufficient income;
- This proportion falls to 24% where both parents work full-time; these families, moreover, constitute only 0.2% of very disadvantaged families.
- Where one parent works part-time, the proportion becomes to 36% and 42%, according to whether it is the mother or father who reduces the hours at work.
- Where only the father works full-time, the proportion in the three categories reaches 59%; thus, for the majority of these families, the budget is tight, while for one-quarter of them it is insufficient.
- Where the employment of both parents is reduced or non-existent, the proportions reach 78% and 97%; among these disadvantaged families, the proportion whose resources are markedly inadequate varies: from 46% where both parents work part-time to 81% where both are unemployed. It is worth recalling that these two categories

Figure 3.1 Distribution of two-parent – mother (M) and father (F) – families (%) by labour force participation – full-time (FT), part-time (PT), or unemployed (U) – and income adequacy, Canada.

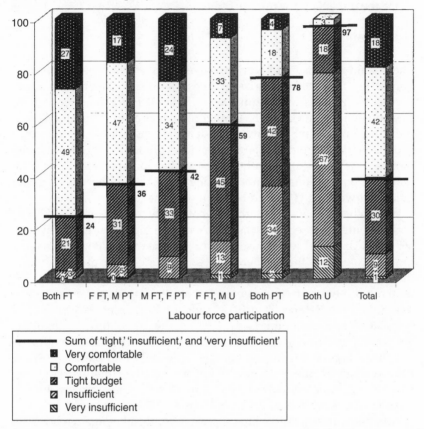

Labour force participation

Sum of 'tight,' 'insufficient,' and 'very insufficient'
■ Very comfortable
□ Comfortable
▨ Tight budget
▨ Insufficient
◩ Very insufficient

Source: NLSCY 1994–95

constitute only 6% of all families with children aged 0 to 11 years.
• Furthermore, the proportion of the most financially comfortable families does not exceed 30% in any employment/no employment category.

In sum, it is evident that families in which only the father is employed have lower incomes than those where both parents are in the workforce, but they are also more likely either to have just enough to meet their needs or to have insufficient resources. If this situation results from a strategy for maximizing family time, it turns out that there is a high price to be paid in terms of the standard of living. It will be interesting to see the impact on the quality of life.

Work Schedules and Variations in Family Income

The second dimension of work arrangements which especially affects family time is related to work schedules. Here are the ten relevant categories: two parents with regular work hours (24%); the father regular, the mother atypical (13%); the mother regular, the father atypical (19%); the father and the mother atypical, identical schedules (7%); the father and the mother atypical, different schedules (9%); the father regular, the mother at home (11%); the father atypical, the mother at home (11%); the mother regular, the father not working (1%); the mother atypical, the father not working (1%); and both not working (3%).

Work schedules also affect the level of family income. Families where both parents have regular schedules earn the highest average income: $67,148. Compared with those families, all the other categories have a lower income. For those where only one parent works atypical hours, the reduction is 7% or 11%, according to whether it is the father or mother who works in the evenings, at night, or during the weekends. The negative difference is also 12% when both parents have identical atypical schedules, but it is larger (18%) in the case of those with different schedules. Moreover, in comparison with families where both parents have regular schedules, families with only one parent working have average incomes that are 31% lower when the father works at regular hours, 36% lower when he has atypical schedules; the corresponding differences are 45% and 52% when the mother is at work.

To explore these relationships in greater depth, let us again rely on the indicator of family income adequacy. Three groups of families will be considered: families where both parents work full-time (44.7%); families where the father works full-time and the mother part-time (25.3%); and families where only one parent works full-time and the other does not work (23.6%). These three groups include the vast majority of families and reflect the major alternative models for reconciling family and labour force participation. The excluded two-parent families, where the link to the labour force is non-existent or very weak, are few (6.4%) and doubtless exhibit particular characteristics that cannot be taken into account here.

Figure 3.2 Distribution of families (%) where both parents – mother (M) and father (F) – work full-time (FT) by work schedules – regular (R) and atypical (A), identical (I) or different (D) – and income adequacy, Canada.

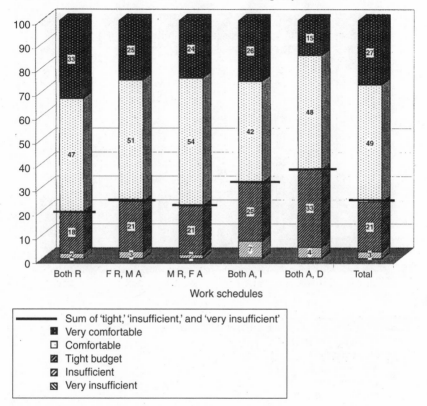

Source: NLSCY 1994–95

Figure 3.2 shows the distribution of families where both parents work full-time. On the whole, only 24% of these families have a restricted or insufficient budget. This proportion drops to 20% where both parents have regular schedules. It rises slightly where one of the two has an atypical schedule. The proportion is, however, substantially higher when both schedules are atypical: 32% for the identical schedules, 37% for different schedules. Moreover, it is noteworthy that the proportion of most financially comfortable families is only 15% for

Figure 3.3 Distribution of families (%) where the father (F) works full-time (FT) and the mother (M) works part-time (PT), by work schedules – regular (R) and atypical (A), identical (I) or different (D) – and income adequacy, Canada.

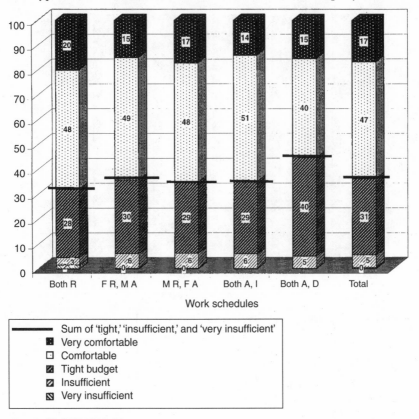

Work schedules

Sum of 'tight,' 'insufficient,' and 'very insufficient'
■ Very comfortable
□ Comfortable
▨ Tight budget
▧ Insufficient
◩ Very insufficient

Source: NLSCY 1994–95

those where both parents have different atypical schedules, in comparison with 25% among other families who cope with one atypical work schedule, and 33% where both parents have regular schedules.

Figure 3.3 focuses on families where the father works full-time and the mother part-time. The picture is appreciably the same as for families where both parents work full-time, but the proportion of families with tight budgets and in difficulty is higher, around 36%. This proportion, which is slightly lower for families where both parents work reg-

Figure 3.4   Distribution of families (%) where one parent – mother (M) or
father (F) – only is working full-time (FT) and the other is unemployed (U),
by work schedules – regular (R) and atypical (A), identical (I) or different (D) –
and income adequacy, Canada.

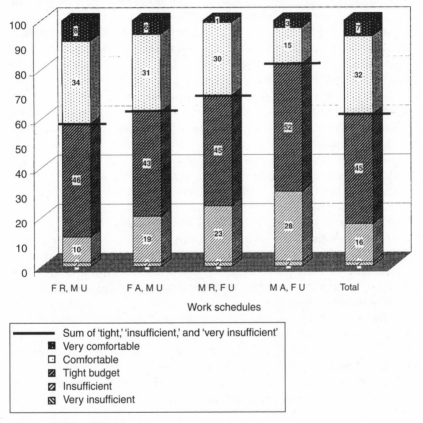

Source: NLSCY 1994–95

ular hours (33%), increases dramatically for families where the two
atypical work schedules are different (45%). The proportion of financially very comfortable families varies only slightly among those
whose work schedule is atypical (from 14% to 17%).

Finally figure 3.4 shows families where one parent is employed and
the other stays at home. In this case, as one might have expected, the

proportion of families with a tight or insufficient budget reaches 58% to 82%. When it is the father who works, the increase related to atypical hours is 6 percentage points (from 58% to 64%), while when it is the mother, it is 12 points (from 70% to 82%).

To interpret these results accurately, we must bear in mind that the regularity of working hours is doubtless partly the result of a free choice by individuals, but that this liberty is restricted by the requirements of the occupation itself. One could maintain that individuals are expressing their choice primarily at the time of selecting the occupation by which they hope to earn a living. Once the choice is made, men and women must find employment and submit themselves to the requirements of the labour market. The latter may, moreover, accommodate individual wishes, but they also constitute constraints which are often inescapable. Thus, certain sectors will offer few jobs outside regular work hours, whereas others, in contrast, will offer few which do not necessitate working evenings, nights, or during the weekend (Lapierre-Adamcyk et al. 2002; 2004; Presser 1999; Beaujot 2000). However, parents, most often mothers, may very well choose to work in a field because it offers positions with atypical schedules; this is often possible when the required qualifications to work are less specialized. From this perspective, it is worth examining employment sectors in which parents earn a living, since 60% of the families doubtless see their family time reduced by the atypical work schedule of at least one of the parents.

When both parents work, the proportion of fathers whose schedule is atypical does not vary appreciably from families where only the father works, overall, 48% instead of 50%. Taking into account the work schedules of mothers evidently increases the importance of non-standard work across families (data not shown). While 66% of families where both parents are employed are affected by this type of schedule, this proportion varies as a function of the father's employment sector. It is only 48% when the father is in education, but exceeds 75% in the health sector, in the services, and the primary sector. Where the mother's occupation is used to categorize the families, the picture that emerges is consistent with that derived from an examination of the fathers' employment sectors; certain employment sectors have a strong influence on the adoption of atypical schedules.

We note that in the families where the father has employment with standard work hours, 30% to 40% will see their family time reduced by the mother's atypical schedule. When the mother has standard work hours, these percentages increase and vary from 35% to 50%.

From this descriptive analysis, the following results emerge: the participation of both parents in the workforce allows them to obtain a higher standard of living. Families where both parents work full-time are in the most favourable position, whether one considers the average income or the indicator of income adequacy. On the contrary, families where only one parent works, usually the father, see their average income diminish, and the percentage of families with a tight or insufficient budget grows. Thus, part-time work appears to be a means of permitting most families to attain or preserve a certain financial comfort, because it allows them to maintain an income not very different from that of better-off families and to maintain a comfortable budget in 60% of the cases. This picture becomes more complex when one considers the schedules of work. Standard work hours are linked to higher income and permit a greater proportion of families to attain financial comfort. When two parents must adopt atypical hours, they are strongly disadvantaged, above all when the schedules are different.

Relative Importance of Employment Patterns and Work Schedules on Adequacy of Family Income

Given that work schedules and employment sectors appear to be related, one needs to control for both variables when assessing the impact of work arrangements on access to financial well-being. Multivariate analysis allows us to do so. Table 3.1 displays the results of a logistic regression analysis conducted separately on families where both parents work full-time and on those where the father works full-time and the mother part-time. In the former group of families, the gross coefficients confirm the results of the descriptive analysis. Compared with parents who both have standard shifts (reference category), we see that the adoption of an atypical schedule has a negative impact on access to financial well-being, resulting in a reduction by 21 percentage points of the probability of being in the more comfortable financial categories when one of the parents has an atypical schedule. The reduction is considerably greater when both parents work outside of regular hours, especially when their schedules are not the same. The introduction of control variables related to the mother and family char-

TABLE 3.1 Impact of Parents' Work Schedules on the Probability of Being in Financially Comfortable Categories. (Logistic Regression: Odd ratios)

Schedules	Model A	Model B[a]	Model C[b]
Families where both parents work full-time			
2 regular	1.000	1.000	1.000
1 regular, 1 atypical	0.791***	0.847*	0.983
2 atypical, but the same	0.495***	0.565***	0.815
2 atypical, but not the same	0.389***	0.442***	0.674***
Families where father works full-time and mother part-time			
2 regular	1.000	1.000	1.000
1 regular, 1 atypical	0.859	0.891	1.000
2 atypical, but the same	0.915	1.060	1.270
2 atypical, but not the same	0.603***	0.663***	0.766*

Source: NLSCY 1994–95.
[a] Controlled for age of children, mother's age and educational level, type of family (intact or step).
[b] Controlled for age of children, mother's age and educational level, type of family (intact or step), parents' employment sectors.
*$p < .05$; **$p < .01$; ***$p < .001$.

acteristics diminishes the impact of atypical shifts slightly, but all the coefficients still remain strongly significant. Nonetheless, the addition of parents' employment sectors into the analysis emphatically reduces this effect, and it only remains significant when the parents' schedules differ. Thus, it is principally through the effect of the employment sector, which is associated with the regularity of work schedules, that the repercussions of atypical work on income adequacy are felt.

In the second group of families, those where the father works full-time and the mother part-time, the negative effect of atypical work arrangements on the access to financial well-being is only significant when both parents work different shifts. In effect, the latter see their prospects of attaining financial well-being reduced by 23% compared to with parents with regular schedules, once the control variables, including employment sectors, are taken into account. These results would indicate that parents, in their search for economic well-being, must make sacrifices in terms of family time. But, these sacrifices could well have positive effects on parental time since, when schedules differ, we may suppose that at least one of the parents remains with the children.

Parents' Work Arrangements: The Result of a Family Strategy?

The examination of the relationships between the working arrangements adopted by parents of young children and the economic well-being of their family leads to the question of whether, in many families, work arrangements result from the deliberate choice of parents who, while pursuing their economic goals, aim to ensure an optimal parental presence for their children. These families would attempt to maximize either parental time by ensuring the presence of one of the parents, or family time by favouring schedules that allow all members of the family, parents and children, to be together for joint activities. Consideration of the number and age of children allows us to develop several hypotheses in this regard.

Table 3.2 presents the distribution of families according to the number and age of the children; the upper half of the table presents this information according to parents' full-time or part-time employment status, and, the lower half according to parents' work schedules. At first glance, both parents' full-time employment appears to be strongly correlated to the number of children in the family – the higher the number of children, the lower the proportion of families with both parents working full-time. Larger families are also more likely to have a mother at home. Furthermore, the age of the children also plays a role, though a modest one. Within categories defined by the number of children, we observe an increase in the proportion of families with both parents working full-time as the age of the children rises: for example, it increases from 50.4% (children's age, 0–5 years) to 58.2% (children's age, 6 or older) among families with only one child. This is particularly noticeable among families with three children or more, as the proportion rises from 24.4% when the children are all under 6 to 37.9% when they are all 6 or older. In the second part of Table 3.2, we also observe such a relationship between parents both working regular shifts and family composition. The proportion of families with two regular work schedules is lower among families with three children or more than where families are smaller. The age of the children also appears to be significant as this proportion is higher when there are children 6 or older, especially when all the children are 6 or older. Do these correlations indicate a strategy at work?

In examining the persistence of these relationships through a more in-depth multivariate analysis, we may detect indications that parental behaviour is geared towards safeguarding family life through optimiz-

TABLE 3.2 Distribution (%) Two-Parent Families, According to Number and Age (in years) of the Children, Parents' Full-Time (FT) or Part-Time (PT) Employment, and Work Schedule of Both Parents.

	One child (age)		Two children (age)			Three or more children (age)			
Parents working FT or PT	(0–5)	(6–11)	(All 0–5)	(0–5 and 6–11)	(All 6–11)	(All 0–5)	(0–5 and 6–11)	(All 6–11)	Total
Two parents, FT	50.4	58.2	42.8	42.8	48.1	24.4	35.0	37.9	44.7
Father FT, mother PT	22.5	15.9	23.1	26.4	28.0	25.0	25.6	33.1	25.3
Mother FT, father PT	2.7	1.8	1.7	1.6	1.3		1.1	0.6	1.6
Father FT, mother not employed	17.8	16.2	26.9	23.5	17.4	47.0	29.9	21.2	22.0
Two parents PT, or 1 PT and 1 not employed	3.2	5.8	3.3	3.0	3.4	1.2	4.4	3.8	3.6
Two parents not employed	3.3	2.1	2.2	2.6	1.8	2.4	4.1	3.4	2.8
Total	100.0	100.0	100.0	100.0	100.0	100.0	100.0	100.0	100.0
Parents' Work Schedules									
Two parents, R	25.6	26.0	20.7	24.3	28.5	11.4	19.7	26.0	24.4
Father R, mother A	13.6	15.6	12.6	13.5	14.7	13.8	10.8	12.4	13.3
Mother R, father A	20.9	20.6	18.7	16.3	19.8	9.6	16.4	16.8	18.6
2 A same	7.2	6.7	6.6	6.8	6.9	7.8	6.5	8.2	7.0
2 A not the same	9.6	7.5	9.6	10.8	7.9	7.8	9.3	9.1	9.1
Father R, mother not employed	8.1	8.4	14.9	13.5	9.1	27.5	14.1	12.0	11.5
Mother R, father not employed	0.6	2.2	1.2	0.6	1.8		0.8	0.7	1.1
Father A, mother not employed	10.2	8.5	13.1	10.7	8.5	19.8	17.4	10.7	11.4
Mother A, father not employed	0.9	2.2	0.5	0.9	1.1		0.9	0.7	0.9
Two parents not employed	3.3	2.1	2.2	2.6	1.8	2.4	4.1	3.4	2.8
Total	100.0	100.0	100.0	100.0	100.0	100.0	100.0	100.0	100.0

Source: NLSCY 1994–95.

A = atypical schedules; R = regular schedules

ing a parental presence in their children's lives. A first step consists of examining all families with the help of logistic regression, whereby the probability that both parents work full-time in regular shifts can be compared for the various categories that define family composition (table 3.3A). Odd ratios less than 1 confirm what the descriptive analysis demonstrated, namely, that larger families are less likely than families with one child to have both parents working full-time at regular schedules. Hence, when control variables are taken into account, the coefficient of 0.530 indicates that parents of three children or more are 47% less likely to both work full-time at regular schedules. Similarly, the parents of families comprising only children under 6 are 25% less likely to both be working full-time at regular shifts. These results offer a preliminary indication that family composition affects forms of labour force participation through reducing the propensity of families with two children or more and of those with young children to work full-time at regular hours, and hence to maximize their income and access to economic security. There appears to be a tension between the demands of family life and the search for financial well-being.

In restricting the analysis only to families where both parents are in the labour force, we observe that the effect of children's ages on the probability that both parents are employed full-time with regular work schedules is no longer significant, once one takes into account the mother's and the family characteristics (table 3.3B column). This suggests that the effect of age noted earlier was, in large part, due to families with very young children, those more likely to opt for a strategy where the mother stays home for a while. As for families where both parents choose to work, having more children continues to exert a negative effect on the tendency to have both parents working full-time with standard schedules: the likelihood to do so is reduced by 19% among families with two children and by 38% among those with three or more children, in comparison with families with only one child. When control variables are taken into account, the effect is slightly diminished, but it remains statistically significant. This result indicates that part-time work and/or atypical schedule (reference category) may correspond to a parental decision that one parent devote more energy to family life.

One final verification is required (tables 3.3, columns C, D, and E). This consists of a three-step investigation of whether the adoption of an atypical work schedule in families where both parents work is due to a deliberate family choice. Table 3.2 suggested the existence of a link

TABLE 3.3 Impact of Family Composition on Various Parents' Work Arrangements, Canada. (Odd Ratios of Various Models of Logistic Regression)

Work arrangements	All families (A) 2 parents FT R / other families (reference)		Families with 2 parents employed (B) 2 parents FT R / other families (reference)		Families with 2 parents employed (C) 1 parent A / 2 parents R (reference)		Families with 2 parents employed (D) Mother PT with A / other families (reference)		Families with 2 parents employed: mother working PT only (E) Mother A / mother R (reference)	
	Gross[a]	Net[b]	Gross[a]	Net[c]	Gross[a]	Net[c]	Gross[a]	Net[d]	Gross[a]	Net[d]
Family composition Children (n)										
1	1.000	1.000	1.000	1.000	1.000	1.000	1.000	1.000	1.000	1.000
2	0.716***	0.761***	0.806***	0.846*	1.042	1.005	1.423***	1.344***	1.077	1.022
≥3	0.493***	0.530***	0.621***	0.701***	1.096	0.973	1.809***	1.581***	0.993	0.930
Age of children (years)										
All ≥6	1.000	1.000	1.000	1.000	1.000	1.000	1.000	1.000	1.000	1.000
0–5 and ≥6	0.941	0.871*	0.957	1.012	1.128‡	1.030	1.223***	1.294***	1.369***	1.499***
All 0–5	0.858*	0.749***	0.818***	0.948	1.240***	1.038	1.384***	1.154	1.593***	1.290*

Source: NLSCY 1994–95

[a] Effect of family composition (number of children and age of children) without control variables.

[b] Effect of family composition (number of children and age of children) controlling for the effect of mothers' age and level of education and of the type of family (intact or step).

[c] Effect of family composition (number of children and age of children) controlling for the effect of mothers' age and level of education, type of family (intact or step), employment status, and parents' employment sector.

[d] Effect of family composition (number of children and age of children) controlling for the effect of mothers' age and level of education, type of family (intact or step), and parents' employment sector.

FT = full-time; PT = part-time; A = atypical schedule; R = regular schedule.

$*p < .05$; $**p < .01$; $***p < .001$; $‡p < 0.1$.

between the proportion of parents working regular shifts and family composition. An initial test (table 3.3 column C) allows us to assess the probability that at least one of the two parents holds a job with atypical hours compared with the category where both parents work standard hours. The analysis reveals that where all the children are under 6 families are significantly more likely to adopt atypical schedules, even when one controls for full-time and part-time employment (data not shown), but it is no longer significant when control variables are included. On the other hand, another test (table 3.3 column D) allows us to verify the probability of the mother working part-time with an atypical schedule, compared with other families where both parents work. Family composition here appears to have a strong effect. The likelihood of mothers to hold a part-time job with an atypical schedule is 34% higher among families with two children, compared with those with only one, and 58% higher among those with three children and more. It is 29% higher among families who also have young children compared with those comprising only children age 6 or older. Finally, to separate the net effect of part-time work and of atypical schedules, a third test (table 3.3 column E) only considers mothers working part-time, and examines their prospects of having employment with an atypical schedule rather than a standard shift. In this case, the number of children does not appear to play a significant role, but mothers with children under 6 are 30% to 50% more likely to work atypical shifts. This result might well be related to a decision aimed at optimizing parental time. Mothers working only part-time may devote more time to their preschool-aged children during the day, while fathers can take over at night or on the weekend, when the former are making their own economic contribution. Such a family strategy is directed at maintaining both a certain standard of living and parental time, if not family time.

Clearly, the existence of a family strategy is demonstrated, in particular, in the reduced number of work hours that mothers achieve, either through part-time employment or through withdrawing from the labour force altogether, especially when there are more and younger children. Juggling atypical work schedules also seems to constitute a means by which families maintain their standard of living. However, one cannot deny that this interferes with family time. Doubtless, the labour market itself determines the possibilities of recourse to a nonstandard work schedule. Still, one might emphasize that if the type of employment held during the year under observation is generally the result of a professional choice made in the course of one's youth, it may also represent, at least for the many jobs which have less demanding qualifications and which offer atypical schedules, a choice inspired by the desire of families to have at least one of the parents look after the children.

Parents' Work Arrangements and the Family's Quality of Life

The second dimension of this analysis of labour force participation among parents with young children is concerned with the impact of employment arrangements on the quality of family life. This is an extremely complex question. First of all, defining the quality of life poses a conceptual problem, the solution to which varies according to the observer's viewpoint and the scientific approach favoured. A sociologist, an economist, and a psychologist will each define quality of life differently. Furthermore, the quality of life is not necessarily the same for parents and children. As our analysis is focused on the question of mothers' increased labour force participation and our results tend to confirm the existence of a family strategy based on mothers' employment, a measure of mothers' stress may offer insight into a fundamental dimension of the quality of family life. Psychological indicators together with measures of respondents' and their partners' labour force participation are rarely encountered in a single data source. However, the NLSCY includes a measure of mothers' psychological depression, which seems pertinent. This indicator, based on a set of statements deemed significant by specialists, classifies mothers along a continuum ranging from 0 to 36. The majority of respondents have the weakest scores, corresponding to the absence of signs of depression: 56% of mothers have a score of 3 or lower. In comparison, only 10% have scores higher than 10. (For more details on this measure, see Somers and Willms 2002).

Labour Force Participation and Variations in the Mother's Depression Index

The mean index of depression for mothers varies according to parental labour force participation.[1] When all families are considered, the average is 4.3, and it varies little when both parents are working. Compared with families where both parents work full-time (4.0), the index is slightly higher among mothers in families where the father is the sole breadwinner (an increase of 14% compared with parents who both work full-time) and is much higher in families where labour force participation is weak (an increase of 52%) or non-existent (79%). Doubtless, this depression is related to poverty or other difficult situations. Nonetheless, it must be recalled that these families constitute a mere 6% of the total sample.

Parental Employment Schedules and Variations in the Mothers' Depression Index

How is this related to work schedules? The first column of Table 3.4 presents the average depression index of mothers, according to the work schedules of both parents. The results show a slight increase in the average depression index when one of the two parents works irregular hours, and a larger one when both parents do so, particularly when their schedules differ. Hence, the index ranges from 3.9 and 4.1 when only one parent has an atypical schedule to 4.8 when both parents have atypical schedules that differ. When only one parent is employed (data not shown), mothers' depression index is 4.8 overall, that is, 20% higher than among mothers of families where both parents work full-time. When the mother is at home, this indicator rises to 4.6 or 4.7, according to whether the father's schedule is standard or atypical. When only the mother is employed, the depression index reaches 5.1 if her schedule is standard, and 6.7 if it is atypical. In the latter case, the stress would result, not only from the effects of her schedule, but also probably from the financial insecurity created by the fact that the father does not work, while the mother alone must shoulder the burden of ensuring the family's economic survival, in addition to her other family responsibilities.

The next two columns of Table 3.4 compare families where both parents are employed full-time with those where the father works full-time and the mother part-time. Here, one observes the same tendency for both groups, namely, a slight increase in the average depression index associated to atypical schedules. We notice, however, that if the tendency is the same for both groups of families, the average indices for mothers working part-time are a little weaker, suggesting that the compensation they reap for their sacrifice in terms of their standard of living (discussed previously) might be a less stressful quality of life.

It seems appropriate to determine whether the observed differences persist when we control for family composition and other factors. Table 3.5 shows the coefficients of various linear regression models.

TABLE 3.4 Average Depression Index of Mothers in Two-Parent Families, According to Parents' Work Schedules, Canada.

Parents' work schedules	All familes	2 parents FT	Father FT / mother PT
2 parents, R	3.8	3.8	3.5
Father R, mother A	3.9	3.8	3.9
Mother R, father A	4.1	4.1	3.7
2 A the same	4.2	4.3	4.1
2 A not the same	4.8	4.9	4.8
Father R, mother not employed	4.6	–	–
Mother R, father not employed	5.1	–	–
Father A, mother not employed	4.7	–	–
Mother A, father not employed	6.7	–	–
2 parents not employed	7.2	–	–
Total	4.3	4.0	3.9

Source: NLSCY 1994–95
FT = full-time; PT = part-time; A = atypical schedule; R = regular schedule.

Families where both parents work regular hours at full-time jobs, which serve here as the reference category, should be among those where the level of stress is the weakest. In that respect, families where both work schedules are standard, but one of the parents, most frequently the mother, works part-time do not differ significantly from the reference category. When both parents have different work schedules, the level of stress is likely to increase, and more so when they both work atypical hours. Hence, mothers' depression index significantly increases when both parents work full-time but have different schedules, one regular, the other atypical. When both parents have identical atypical schedules, mothers' level of depression is not higher than that if both parents work full-time regular schedules; only when the atypical schedules differ do mothers display a significantly higher depression index. Furthermore, families where one of the two parents does not work show significantly higher depression index levels than families where both parents work full-time at regular hours. Here, the stress revealed in depression is doubtless correlated to economic issues. We should recall that these families are more likely to be financially disadvantaged than others. This situation might result from a deliberate choice to safeguard family time or the inability to find work. It thus seems that the price to pay is not only economic, but that it equally affects the quality of life in certain families.

TABLE 3.5 Impact of Parents' Work Arrangements in Two-Parent Families on Mothers' Quality of Life, as Measured by a Depression Index, Canada. (Coefficients B from Various Models of Linear Regression; Reference Category: Two Regular Schedules, Two Full-Time)

Parental working arrangements	Model 1[a]	Model 2[b]	Model 3[c]	Model 4[d]
2 R: 1 FT, 1 PT	−0.102	−0.083	−0.083	−0.088
1 R, 1 A, both FT	0.178*	0.175*	0.159*	0.092
1 R, 1 A – 1 FT, 1 PT	0.110	0.159	0.111	0.076
2 A identical – 2 FT	0.084	0.070	0.064	−0.032
2 A not the same – 2 FT	0.720***	0.718***	0.718***	0.625***
2 A identical – 1 FT, 1 PT	0.141	0.163	0.146	0.032
2 A not the same – 1 FT, 1 PT	0.631***	0.666***	0.631***	0.535***
1 R – FT, 1 not employed	0.269***	0.281***	0.241***	0.130
1 A – FT, 1 not employed	0.512***	0.506***	0.467***	0.314***
2 PT or 1 PT, 1 not employed	1.052***	1.032***	1.010***	0.823***
2 not employed	1.115***	1.121***	1.102***	0.732***

Source: NLSCY 1994–95
[a] Gross: without any control.
[b] Controlled for number of children.
[c] Controlled for number and age of children.
[d] Controlled for number and age of children, mother's age and education, and family type (intact or step).
FT = full-time; PT = part-time; A = atypical schedule; R = regular schedule.
$*p < .05$; $**p < .01$; $***p < .001$; $\ddagger p < 0.1$.

When one includes in the model indicators of family composition (Models 2 and 3), such as the number and age of children, the effects associated with different work schedules and not being employed remain statistically significant. Depression indices are significantly higher among families displaying these work patterns. These results hold when taking into consideration the mother's age and education level, as well as the type of family (intact or with step children), except for two situations: the coefficients associated with families where both parents work full-time but one has an atypical schedule, and with those where the father works full-time and regular hours while the mother is at home, no longer significantly differ from the reference category. Mothers who are under age 35, less educated, and part of a stepfamily are affected by significantly higher depression indices (data not shown).

These results merely touch on the influence of work arrangements on families' quality of life, because the depression index employed is only one of the possible indicators of the stress that families experience, and it detects particularly difficult conditions. If atypical differing employment schedules are clearly associated with greater depression among mothers, while other types of links to the labour force seem more favourable, one still cannot conclude that these other forms of labour force participation always have a positive effect on quality of life and family time.

Conclusion

A key challenge of contemporary developed societies has to reside with the way families are allowed to respond to their dual responsibilities as workers and income earners, as well as parents in charge of raising children. Time for work and time for family are two pressing issues that today's families have to deal with, while gathering an adequate income to assure the fulfilment of their needs.

Indeed, Canadian parents with young families are torn by a need to balance family time, on the one hand, and economic well-being, on the other. Much of the evidence put forward in this chapter brings the observer to conclude that many parents adjust their work schedules in response to the need to look after their children, but that the search for economic well-being leads a relatively high proportion among them to give up some of their family time to maintain their standard of living. One of the most notable aspects of this tension between financial needs and family time relates to the diversity and complexity of working arrangements. While combining full-time employment and part-time work, parents have to adjust to various work schedules, often imposed by the workplace, but at times chosen to accommodate family needs. Mothers' employment is, in many cases, affected by the number and age of their children. When they have young children, mothers are more inclined to care for them themselves. Thus, they may either withdraw from the labour force or resort to part-time work. Such is rarely the case for young fathers.

Of course, one must also consider the availability of affordable childcare services. The absence of such services may well play a role in the choice of complex work arrangements, when parents deliberately choose atypical and/or different work schedules. In this case, the attainment of economic well-being is not as easily reached, and negative effects on the quality of family life may be observed.

One may ponder on the very definition of family time, which was referred to as those moments when all family members are available for common activities. While intuitively interesting, this notion remains rather vague and cannot be measured in a precise fashion with the available data, even with existing time-use surveys. When considering work arrangements as part of a family strategy, the picture remains 'impressionistic': it requires refinement, not only to measure family time more accurately but also to better understand its significance. The notion that the amount of family time constitutes a positive element for the equilibrium of family members seems readily acceptable, but this has not been demonstrated in a thoroughly satisfactory manner. However, other studies have shown that 'parental time' (a concept used by Benoît Rapoport and Céline Le Bourdais in chapter 4 of this volume), defined as the time each parent allows for the care of his or her children, could be another indicator of good family functioning. To better understand their significance, these indicators should be studied in connection with children's development, academic success, and community integration.

Parents' work arrangements have repercussions not only for children's lives, but also for those of adults, and doubtless give rise to adjustments in the parental sharing of the tasks of childcare and childrearing. Though increasingly both parents are found in the workforce, it seems that the traditional family model persists in a 'weakened version.' When only one parent works, it is the father. When only one parent works part-time, it is the mother. This suggests that an egalitarian sharing of responsibilities has yet to be attained, and that women continue to pay the price in terms of income and eventually of less comfortable retirement conditions. These questions are particularly relevant in the context of conjugal instability that prevails and of the new types of families that ensue.

The research presented here has highlighted the fact that the complexity of work arrangements chosen by parents does not necessarily lead to a satisfying standard of living. Indeed, economic well-being seems to be inversely proportional to the complexity of working arrangements. Other studies should attempt to pinpoint to what degree occupational choices and the labour market itself inevitably determine not only work arrangements, but also standards of living. In addition, it should be noted that the definition of work arrangements used here does not encompass all the elements that could serve to characterize a worker's precarious status. This dimension is certainly not foreign to families' quality of life and deserves to be included in future research.

As the presence of both parents in the labour force now appears essential for attaining an acceptable standard of living, society is confronted by the need to re-examine the role that public authorities should play in assisting parents to look after their children. Family needs are diverse and vary as a function of the number and age of children. The development of family and social policies must place this reality at the heart of the principles guiding decision-making.

Finally, the workplace has profitability requirements that must be respected to ensure economic growth. But it should also recognize its responsibility to assist workers in their role as parents. From this perspective, the state certainly has an active role to play, be it by incitement or by coercion, in enacting labour laws that take into account the dual responsibilities of men and women, who must work to assure the economic well-being of their children, as well as find the time and energy needed to raise them.

NOTE

1 In this section, labour force participation and work schedules were measured at the time of the survey rather than during the course of the previous year. This decision was necessary to facilitate collecting the relevant employment information as closely as possible to the time when the index of depression was gauged.

REFERENCES

Beaujot, R. 2000. *Earning and Caring in Canadian Families*. Peterborough, ON: Broadview Press.

Bianchi, S. 2000. 'Maternal Employment and Time with Children: Dramatic Change or Surprising Continuity?' *Demography* 37(4): 401–14.

Bielby, W.T., and D.D. Bielby. 1989. 'Family Ties: Balancing Commitments to Work and Family in Dual-Earner Households.' *American Sociological Review* 54(5): 776–89.

Lapierre-Adamcyk, E., and N. Marcil-Gratton. 1995. 'Prise en charge des enfants: stratégies individuelles et organisation sociale.' *Sociologie et société* 19(1): 33–51.

Lapierre-Adamcyk É., N. Marcil-Gratton, and C. Le Bourdais. 2002. 'Temps de travail et temps familial. Comportements des mères et des pères dans une économie en changement.' Actes du Colloque *Avenirs démographiques et mondialisation: Enjeux politiques*, 149–63. Fédération canadienne de démographie. Ottawa: Carleton University.

– 2004. 'Régimes de travail: équilibrer temps familial et bien-être économique.' In J. Véron, S. Pennec, and J. Légaré (eds.), *Age, générations et contrat social.* Les Cahiers de l'INED no 153, 263–76. Paris: Les Éditions de l'Institut national d'études démographiques.

Marcil-Gratton, N., and C. Le Bourdais. 2000. 'La conciliation famille-travail comme facteur de stress: multiplicité des situations et diversité des besoins de soutien des familles au Québec.' Presented at the Comité de priorité sur les ruptures d'unions, Partenariat Familles en mouvance et dynamiques intergénérationnelles, Institut national de la recherche scientifique – Urbanisation, Culture et Société, Quebéc, 15 March.

Presser, H. 1989. 'Can We Make Time for Children? The Economy, Work Schedules, and Child Care.' *Demography* 26(4): 523–43.

– 1995. 'Job, Family, and Gender: Determinants of Nonstandard Work Schedules among Employed Americans in 1991.' *Demography,* 32(4): 577–98.

– 1999. 'Towards a 24-Hour Economy.' *Science,* 284 (June), 1778–9.

Somers, M.-A., and J.D. Willms. 2002. 'Maternal Depression and Childhood Vulnerability.' In J.D. Willms (ed.), *Vulnerable Children,* 211–28. Edmonton: University of Alberta Press.

Statistics Canada. 1997. National *Longitudinal Survey of Children and Youth (NLSCY) 1994–95: User's Guide.* Ottawa: Statistics Canada.

4 Parental Time, Work Schedules, and Changing Gender Roles

BENOÎT RAPOPORT AND CÉLINE LE BOURDAIS

The economic and demographic changes observed in the past few decades have profoundly altered the family life of individuals in Canada, as well as in most western societies. Around 1965 these societies entered their 'second demographic transition' (Van de Kaa 1987), and successively experienced a sharp reduction of fertility, an increase of divorce that was followed by a decline in marriage, and the rise of cohabiting unions, first, as a way to start conjugal life and, then, to form families. As a consequence, in today's families there are a smaller number of children than in those existing some thirty-five years ago, and they are more at risk of experiencing a breakdown, as entry and exit from relationships has become more flexible, as shown by the rise of divorce and cohabitation (Beaujot 2000).

The increased participation of women, and especially of mothers of young children, in the labour market has also led to a reorganization of family time. This movement was first encouraged by the development of a service economy that required additional new workers. With fewer children to take care of and the needed qualifications to fill these new jobs, a large proportion of mothers moved into the service sector; this, in turn, led to a rising demand for non-standard employment schedules, as the increased participation of women in all sectors and the rise of dual-earner families generated a growing demand for extended shopping hours and homemaking services (Presser 2002; Beaujot 2000). Oppenheimer (1994) also suggests that the deteriorating working conditions of young men have encouraged women to increase their participation in the labour market, as a family strategy to cope with the rising risk of unemployment faced by young males, and thereby avoid poverty.

These macro-changes in demographic and economic behaviours have doubtlessly modified the amount of time and the type of relations that family members have with one another within the home. Past research has insisted on the importance of the quality of the parent-child relationship for children's development and well-being (Amato 1994; Amato and Gilbreth 1999; Carlson 2000). However, studies focusing on the determinants of the amount of time that parents spend with their children are recent and go back to a dozen years at most. Yet, one could argue that the quantity of time spent by parents, which can be measured with less subjectivity, is as important as its quality for children's development, and that the two are closely related.

Studies documenting parental time have started to emerge, but their conclusions are sometimes contradictory. Whereas one would expect that the changing faces of families and the increased participation of women in the labour market would yield a reduction in the average time spent by parents with children, recent American studies have shown that maternal time has not changed much (Bianchi 2000), and that parental time has even increased in two-parent families in the past two decades (Sandberg and Hofferth 2001). Some of the explanations advanced to account for such findings are the overestimation in the past of the time that at-home mothers actually spent with their children, the smaller than expected effect of employment on maternal time, and changes in men's behaviour.

Not only is the presence of women in the labour market likely to affect parental time; the patterns of employment of parents are also likely to play a substantive role. In increasing numbers, men and women are taking jobs involving late or rotating hours or work on weekends. 'Non-standard' employment is on the rise. In Canada, for instance, one-third of workers were in non-standard jobs (i.e., had part-time or temporary work, held multiple jobs, or were self-employed) by the mid-1990s, compared with 28% in 1989; only half of the employed population was working 'full-time full-year,' and only one-third did so through regular day shifts (Beaujot 2000). The figures are somewhat similar in the United States where, according to Presser (2002), 45% of the employed Americans in 1997 worked non-standard schedules, that is, in the evenings or at night, on weekends, or on rotating days or hours. The proportion of individuals affected by atypical schedules is even higher when one takes as the unit of analysis dual-earner couples, in which both partners are at risk of experiencing such work patterns. Evidently, one can expect the work patterns held by both parents to influence the extent and organization of family time. Presser (1994; 2002) is one of the few researchers who have directly examined this issue.

To what extent have the complementary roles of men and women in providing for their family been accompanied by an increasing sharing of domestic activities? And, more specifically, how have changes in the family and the economy influenced the way in which family members interrelate with one another and, in particular, how do they affect the time that parents spend with their children? These questions constitute the main thread of this chapter. In the next section, we briefly describe the data and the subsample used in the analysis, and we define our concepts. Then follows a section describing total parental time and its allocation across activities for both fathers and mothers living in one-parent and two-parent households. The next section distinguishes parental time spent only in the presence of children and that spent doing a common activity with the other parent in two-parent households. In the section after that, we present the results of a multivariate analysis of parental time that focuses on the effects of work schedules on time spent with children among employed parents. The last section presents our conclusions.

Data

In the following analysis we use the 1992 and 1998 Canadian General Social Surveys (Statistics Canada 1992 – Cycle 7, hereafter GSS92; and 1998 – Cycle 12, hereafter GSS98), which collected information on Canadians' time allocation. Besides answering several sociodemographic questions, 10,749 respondents aged 15 years and older (coming from 10,749 separate households) in 1998, and 8,996 respondents in 1992, representative of the non-institutionalized population in Canada,[1] were asked to report on how they used their time during a given 24-hour period. Individuals were interviewed either on a weekday or during the weekend, and interviews were conducted through a complete year, so that every month and every day could equally be represented in the survey. This type of approach is important since respondents' time use greatly differs between weekend and weekdays, as well as between months.

For a 24-hour period starting at 4 o'clock in the morning, respondents had to report and describe each of their activities, and to indicate where and with whom they did these activities. Activities were selected from a wide list of about 200 items (e.g., 'Work for pay at main job,' 'Food (or meal) cleanup,' 'Grocery shopping,' 'Restaurant meals,' 'Night sleep / Essential sleep,' 'Attending art gallery').[2] Statistics Canada (1999) provided a description of Canadians' time use in 1998, along with different characteristics of respondents and of households (also see Lefebvre and Merrigan 1999, for a comparison of 1986 and 1992 results).

For each activity, respondents had to indicate whether the activity was done alone or together with another person and, if so, to identify their relationship to that person. Moreover, children younger than 15 years old living in the respondent's household were mentioned as soon as they were present in the same room as the respondent, even though their activities could differ.

The different activities were first grouped into twenty-four categories[3] in the public data file released by Statistics Canada (1999). We further grouped them into ten main categories for our analysis:

1 Work and school activities (categories 1–3 and 11: paid work, activities related to paid work, commuting, education and related activities)
2 Domestic work (4–8: cooking/washing up, housekeeping, maintenance and repair, other household work, shopping for goods and services)
3 Childcare (9)
4 Voluntary activities (10: civic and voluntary activities)
5 Personal care (14: other personal activities)[4]
6 Meals at home (13: excluding restaurant meals)
7 Social activities (15–17: restaurant meals, socializing (in homes), other socializing)
8 Media (18–20: watching TV; reading books, magazines, newspapers; other passive leisure)
9 Entertainment events (21: sports, movies, and other entertainment events)
10 Active leisure (22 and 23: active sports, other active leisure)

Definitions

We refer to *parental time* as the total amount of time spent either by the father or the mother in the presence of their children. In both the 1992 and 1998 surveys, children less than 15 years old were systematically reported as soon as they were present in the room of the respondent. However, in 1992 (and in contrast to 1998), time spent with children younger than 15 and that spent with those older than 15 were not distinguished in the public data file. Consequently, we use a heterogeneous measure of parental time that combines time spent with children less than 15 years old, no matter if the activities of the parent and of the child differ, and time spent with children more than 15 years old, but only when children and parents were doing the same activity. This is the only way in which we can use both the 1992 and 1998 survey data.

Maternal time and *paternal time* refer to the amount of time that mothers and fathers respectively spent with their children. One should note that we do not have measures of both paternal time and maternal time within a given family, since only one person per household was asked to fill a diary.[5]

Finally, we define *family time* as the time spent simultaneously by both parents with their children; as noted before, only when parents were doing the same activity was the presence of the other parent recorded. For example, if both parents were present in the kitchen, with the respondent supervising children's homework and the other parent cooking dinner, we would not know that both parents were present in the same room; on the contrary, if both parents were preparing a meal while their children were reading comics in the kitchen, we would know that both parents were doing this activity together while their children were present in the same room, but we would not know what the children were doing. We will have to keep this in mind when interpreting the results.

The Subsample

Since we are focusing on parental time, our sample comprises only respondents who were living with at least one of their[6] children who was less than 15 years old at the time of the survey.[7] As some information is missing for certain respondents in the survey, our final sample contains 5,657 observations (2,501 mothers and 2,234 fathers living in two-parent families; and 819 mothers and 103 fathers living in one-parent families). The total subsamples consist of the combined respondents of the 1992 and 1998 Canadian General Social Surveys on time use.

Parental Time in Canadian Families

Figure 4.1 presents the allocation of paternal and maternal time among the different activities retained, according to the structure of the family

Figure 4.1 Parental time by activity and type of household.

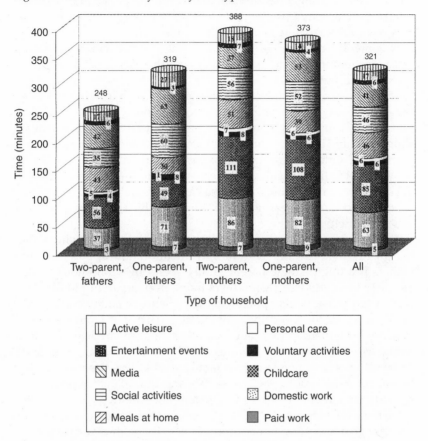

Source: Statistics Canada. *General Social Survey* (1992, Cycle 7) and (1998, Cycle 12).

in which the respondent lived. On average, parental time (for fathers and mothers combined) amounts to 5 hours and 21 minutes (321 minutes) a day. Direct childcare constitutes the main activity that parents do in the presence of their children (85 minutes). They devote approximately one hour (63 minutes) to domestic work with their children present around them. Eating meals at home, having social activities, and reading or listening to media each occupy around three-quarters of an hour a day of parental time. Playing sports or doing another active leisure activity in the presence of children occupy 17 minutes a day, while attending entertainment events, doing personal care or voluntary activities are less often pursued with children, and each require only 6 minutes. Work-related activities done in the presence of children only represent on average 5 minutes a day, which is not surprising since most parents do not work at home or they work while their children are in school.

The amount and allocation of time spent with children vary significantly between mothers and fathers. Mothers living in two-parent families spend a total of 388 minutes a day (about 6.5 hours) with their children, only 15 minutes more than single mothers do. The allocation of maternal time between activities only slightly differs with the type of household. In particular, mothers living in single-parent families devote more time listening to media (mainly watching TV) with their children and less time eating meals at home, which appears to be more of a family activity.

The differences are greater for fathers, for whom living with a partner greatly modifies the amount and the allocation of parental time. Fathers heading a single-parent family spend over one hour more a day with their children than fathers living in two-parent families. The main activity that fathers pursue in the presence of children consists of domestic work for those living without a partner (71 minutes vs 37 minutes for fathers in two-parent families), and of childcare for those living with a partner (56 minutes vs 49 minutes for single fathers). Fathers living in a single-parent family devote less time to meals at home, but more time to social activities and leisure (active leisure and media) than fathers living in a two-parent household.

On the whole, the differences in the amount and allocation of parental time are greater among fathers and mothers living in two-parent families than between single fathers and mothers. Time devoted to direct childcare is one exception; in this case, the difference is slightly greater between fathers and mothers in single-parent than in two-parent households. This partly reflects the fact that single-parent families headed by a man do not have the same composition in terms of the number and age of children as those headed by a woman. Hence, very few single fathers live with young children, whereas this is often the case for mothers. This also explains why time devoted by fathers to direct childcare is so low, and that devoted to leisure so high, in one-parent households. Finally, it is interesting to note that, on average, fathers devote more parental time to leisure (in particular to media) than mothers.

Parental Time and Family Time

Although studies on parental time are numerous, few scholars have examined family time, that is, periods during which all family members spend time together (for an exception, see Lapierre-Adamcyk et al. 2001). In this section, we separate the total amount of time that mothers and fathers living in two-parent families spent in the company of their children into two components: *family time* that was spent in the presence of their partner while doing a common task, and that spent without doing an activity with the partner (figure 4.2). First, it is interesting (and reassuring) to note that the amount of family time reported separately by fathers and by mothers coming from different households is, on average, very similar: 157 minutes for fathers, as compared with 158 for mothers. However, the allocation of family time declared by men and women slightly differs. Part of the explanation for this difference could be due to the fact that multiple activities were not reported in the survey (see Rapoport and Le Bourdais 2002b); respondents had to declare only their 'main' activity. Past research has shown that mothers are more likely than fathers to do several tasks at once. Activities related to the preparation of meals and cleaning up afterwards cannot always easily be distinguished from domestic work, and that could explain why mothers report slightly more family time devoted to domestic chores, and fathers slightly more time devoted to meals at home.

The ratio of family time to total parental time provides the percentage of activities done with the other parent in the presence of children. Figure 4.2 indicates that only 37% of paternal time (92 minutes out of a total of 249[8]) is spent without the partner, whereas 59% of maternal time (229 out of 387) is carried out without the father. In other words, fathers spend close to two-thirds of the time devoted to their children while doing activities jointly with their partner, while mothers only spend 40% of theirs this way. Clearly, fathers' interaction with their children appears to be largely mediated by the women with whom they live (Fox 2001). On the whole, fathers spend only one hour and a half (92 minutes) alone with their children, less than half the time spent by mothers. Domestic work is an activity that rarely involves fathers, either alone or with their partner. It remains a female task that occupies an important fraction (27%) of the time that mothers spend alone in the presence of their children. Direct childcare is the only activity that fathers accomplish alone with their children for more than 16 minutes

Figure 4.2 Parental time and family time for mothers and fathers in two-parent households.

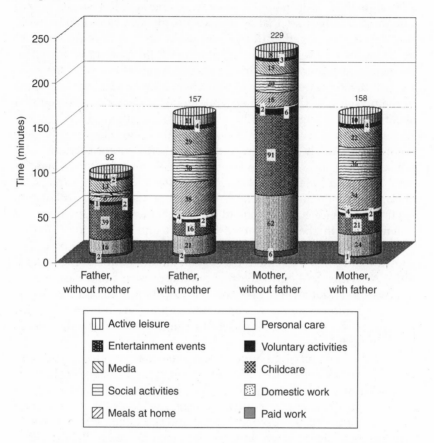

Source: Statistics Canada. General Social Survey (1992, Cycle 7) and (1998, Cycle 12).

a day, and it also occupies the largest period of time that mothers spend alone with their children. This suggests that direct childcare is the only activity for which fathers and mothers highly substitute parental time, and it seems to indicate that fathers and mothers achieve arrangements mainly to provide the highest possible amount of direct childcare to their children. Others activities would appear to be more 'social' and, perhaps, less important to them.

Parental Time and Work Schedules

Fathers participate in higher proportion than mothers to the labour market, and they also tend to work longer hours; that probably accounts partly for the smaller amount of time they spend with their children. Most studies focusing on parental time, and in particular those aiming to estimate the impact of the increasing participation of women in the labour market, strive to take into account the number of hours worked by parents. These studies usually distinguish parents who are not working from those who are working full-time and part-time (e.g., see Lefebvre and Merrigan 1999), but, as noticed by Presser (1994), they generally ignore when these hours are worked. Yet, work schedules are important inasmuch as children are not available all day, which constrains the timing of parental time.

Recent research (Bogen and Joshi 2002; quoted by Presser 2002) suggests that young children in low- and moderate-income American families tend to have more behavioural problems when their parents work non-standard rather than standard schedules. This finding is not without consequences, as the economy is moving towards a '24-hour economy' that implies the multiplication of non-standard schedules (Presser 1999). Working hours and schedules constitute an important determinant of family and social relationships (Hamermesh 1998). Hence, recent studies suggest that couples try to coordinate their work schedules in order to enjoy leisure at the same time (Hamermesh 2002). However, there exists some evidence that couples with children have more dissimilar work schedules than do childless couples, and that this dissimilarity increases with time devoted to childcare (Chenu and Robinson 2002; Presser 2002).

The few studies that introduced some measures of work schedules in the analysis of parental time reckon only from the end of the 1980s, and remain rather scarce. These studies show that fathers were more likely to be in charge of childcare or to spend more time with their children when their spouses did work at night or in the evening,[9] but also paradoxically, when the mothers worked part-time rather than full-time (Presser 1988; 1989; Nock and Kingston 1988). Moreover, fathers who worked during the weekend were less likely to be in charge of their children, whereas fathers who worked at night were more likely to be in charge of their children when their partner was not at home (Nock and Kingston 1988; Casper 1997; also see Brayfield 1995, for further references). Neither the total number of hours worked by fathers, nor their work schedules seemed to have any effect on their propensity to be in charge of children, once the number of fathers' and mothers' working hours that overlap was taken into consideration (Brayfield 1995); only the fact of having non-regular schedules had a negative and significant effect on paternal time. In contrast, mother's working hours and schedules were shown to have a substantial impact on the likelihood of fathers to be in charge of their children.

Most studies investigating the effects of work schedules on parental time have generally used dichotomyous ('dummy') variables to control for work schedules (see, e.g., Brayfield 1995). The work of Nock and Kingston (1988) is an exception. These authors distinguished hours worked: between midnight and 9 a.m.; between 9 a.m. and 3 p.m.; between 3 p.m. and 6 p.m.; and between 6 p.m. and midnight. This strategy allowed them to study more precisely the effect of one additional hour worked at any particular moment of the day on parental time; however, the authors could not differentiate among hours worked at night and those worked during the evening. We followed a similar approach in a previous report in which we described the effects of work schedules on parental time by distinguishing among hours worked during the day, at night, and in the evening (Rapoport and Le Bourdais 2002a). In the multivariate analyses, we take a slightly different approach. We divide the day into four-hour periods, and we estimate the time devoted to different activities with children by using dummy variables that indicate whether the respondent has worked at least some time within a given period.

Work Schedules and Parental Time

Figure 4.3 displays the average time that fathers and mothers, living in one- and two-parent families, spent with their children depending on whether they had worked during the day, in the evening, and/or at night on the day they were interviewed in 1992 and 1998. Because of the small size of the sample, we had to collapse certain categories for this graphic presentation. When moving from left to right on Figure 4.3, the retained categories are: on day of the survey (the Designated Day), the respondent (1) did not work; (2) worked in the evening and/or during the night (but not during the day); (3) worked during the day only; (4) worked both during the day and night (but not in the evening); (5) worked both during the day and in the evening (but not during the night); and (6) worked during the day, evening, and night.

Figure 4.3 Parental time, by sex and work schedules, 1992 and 1998.

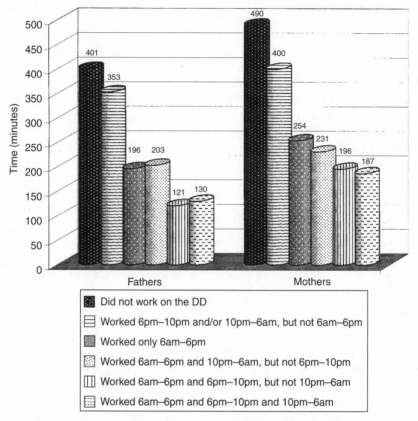

Source: Statistics Canada. *General Social Survey* (1992, Cycle 7) and (1998, Cycle 12).

In line with the results presented earlier, Figure 4.3 shows that whatever their labour market status and work schedules are, mothers spend more time with their children than their husbands do.[10] The difference ranges from half an hour, when comparing mothers and fathers who have worked both during the day and night, but not in the evening (203 minutes for fathers compared with 231 for mothers), to one hour and a half for parents who did not work during the Designated Day (401 vs 490 minutes). The impact of work schedules appears to be slightly greater for mothers than for fathers. In particular, fathers who worked daytime schedules reduced the amount of time spent with children by 205 minutes compared with those who did not work on the

Designated Day (196 vs 401 minutes), whereas mothers reduced theirs by 236 minutes.

Moreover, parents whose working hours on the Designated Day cut through more than one period spent significantly less time with their children than other parents and, as expected, especially than parents who did not work during that day.[11] This observation is particularly true for parents who worked both during the day and during the evening (no matter if they worked at night). However, we do not control here for the number of hours worked on the Designated Day. We expect parents who worked both during the day and in the evening to have worked longer hours than those who worked only within a given period, which would reduce the time they were available for their children. A similar argument can be advanced for parents who worked in the evening and/or at night, but not during the day. These parents spent a large amount of time with their children compared with the other employed parents, and this could be due to the fact that they worked a smaller number of hours on the Designated Day. Further analyses that control for the number of working hours are thus necessary if we are to correctly assess the impact of work schedules on parental time.

Predicting Parental Time: Multivariate Analysis

We now turn to multivariate analyses to measure the impact of parents' work schedules on the total amount of time they spend with their children and on the time they devote to specific activities. In this analysis, workdays are broken down into six equal four-hour periods, starting from 6 a.m. This approach is essential if we wish to compare the marginal effects of working within a given period on parental time. Activities done in the presence of children have been grouped into five categories: (1) domestic work; (2) direct childcare; (3) social activities (social activities and voluntary activities); (4) meals at home; and (5) leisure (active leisure, personal care, entertainment events, and media). Work-related activities have been excluded from the analysis, since they are very rarely conducted in the presence of children. Multiple regression models are run separately for total parental time and for each type of activities. Each equation, aiming to predict parental time devoted to a given type of activities, uses a set of independent variables for both working and non-working respondents (for a more detailed discussion of the method, see the Appendix). In this chapter, we present results only for working people, as our main interest focuses on the impact of work schedules on parental time (table 4.1).

Table 4.1 presents the effects of work schedules on parental time, for various categories of activities and different subgroups of parents, when a series of other characteristics are controlled.[12] In this table, the category 'Has worked 6 a.m. – 9 a.m.' means that the respondent has worked at least some time between 6:00 a.m. and 9:59 a.m. A positive coefficient attached to this category indicates that working in the morning increases the amount of time spent with children, while a negative coefficient reduces it. For individuals who worked through more than one period, the effect of each coefficient needs to be added to one another. Suppose, for example, that we want to compare the effect of work schedules between two fathers living in two-parent families, who have the same characteristics and have both worked eight hours, but through slightly different schedules. The first one A worked from 8 a.m. to 5 p.m., while the second one B worked from 10 a.m. to 7 p.m. The difference in total parental time between these two fathers, net of other characteristics, is calculated by adding the appropriate coefficients[13] and it amounts to +0.457, which means that A spent almost half an hour more with his children, when compared with B.

Not surprisingly, table 4.1 shows that total parental time decreases as the number of hours worked by the respondent during the Designated Day increases. The coefficient of –0.389 observed for all combined working fathers and mothers indicates that each additional hour worked reduces by 23 minutes (0.389 × 1 hour) the total amount of time spent with children. The comparison of coefficients among subgroups of parents reveals that the effect of substitution between work and parental time is slightly higher for fathers than for mothers in two-parent households (coefficients of –0.436 and –0.407), and higher for mothers than for fathers[14] in one-parent households (the coefficient is not, however, significant for fathers in one-parent households). Furthermore, for each additional hour worked, parents living in two-parent households also reduce more significantly the total time spent with children than those in one-parent households, and this holds for both fathers and mothers. These results suggest, first, that mothers are slightly more likely than fathers to manage time with their children and, second, that parents – generally mothers – living in one-parent families are more time constrained than parents living in two-parent households. Put differently, these results indicate that couples' work schedules are often complementary, which allows them to spend more time with their children.

TABLE 4.1 Work Schedules and Parental Time, by Activity, for Respondents and Their Spouses at Work, Respectively, on the Designated Day (DD) and during the Week Preceding the Survey

At Work	Total	Domestic tasks	Direct childcare	Social activities	Meals	Leisure
All Types of Households, Fathers and Mothers (5,657 households)						
DD	−0.389***	−0.201***	−0.211***	−0.280***	−0.067***	−0.208***
6 am–9 am	0.067	0.233	0.239*	0.215	0.013	0.187
10 am–1 pm	0.044	−0.319*	0.463***	0.022	0.144**	0.115
2 pm–5 pm	−0.220	0.025	0.322**	−0.140	0.052	0.312
6 pm–9 pm	−0.577***	−0.209	0.044	−0.125	−0.028	−0.956***
10 pm–1 am	0.436**	0.759***	0.390***	−0.293	0.083	0.188
2 am–5 am	−0.200	−0.378*	0.081	0.390	−0.013	0.201
One-Parent Households, Mothers (819 households)						
DD	−0.247**	−0.108	−0.041	−0.436***	−0.025	−0.171
6 am–9 am	−0.799	−0.713	0.426	0.505	−0.229	−0.890
10 am–1 pm	0.119	−0.415	0.296	−0.095	0.272	1.290*
2 pm–5 pm	−1.490**	−0.007	−0.870*	1.292*	−0.141	−0.741
6 pm–9 pm	−0.806	0.019	−0.182	0.148	−0.089	0.263
10 pm–1 am	0.173	−0.499	−0.054	0.400	0.232	−0.840
2 am–5 am	−1.279	−0.404	−0.306	0.718	0.153	0.289
One-Parent Households, Fathers (103 households)						
DD	−0.154	−0.021	0.231	−1.557***	0.091	−0.404
6 am–9 am	1.274	−1.009	−0.459	−2.932	−0.655*	0.963
10 am–1 pm	−4.220*	0.551	−0.107	3.630	0.849*	−2.869
2 pm–5 pm	1.215	−1.006	−0.820	2.414	0.714	3.476*
6 pm–9 pm	−3.770**	−2.093**	−2.237***	5.985***	−1.272***	−4.614***
10 pm–1 am	−0.092	0.397	1.087**	0.816	0.538	−0.830
2 am–5 am	−4.774**	−2.102*	−0.390	2.247	−1.114***	−0.235
Two-Parent Households, Mothers (2,501 households)						
DD	−0.407***	−0.224***	−0.163***	−0.260***	−0.063***	−0.163***
6 am–9 am	0.397	0.664**	0.058	0.168	0.031	−0.048
10 am–1 pm	−0.412	−0.223	0.427**	−0.390	0.071	−0.006
2 pm–5 pm	−0.041	−0.225	0.139	0.304	0.071	0.551
6 pm–9 pm	−0.713***	−0.212	−0.017	−0.900***	0.010	−0.978***
10 pm–1 am	0.444	−0.797**	0.208	−0.174	0.084	−0.072
2 am–5 am	−0.673	−0.541*	−0.035	0.241	0.064	−0.099
Spouse						
6 am–5 pm	0.127	0.200	0.183	0.138	0.035	−0.201
6 pm–9 pm	0.633***	0.439**	0.272**	−0.469	0.001	0.197
10 pm–5 am	−0.461	−0.082	−0.192	−0.214	−0.028	−0.305

TABLE 4.1 (Concluded)

At Work	Total	Domestic tasks	Direct childcare	Social activities	Meals	Leisure
Two-Parent Households, Fathers (2,234 households)						
DD	−0.436***	−0.181***	−0.280***	−0.361***	−0.082***	−0.274***
6 am–9 am	0.060	−0.118	0.305	0.576	0.041	0.608*
10 am–1 pm	0.590	−0.505	0.606**	0.600	0.202*	0.253
2 pm–5 pm	−0.145	0.336	0.730***	−0.509	0.065	0.172
6 pm–9 pm	−0.397**	−0.339*	0.120	0.384	−0.010	−0.971***
10 pm–1 am	0.734***	0.901***	0.544***	−0.072	0.086	0.651
2 am–5 am	0.269	−0.283	0.294	0.531	−0.013	0.318
Spouse						
6 am–5 pm	0.456**	0.475***	0.446***	0.116	0.034	0.062
6 pm–9 pm	0.883*	0.211	1.023**	0.561	−0.089	−0.887*
10 pm–5 am	−0.573	−0.206	−0.228	−1.149	0.127	0.561

Source: Statistics Canada, General Social Survey (1992, Cycle 7) and (1998, Cycle 12).
*$p < .1$; **$p < .05$; ***$p < .01$.

Working hours reduce significantly ($p < .01$) all activities spent with children, both for mothers and fathers in two-parent households, whereas only time devoted to social activities is significantly reduced in one-parent households. When considering together all types of households, the effect of working hours on parental time is similar in magnitude across all the different activities (coefficients ranging from −0.201 for domestic task to −0.280 for social activities), except for time devoted to meals (−0.067). However, there are some substantial differences between types of households and between genders. The effect of the number of hours worked is stronger for fathers than for mothers in all activities except for domestic tasks, and this is also true in one-parent households (however, the coefficients are not significant in the latter). This indicates that paternal time is more sensitive to working hours than maternal time is for most activities. Moreover, in single-parent families, leisure time and, above all, social activities done with children are the first activities with children that parents sacrifice because of work. This last result supports the idea that it is for direct childcare that parents substitute more directly for one another in two-parent families (see Rapoport and Le Bourdais 2001).

Work schedules exert various effects on parental time across activities, genders, and types of families. It is in one-parent families (in particular, in single-mother families) that parental time is less sensitive to work schedules, and it is the evening schedules (between 6 p.m. and 10 p.m.) that have the largest effect across household types. When controlling for number of hours worked, work in the evening sharply decreases total parental time, except for mothers living alone (the coefficient is large but not statistically significant). The activities that are most severely reduced by evening schedules are those related to leisure. In fact, leisure is the only activity (with, but to a lesser extent, domestic tasks) that fathers living in two-parent families who work in the evening significantly reduce; this result is not surprising since, as we have seen before, leisure is the only activity for which fathers spend proportionately more time with children than mothers. Mothers living in two-parent families also greatly reduce parental time devoted to social activities when they work in the evening.

In general, parents who work in the beginning of the night (between 10 p.m. and 2 a.m.) spend significantly more time with their children than others (the coefficients in table 4.1 are positive). This positive effect is found mostly among fathers in two-parent households, and it concerns only domestic tasks and childcare. This result is interesting in that it suggests that atypical schedules can benefit fathers who wish to spend more time with their children: they work while their children sleep, and they probably sleep when their children are absent; these fathers are also more likely to be in charge of domestic tasks. Similarly, fathers living in couples devote more time to childcare when they work a regular mid-day schedule (10 a.m. to 2 p.m.).[15]

Working in the evening appears to be especially damaging for parental time among fathers living in one-parent households. Almost all activities with children are greatly reduced, except social activities, which significantly increase.[16] For mothers living in one-parent households, number of hours of work and work schedules have almost no impact on the amount of time they spend with their children, except for two situations: first, total parental time (mainly time devoted to social activities) decreases as the number of hours worked increases, and second, these mothers significantly reduce total parental time (mostly direct childcare) when they work in late afternoon (between 2 p.m. to 6 p.m.). This can be interpreted as a result of the time constraints experienced by mothers living in single-parent families: like their male counterparts, single mothers cannot rely on any help from their partner, but in contrast to single fathers, their children are generally younger and need more care.

In regressions based on two-parent households, we also controlled for the work schedules of the other parent. These variables were reported by respondents and not by their partner; consequently, they are less precise, and we have thus chosen to only distinguish between day, evening, and night schedules. We do not control for the number of hours worked by the partner, so that the three variables, whose effects are reported in table 4.1, fully describe their work schedules.

Mothers spend more time with their children when their spouses work during the evening, but this affects only domestic tasks and direct childcare. In the same way, paternal time increases when the mother works during the day or during the evening; once again, only domestic tasks (when the mother works during the day) and direct childcare are concerned. Again, this result can be interpreted as an indication that maternal and paternal time substitute for one another, but mainly concerning tasks and not for leisure or social activities. Further investigation (see Rapoport and Le Bourdais 2002a) also shows that paternal time is more responsive to the work schedules of the partner than maternal time is, as was observed in previous studies (Brayfield 1995; Presser 1988; 1989). In particular, fathers whose partners did work in the evening tended to reduce leisure activities with children and to increase time devoted to direct childcare.

Other variables related to work schedules only have a modest impact on parental time. For instance, working rotating shifts does not significantly affect time spent with children, except for single mothers who tend to reduce time devoted to leisure (data not shown). The fact of having flexible schedules is linked to a reduction of the time devoted to leisure for mothers (but not for fathers) living in couples, and for single fathers, who also reduce the amount of time devoted to domestic tasks. Finally, parents who sometimes work at home spend more time with their children, especially for those living in two-parent households: social activities are the main activity concerned, together with domestic tasks for mothers and meals at home for fathers.

Other Results

We now briefly comment on the effects on parental time of the other control variables included in the analysis, in particular, the effects of the number and age of children, education, and the differences across regions. More detailed discussion is available in Rapoport and Le Bourdais (2001; 2002a).[17] First, as expected, parental time is higher during weekends than on weekdays. On weekends mothers and, to a lesser extent, fathers increase the amount of time devoted to social activities and to leisure at the expense of direct childcare, probably because parents do not have to prepare and accompany children to school and to supervise homework. These effects are not significant among parents living in one-parent households, and again, this confirms that the latter are highly time constrained. Furthermore, fathers living in two-parent households do not significantly decrease time involved in direct childcare, and they only marginally ($p < .01$) increase time devoted to leisure, which is related to the fact that they already spend a relatively large amount of time in leisure activities.

Not surprisingly, the younger and the more numerous the children, the higher the amount of parental time. Instead of introducing two continuous variables for the number of children and for the age of the younger child as commonly done, we choose to more fully describe the family structure by using a set of dummy variables that summarize the number and the age of the children.[18] This allowed us to show that the effects of age and number of children are non-linear, and that these effects differ across the various activities. Time devoted to direct childcare decreases as the age of children increases, and it generally increases with their number, whereas leisure activities with children increase with age, especially among fathers. Meals and social activities appear to be rather insensitive to the age or number of children.

Despite the fact that total parental time is, on average, higher for mothers and lower for fathers, neither paternal nor maternal time appears to statistically differ between one-parent and two-parent households, once we control for all the other variables included in the analysis. The only differences that are statistically significant ($p < .01$) concern time devoted to domestic work in the presence of children, which is lower in two-parent households, and time devoted to meals, which is higher in those families. Respondents' total parental time tends to increase as the time spent in childcare activities by their partners increases.[19] More precisely, it is the amount of time devoted to leisure and social activities with children that significantly increases with the partner's involvement in childcare. This result suggests that paternal and maternal times are complements rather than substitutes; in other words, the partner's involvement in childcare frees time for leisure and social activities – activities that are more commonly pursued together by parents. However, this effect is significant only for mothers.

Total parental time tends to increase with the respondents' completed level of education. The difference mostly opposes less educated respondents (i.e., those with less than a high school diploma) to those who achieved different levels of schooling. The effect of education is noticeable only among working respondents, who tend to be more educated than those who are not employed, and it concerns predominantly two types of activities: direct childcare and leisure.

The last point that deserves mention concerns the differences across regions. On the whole, parents spend significantly less time with their children in Quebec than in the other regions.[20] This is particularly true for women (although there is no significant difference between Quebec and British Columbia). Besides the differences in total time, the allocation of parental time also differs among regions. More precisely, mothers spend significantly less time in most activities in Quebec than in most other regions, and fathers devote less time to childcare in Quebec than in Ontario. On the contrary, both fathers and mothers spend more time while eating meals with their children in Quebec. As meals constitute a typical family activity, it could be interpreted as an indication that Quebeckers have some preference for family activities.

Conclusion

This chapter examined to what extent changes in family and work patterns have influenced the time that parents spend with their children. Like other studies, our analysis shows that mothers, on average, spend more time than fathers (approximately two hours more per day) in the presence of their children. Mothers living in two-parent families spend a large share of their parental time pursuing activities alone with their children, while fathers tend to devote a greater fraction of their time conducting activities jointly with their partner. This result partly explains the paradox observed in previous studies, namely, that the increased participation of fathers in childcare does not significantly reduce the amount of time that women spend with their children. It does, however, yield an augmentation of the amount of family time, that is, time that both parents spend doing common activities in the presence of their children, and that in itself probably represents a positive outcome, even though it did not necessarily help to alleviate the double burden of mothers. Indeed, family time constitutes privileged moments during which family members establish and develop close relationships with one another, moments which, to paraphrase Beaujot (2000), 'make family' life (also see De Vault 1991, who used this concept).

Our analysis showed that parental time differs between men and women, across family types, and with work schedules. On average, mothers spend approximately the same amount of time with their children, no matter if they live in a one-parent or two-parent family. The difference is quite large among fathers: those heading a single-parent family spend over one hour a day more with their children than those living in two-parent families. Evidently, children require a minimal amount of time and care, and when there is no partner with whom to share the tasks, single parents have to find ways to make ends meet. In other words, parental time is much more constrained in one-parent than in two-parent families. No matter the type of family, mothers tend to devote a greater amount of time to domestic work and direct child-care, and fathers to leisure activities.

Work patterns have a strong impact on the quantity and type of activities that parents pursue in the presence of their children, but again, this impact varies according to the sex of parents and the family structure in which they live. Parental time appears to be negatively linked to the amount of time worked, that is, it decreases as the number of hours worked increases. The effect of working hours is especially strong among two-parent households, where each additional hour worked contributes to significantly reduce all types of activities conducted by parents in the presence of children. This result suggests that parents living in couples have complementary work schedules, which maximizes the total amount of time that is spent with children. In one-parent families, parental time is more constrained, and only time devoted to social activities is significantly cut as the number of hours worked increases.

Work schedules also appear to have a smaller impact on parental time in one-parent than in two-parent families. Evening schedules exert the strongest and most detrimental effect on parental time: mothers and fathers living in couples end up spending 45 and 25 minutes, respectively, less per day with their children when they work between 6:00 p.m. and 10 p.m., that is, during the period in which school-aged children are the most likely to be available at home. Leisure activities are, by far, the most severely reduced when parents work in the evening. By contrast, fathers in two-parent households who work in the beginning of the night (from 10:00 p.m. to 2 a.m.) tend to spend more time with their children and to be more involved in direct childcare and domestic activities.

If evening schedules are detrimental to parental time per se, they do tend to significantly increase the participation in childcare of the other parent living in two-parent families. Hence, when fathers work during the evening, mothers spend more time with their children; this affects primarily domestic and childcare activities. Conversely, when mothers work during the evening, parental time also increases; in this case, fathers reduce the time devoted to leisure activities in favour of direct childcare to which they contribute an increased amount of time.

These results are disquieting in the context of rising non-standard employment, which has been observed recently. If female work in the evening can lead to a greater involvement of fathers in direct childcare, it does compete directly with family time, by making mothers unavailable when other family members are present in the home. The development of late, rotating, or weekend work schedules, in order to provide services on a 7 day / 24-hour basis, is particularly troubling in that children risk suffering from this evolution. Recent research has shown that conjugal separation is more frequent among parents who have atypical work schedules than among those working regular day hours (Marcil-Gratton and Le Bourdais 2000; Presser 2000). The increasing flexibility of work appears to be more of a constraint than a means chosen by parents to more easily balance family and work. More refined analyses are required if we are to better understand the strategies adopted by parents to cope with work and family needs. Preferably, these analyses should be based on longer periods of observation than the one-day diaries that we have used here, and they should involve data describing the time uses of different family members and not solely that of the respondent. Hence, the fact that parents did not devote time to a particular activity with their children on a given day does not preclude them from doing it another day. Similarly, while we made inferences about how parents substitute or complement one another in time spent with their children from the separate analyses conducted for fathers and mothers, only a joint analysis of father's and mother's behaviours within a family would bring more conclusive results.

Finally, one question needs to be addressed given the polarization of work and income that is observed in many western societies. Will the most educated parents have more freedom in choosing regular 9-to-5 work schedules thereby allowing them to spend more time with their children and partner, than the less highly educated ones, who will be more time constrained and, thus, who will have less time to devote to their children? As a recent study suggests, the combination of both the quantity and quality of time spent in parent-child interaction appears to affect the intellectual development of preschool children (Gagné 2003), which could lead to rising inequalities among children.

Appendix 1: Technical Notes and List of Control Variables

Multiple regression models are used to measure the impact of parents' work schedules on the amount of time they spend with their children for different sets of activities. Each equation, run for a given set of activities, is estimated by using a switching regression model. The main reason for using such a method is that we suspect that the fact of working and the amount of time devoted to children (and its allocation between different activities) are not independent from one another. This method allows us to simultaneously estimate the probability of participating to the labour market and parental time, both for working and non-working respondents, using, of course, different sets of regressors (see the lists below); for more details, see Rapoport and Le Bourdais (2002a). The principle of this method is quite simple: it assumes that the determinants of parental time are not necessarily the same among working and non-working individuals, and that they might exert different effects on parental time. The model contains three sets of equations: one predicting the probability of respondents for being employed, and two describing parental time for working and non-working respondents.[21] These three equations are simultaneously estimated by using maximum likelihood. One other technical point needs to be mentioned. For some parents, parental time (and especially that devoted to a given activity) might be equal to zero on the day they were interviewed. For this reason, all endogenous variables have been treated as censored variables; in other words, we have taken into account the fact that for a given activity, the observed distribution is normally distributed but truncated, which would not be the case if the observation period had been long enough.[22]

Variables Predicting Parental Time for Both Working and Non-Working Respondents

- Parental time (in minutes)
- Respondent interviewed on Saturday or Sunday: dichotomous
- Age of respondents: continuous (by five-year groups)
- Female respondent: dichotomous (only for regressions for all types of households)

FAMILY AND HOUSEHOLD COMPOSITION
- Number and age of children: polytomous (one 0- to 2-year-old child; one 0- to 2-year-old child and one 3- to 4-year-old child; one 0- to 2-

year-old child and one more than 4-year-old child; one 0- to 2-year-old child and several more than 4-year-old children; one 3- to 4-year-old child; one 3- to 4-year-old child and one more than 4-year-old child; one 3- to 4-year-old child and several more than 4-year-old children; one 5- to 12-year-old child; two 5- to 12-year-old children; one 5- to 12-year-old child and one or several 13- to 14-year-old children; two 5- to 12-year-old children and one or several 13- to 14-year-old children; three 5- to 12-year-old children; one or several 13- to 14-year-old children). Only for regressions for all types of households and for regression for mothers.

- Age of the youngest child: continuous (only for regressions for fathers)
- Number of less than 18-year-old children: continuous (only for regressions for fathers)
- Two-parent household: dichotomous (only for regressions for all types of households)

ACTIVITY AND WORK SCHEDULES

- Respondent's number of hours worked the Designated Day: continuous (in hours)
- Respondent's work schedules: series of dichotomous variables as described in Table 4.1 (only for working respondents)
- Partner's work schedules: series of dichotomous variables described in Table 4.1 (only for regressions for two-parent households)
- Respondent sometimes works at home: dichotomous (only for working respondents)
- Respondent has flexible schedules: dichotomous (only for working respondents)
- Respondent usually works rotating shift: dichotomy (only for working respondents)
- Time spent by the partner with children in the previous week: continuous (only for regressions for two-parent households)
- Time spent by the partner with children is missing: dichotomous (only for regressions for two-parent households)

SOCIOCULTURAL VARIABLES

- Respondent's educational level: polytomous (university diploma; post-secondary diploma, or some (non-completed) university; secondary diploma or some (non-completed) high school; elementary or some (non-completed) secondary (reference); non-stated
- Respondent's professional occupation: polytomous (Standard Occu-

pational Classification, 1980: managerial and other professional (reference); clerical; sales; services; primary occupations; processing, machining, and fabricating; construction trades; transport equipment operating; material handling and other crafts; missing) (only for working respondents)
- Respondent born in Canada: dichotomous
- Respondent's region of residence: polytomous (Atlantic region; Quebec (reference); Ontario; Prairie region; British Columbia)
- Respondent sometimes goes to church: dichotomous

Variables Predicting the Probability of Participating in the Labour Market (Switch Part of the Regression)

- Female respondent: dichotomous (only for regressions for all types of households)
- 1998 survey: dichotomous

FAMILY AND HOUSEHOLD COMPOSITION
- Two-parent household: dichotomous (only for regressions for all types of households)
- Respondent's age: continuous (by five-year groups); square age
- Age of the youngest child: continuous and square age of the youngest child
- Number of less than 18-year-old children: continuous

SOCIOCULTURAL VARIABLES
- Respondent's educational level: (see above)
- Respondent born in Canada: dichotomous
- Respondent's mother born in Canada: dichotomous
- Respondent's father born in Canada: dichotomous
- Homeowner: dichotomous
- Respondent's region of residence: (see above)

NOTES

1 Excluding Yukon and the Northwest Territories.
2 This differs, e.g., from the Swedish household panel study (Household Market and Non-Market Activities; see, Hallberg and Klevmarken 2002) in which no fixed format was used for activities (the respondent's own words

were recorded). See also, e.g., Juster and Stafford (1991) for a discussion on the advantages and shortcomings of the different types of time use surveys.

3 Category 24 concerns residual codes (missing information).

4 Category 12 (sleep) has been excluded, as respondents were not asked with whom they were while sleeping; this is also the case for most personal activities.

5 However, respondents were asked to evaluate the total amount of time spent in childcare by the other parent during the week preceding the survey.

6 Note that biological, adopted, and stepchildren are not distinguished in the public data files.

7 The variables on family composition provided in the 1992 data file do not allow to distinguish among children aged between 13 and 18, whereas children aged 13–14 and 15–18 are differentiated in the 1998 file. However, even in 1992, it is possible to know whether a child younger than 15 lives in the household.

8 The difference of 1 minute observed between figures 4.1 and 4.2 in total parental time is due to the rounding of numbers across categories.

9 However, according to Nock and Kingston (1988), they spend in fact more time watching TV with their children.

10 On average, mothers spend 386 minutes with their children, compared with 250 minutes for fathers.

11 Compared with the means, standard deviations are much larger for the average parental time of respondents whose working hours on the Designated Day cut through more than one period. This indicates that these situations are probably more varied than others.

12 Other controls include among others: day and year surveyed; age and sex of respondents; number and age of children; type of family; work characteristics (flexible schedules, rotating shifts, work at home); sociocultural variables (education, occupation, religious attendance, place of birth, region of residence). Variables are not included when not relevant (e.g., work-related variables are not included for non-working people). Moreover, for respondents living in two-parent households, the number of hours that the partner spent looking after children during the week previous to the survey is included in the models. Finally, some other variables are added for the switch part of the regression (see the Appendix for a detailed presentation of the different variables).

13 The calculation is as follows: [0.060 (A worked from 8 am to 10 am) + 0.590 (A worked from 10 am to 2 pm) –0.145 (A worked from 2 pm to 5 pm)] – [0.590 (B worked from 10 am to 2 pm) –0.145 (B worked from 2 pm to 6 pm) –0.397 (B worked from 6 pm to 7 pm)] = 0.457. See first column of Table 4.1.

14 Results for fathers in one-parent households must be interpreted with caution because of the small size of the subsample (85 fathers).
15 It is important to keep in mind that we reason ceteris paribus, that is, when controlling for the number of hours worked.
16 However, once again, the subsample is quite small.
17 Note that we comment on only the results for working parents, although the model is estimated for both working and non-working parents, as indicated above. See Rapoport and Le Bourdais (2002a) for a comparison.
18 Except for fathers in one-parent households, due to the small size of the sample and to the fact that single fathers with very young children are very rare. For those households, we introduced one variable that measures the age of the youngest child and another that indicates the number of children less than 18 year-old.
19 The amount of time allocated to childcare by the partner is not precisely measured in the survey, as it is estimated by the respondent on a weekly basis.
20 See Rapoport and Le Bourdais (2001; 2002a) for more detailed analyses.
21 Since there were only 18 fathers living in one-parent families who did not work on the day they were interviewed, the model for them is much simpler. Only working fathers were included in the analysis, and we simply used a tobit model.
22 We observed only the conditional distribution which is conditional on the fact that time devoted to the activity is positive.

REFERENCES

Amato, P.R. 1994. 'Father-Child Relations, Mother-Child Relations, and Offspring Psychological Well-Being in Early Adulthood.' *Journal of Marriage and the Family* 56: 1031–42.
Amato, P.R., and J.G. Gilbreth. 1999. 'Nonresident Fathers and Children's Well-Being: A Meta-Analysis.' *Journal of Marriage and the Family* 61: 557–73.
Beaujot, R. 2000. *Earning and Caring in Canadian Families*. Peterborough, ON: Broadview Press.
Bianchi, S.M. 2000. 'Maternal Employment and Time with Children: Dramatic Change or Surprising Continuity.' *Demography* 37: 401–14.
Bogen, K., and P. Joshi. 2002. 'Bad Work or Good Move: The Relationship of Part-Time and Nonstandard Work Schedules to Parenting and Child Behavior in Working Poor Families.' Mimeo.
Brayfield, A. 1995. 'Juggling Jobs and Kids: The Impact of Employment Sched-

ules on Fathers' Caring for Children.' *Journal of Marriage and the Family* 57: 321–32.

Casper, L.M. 1997. 'My Daddy Takes Care of Me! Fathers as Care Providers.' *Current Population Report*, 70–59. Washington, DC: U.S. Bureau of the Census.

Carlson, M.J. 2000. 'Family Structure, Father-Child Closeness and Social-Behavior Outcomes for Children.' Mimeo.

Chenu, A., and J.P. Robinson. 2002. 'Synchronicity in the Work Schedules of Working Couples.' *Monthly Labor Review* 125(4): 55–63.

De Vault, M.L. 1991. *Feeding the Family: The Social Organization of Caring as Gendered Work*. Chicago: University of Chicago Press.

Fox, B. 2001. 'The Formative Years: How Parenthood Creates Gender.' *Canadian Review of Sociology and Anthropology* 38(4): 373–90.

Gagné, L. 2003. *Parental Work, Child-Care Use and Young Children's Cognitive Outcomes*. Ottawa: Statistics Canada, cat. 89-594-XIE2003001.

Hallberg, D., and A. Klevmarken. 2002. 'Time for Children: A Study of Parents' Time Allocation.' *Journal of Population Economics* 16(2): 205–26.

Hamermesh, D. 1998. 'When We Work.' *American Economic Review.* 88(2): 321–25.

– 2002. 'Timing, Togetherness and Time Windfalls.' *Journal of Population Economics* 15(4): 601–23.

Harrington, M. 2001. 'Gendered Time: Leisure in Family Life.' In K.J. Daly (ed.), *Minding the Time in Family Experience: Emerging Perspectives and Issues*, 343–82. New-York: JAI Press.

Juster, F.T., Stafford, F.P. 1991. 'The Allocation of Time, Empirical Findings, Behavioral Models, and Problems of Measurement.' *Journal of Economic Literature* 29:471–522.

Lapierre-Adamcyk, E., C. Le Bourdais, and N. Marcil. 2001. 'Temps de travail et temps familial: comportements des mères et des pères dans une économie en changement.' In *Demographic Futures in the Context of Globalization: Public Policy Issues*, 149–63. 2001 Symposium of the Federation of Canadian Demographers. Ottawa, Carleton University.

Lefebvre, P., and P. Merrigan. 1999. 'Comportements d'utilisation du temps non marchand des familles au Québec et au Canada: Une modélisation sur les microdonnées du budget-temps de 1986 et de 1992.' *L'Actualité économique: Revue d'analyse économique* 75: 625–63.

Marcil-Gratton, N., and C. Le Bourdais. 2000. 'La conciliation famille/travail comme facteur de stress: Multiplicité des besoins et diversité des besoins.' Mimeo.

Nock, S.L., and P.W. Kingston. 1988. 'Time With Children: The Impact of Couples' Work-Time Commitments.' *Social Forces* 67(1): 59–85.

Oppenheimer, V.K. 1994. 'Women's Rising Employment and the Future of the Family in Industrial Societies.' *Population and Development Review* 20(2): 293–342.

Presser, H.B. 1988. 'Shift Work and Child Care among Young Dual-Earner American Parents.' *Journal of Marriage and the Family* 50(1): 133–48.

– 1989. 'Can We Make Time for Children? The Economy, Work Schedules, and Child Care.' *Demography* 26(4): 523–43.

– 1994. 'Employment Schedules among Dual-Earner Spouses and the Division of Household Labor by Gender.' *American Sociological Review* 59(3): 348–64.

– 1999. 'Toward a 24-Hour Economy.' *Science* 284(5421): 1778–9.

– 2002. 'Employment in a 24/7 Economy: Challenge for the Family.' Mimeo.

Rapoport, B., and C. Le Bourdais. 2001. 'Temps parental et formes familiales.' *Loisir et société* 24(2): 585–617.

– 2002a. 'Parental Time and Working Schedules.' Paper presented at the 14th Annual European Association of Labour Economists (EALE) Conference, Paris, Sept.

– 2002b. 'The Allocation of Spousal Time.' Paper presented at the conference Work Time and Leisure Time: Dynamics and Convergence in Changing Contexts of the International Association for Time Use Research (IATUR), Lisbon, 15–18 Oct.

Sandberg, J.F., and S.L. Hofferth. 2001. 'Changes in Children's Time with Parents: United States, 1981–1997.' *Demography* 38(3): 423–36.

Statistics Canada. 1993. *General Social Survey* [Cycle 7]. Ottawa: Statistics Canada.

– 1999. Enquête sociale générale, cycle 12: l'emploi du temps (1998) – Documentation sur le fichier de microdonnées à grande diffusion et guide de l'utilisateur. Ottawa: Statisties Canada.

Van de Kaa, Dirk. 1987. 'Europe's Second Demographic Transition.' *Population Bulletin* 42(1): 1–58.

5 Delayed Life Transitions: Trends and Implications

RODERIC BEAUJOT

In Canada and in a number of other societies, life course patterns of the past forty years have seen delayed transitions associated with home leaving, completion of education, and family formation. This chapter reviews these trends and considers the implications for the various phases of the life course, and for the society as a whole. We will start with the transitions associated with families, that is, home leaving, union formation, and first birth; but these are clearly linked to the transitions of education and work. All of these have undergone delays over the past four decades, which is in marked contrast to the patterns over the previous decades where transitions were occurring at increasingly younger ages on average.

In particular, cohorts born between the world wars experienced a transition to adulthood that was compressed into a relatively short period that included completing formal education, entering the labour force, leaving home, establishing a nuclear household, and having a first child. For subsequent cohorts, not only has this standardization broken down, but the early life course transitions have extended over a longer period, the sequencing is more diverse, and the events themselves are less clearly defined.

A long period of juvenile dependence is part of the uniquely human life course, which also includes a long life span and a substantial period of post-reproductive productivity. From this perspective, the period of adolescence and youth has been extended, as there is need for more investments in skills, for both men and women. From a political economy perspective, the value of youth labour has declined. Demographically, youth have seen their opportunities blocked by the large baby boom generation. As families adopt a two-worker model, there are further complexities in the role transitions of both women and men, in the dual agendas of work and family.

Early Adult Transitions

Home Leaving

The median age at home leaving was youngest for the cohort born in 1951–56, at an average of 21.5 years for men and 19.9 years for women (Beaujot 2000: 97). In their explanation, Lapierre-Adamcyk and her colleagues (1995) pay particular attention to the more difficult economic times since the beginning of the 1980s, and women's labour market interests wherein their strategies would come to resemble those of men, and they would seek to put off family life to give priority to their work status. The 2001 census shows that the trends continue, with 41.1% of those age 20–29 living with their parents in 2001, compared with 27.5% in 1981 (Statistics Canada 2002a: 27). In contrast, the period 1971–81 saw a decline in the proportion of young persons living in their parents' home (Boyd and Norris 1999). Young people are more likely to be living at home if they are studying full-time, are unemployed, or have low income. That is, the economic resources of youth are important to home leaving, but the differences are much larger by marital status, showing a lower likelihood for married or formerly married persons to be living with their parents.

Boyd and Norris (1999) contrast two views on later home leaving. On the one hand, home leaving signals other successful transitions to adulthood, like completion of education, employment, marriage, and childbearing. On the other hand, living at home can benefit young people in making other types of transitions from adolescence to adulthood, especially completing education, experimenting with relationships, and obtaining employment.

In their book entitled *The Changing Transition to Adulthood: Leaving and Returning Home*, Goldscheider and Goldscheider (1999) note especially the instability of the nest leaving transition, with children both leaving and returning home. They observe that leaving home and establishing independent residence is largely seen as a critical step in the transition to adulthood. It clearly marks a shift from some forms of dependence to greater autonomy. On the other hand, they note that early home leaving can mark lower transfers to children.

Most authors focus on the economic factors associated with a delay in home leaving, but there are also cultural factors making parental homes more suitable to older children, as generation gaps have narrowed, and as parents have established more egalitarian relationships with their children. As another example of the importance of values and expectations, Goldscheider and Goldscheider (1993) find that the attitudes of both parents and children matter considerably in the decision to leave home. At the same time, they find little relationship between measures of parental resources and the timing of home leaving, except that home leaving to attend post-secondary education is more likely when parents have more resources (Goldscheider and Goldscheider 1999: 209). Also, parental resources do not predict children returning home; that is, 'parents' willingness to share their home is not a function of their affluence' (ibid.).

A persistent finding is that, on average, children leave home sooner from lone-parent families and from stepfamilies than from intact families (Goldscheider and Goldscheider 1998). When parents separate, children are most likely to live with their mother. However, there is an exception showing that children tend to prefer living with a father who is not in a relationship over a mother who is in a new relationship (Boyd and Norris 1995). These contrasts across family types suggest that there are better transfers to children in intact families. American results show, in particular, that leaving home to pursue further education is more likely to occur in intact families (Goldscheider and Goldscheider 1998).

Many commentators talk about late home leaving in negative terms; for instance, Boyd and Pryor (1989) have used the term *cluttered nest*. In some regards, the delay in home leaving is counter to the 'idea of progress' underlying family trends, as implied especially by the growth of individualism. However, from the point of view of children, early home leaving can pose problems for completion of high school, establishing savings, and receiving transfers from parents. Bernhardt et al. (2003) find that early home leaving is linked to lower educational aspirations and lower educational attainment and that this would be particularly the case when the departure is due to a push factor, such as family conflict. Such early departures lead to a reduction in the quantity and quality of contact with both parents, and have negative consequences not only for successful career patterns, but also for stable families. Based on data from Sweden, Bernhardt et al. (2003) further find that when children are living with a divorced parent and no stepparent, and family conflict is also low, there is not a higher risk of early leaving than in an intact family.

On the other hand, Palomba (2001) finds that the very late departures that occur in southern Europe may be detrimental to the independence of young people. Contrasts across countries suggest that home leaving is later when children depend on transfers within the family, and earlier if there are more state transfers, as in Nordic countries (Reher 1998; Breen and Buchmann 2002; Iacovou 2002). For cohorts born around 1960, the median age at men's home leaving ranges from 26 or 27 years in Italy and Spain to 20 years in Sweden (Billari et al. 2001). There is less possibility of independence from parents at affordable costs when there is a poor housing market and lack of rental accommodation. In contrast, greater social transfers to young people, as occur in Sweden, allow more independence from parents.

Union Formation

The fluidity of the transition associated with home leaving, with the greater predominance of returning home, is matched by that of union formation, which includes not only marriage but also cohabitation. Part of the delay in marriage can be attributed to a larger proportion entering unions through cohabitation. For instance, 63% of first unions among women who were age 20–29 in 2001 were common law rather than marriages (Statistics Canada 2002b).

However, there are delays not only in marriage, but also in union formation. The census shows very strong differences between 1981 and 2001, with the proportion in union at age 20–24 declining from 27% to 14% for men and from 46% to 26% for women (Statistics Canada 2002a). By age 25–29, the majority of women are living in union (57% in 2001) but this figure was three-quarters (73%) in 1981. Of men age 25–29, two-thirds were in union in 1981, but less than half (45%) were in 2001. The median age at first marriage declined from 23.0 years for brides and 26.3 years for grooms in 1941 to just over 21 and 23 years, respectively, for those marrying in the early 1970s and then increased to 28.2 and 30.2, respectively, in 2001 (Beaujot and Kerr 2004: 212; Statistics Canada 2003b).

While common law unions take on a variety of forms, from those that are the equivalent to marriage to those that might better be seen as an alternative to living single, two things are clear. First common law unions are twice as likely to end in separation as are first marriages (Statistics Canada 2002b). Also, cohabitation postpones marriage and is correlated with lower marital stability. Wu (1999) proposes that cohabitation delays marriage not only because people who are marrying have a longer period of premarital relationships, but also because persons who are cohabiting are less likely to be actively searching for a marital partner, which further delays marriage timing if the relationship does not work out.

Becker (1981; 1991) proposes that the delay of marriage can be attributed to fewer gains from marriage when there is less gender specialization in the division of labour of couples. This 'independence hypothesis' would argue, in particular, that women who have higher achieved status would be less likely to marry, because they have less to gain from marriage.

Looking at the situation in the United States before 1980, Goldscheider and Waite (1986) interpret the results as implying that men with more achieved status are more likely to 'buy marriage' as part of the package, while women may use their higher education and occupational status to 'buy out of marriage.' However, with most relationships taking the form of the two-worker model, achieved status has since come to increase the likelihood of marriage for both men and women (Goldscheider and Waite 1991; Sweeney 1997).

Canadian results show similar changes over time, implying shifting dynamics associated with forming relationships. Using the 1995 General Social Survey, Turcotte and Goldscheider (1998) find that more highly educated women from the pre-1950 cohorts were less likely to marry, but the opposite applies for the post-1950 cohorts. For men of both cohorts, education is positively related to entry into unions, but the association has declined in importance. Mongeau and her colleagues (2001) also find that the Becker model applies to older cohorts, where women were more likely to marry sooner if they had more work interruptions. However, in the more recent cohorts, uncertainties at work – as measured through significant work interruptions – reduce men's likelihood of marriage, and they increase the likelihood that women will cohabit rather than marry. Given that union formation increasingly requires the earning power of both partners, we can expect to see an increased importance of education to women's entry into marriage, while working becomes increasingly important to entry into any type of union. In Quebec, where cohabitation is particularly high, women's employment increases their likelihood of forming a common law union (Bélanger and Turcotte 1999).

That is, it would appear that the Becker model does not apply to younger cohorts. That model expected fewer marriages when there were fewer gains associated with gender specialization, and as women became more economically independent. In her alternate 'Theory of Marriage Timing,' Oppenheimer (1988) does not attribute the delay of marriage to fewer gains from marriage, nor to an independence hypothesis wherein women with more status would use that status to remain more independent. Instead, Oppenheimer (1988; 1997) attributes the delay to the difficulty that young men have had in establishing their work lives and to the importance attached to the work lives of both spouses. That is, young adults will search longer for a spouse as their economic future is being defined and while they lack knowledge regarding important characteristics of a potential spouse. In a qualitative survey that asked when it was best to start a union or get married, respondents from London, Ontario, and the surrounding area largely said that it was best to wait until education is completed and work lives are being established (Beaujot and Bélanger 2001). That is, given the importance of work to a couple's lifestyle, the delayed entry into relationships follows on the longer period of education and the difficulty in establishing secure jobs.

Besides these economic questions underlying the theories of both Becker and Oppenheimer, marriage may pose a different priority for young people. In 'Sure, I'd Like to Get Married ... Someday,' White (1999) proposes that there is a 'worldwide retreat from marriage,' as men know that marriage requires greater commitment to a stable work life and as women know that they cannot depend on the stability of the union. However, survey evidence would suggest that young people attach much importance to living in a stable relationship (Lapierre-Adamcyk 1990). Attitudes and values clearly play a role in the entry into cohabitations and marriages, but these attitudes indicate strong expectations and preferences to enter relationships (Milan 2003). That is, the delay would not be associated with a retreat from relationships, but rather with the complexity of achieving two rewarding jobs and a stable relationship.

First Childbirth

While there is a certain fluidity to home leaving and union formation, making the transition difficult to mark, the same does not apply to the transition to parenthood, especially for women. The transition to parenthood involves much change in people's lives, and it is highly significant because of the associated permanence and obligation. One can have ex-spouses and ex-jobs but not ex-children. Even for men, parenthood is one of the most permanent commitments (Rindfuss et al. 1988).

The significance of the transition to parenthood can also be seen in how people use their time over a 24-hour day. The change from being single to partnered brings a small increase in the time spent doing housework for men, and a larger increase for women; in some countries, being partnered brings a decline in the time women spend doing paid work (Gauthier and Furstenberg 2002). The transition to parenthood brings a definite increase in the time women spend in housework and childcare, with a reduction of time in paid work. Men also experience an increase in time spent in housework and childcare (Beaujot and Liu 2005).

The delay in childbearing can be seen in the average age of women at first birth, which has increased from 23.4 years in 1976 to 27.6 in 2001 (Lochhead 2000; Statistics Canada 2003a). In 1976, only 9% of first-time mothers were age 30 or more, but this applied to 34% by 2001.

Over cohorts, the median age of men at their first birth was 26.5 years in the 1941–45 birth cohort, compared with 31.2 in the 1961–65 cohort (Beaujot 2000: 97). For women, this median age increased from 23.3 years in the 1941–45 cohort to 27.8 in the 1966–70 cohort.

The changed age pattern of childbearing, or the delay of fertility, has largely been associated with women's increased education and labour force participation. Particularly in the period 1963 to 1989, Rindfuss and his colleagues (1996) observe that women with college education in the United States experienced dramatic shifts towards later ages at childbearing. Looking at the 'variations in length of male parenting,' Ravanera and Rajulton (2000) find that men of higher status start later and finish sooner. Lochhead (2000: 42) observes that the distribution of first births shifts further to higher ages for women who have more education. He points especially to powerful economic and career incentives to delay childbirth and family formation, for many young women and men. Looking at 'the transition to adulthood in aging societies,' Fussell (2002) attributes both later and less childbearing to more insecurities for men and more labour force participation for women.

However, these economic relationships are not always simple. For instance, Smith (1999) observes that on some questions, such as the contractual protection of employees, insecurity has been reduced. What may have especially increased is people's aversion to risk (Hall 2002). It has also become much more acceptable to refer to lack of security as the reason for not having children.

Just as there is not a simple relationship between economic security and childbearing trends, the relation between fertility and labour force participation is not straightforward. We often pay attention to the period 1960 to 1975, when there were clearly reductions in fertility and increases in women's labour force participation (Beaujot and Kerr 2004: 87). However, women's education and labour force participation were increasing in the 1950s, when fertility was also rising. The period since 1975 has seen reasonably stable fertility but continued increases in labour force participation.

The relation between labour force participation and childbearing probably involves two models. In a model that was more relevant to older cohorts, women who had less labour market integration were more likely to have children. However, in younger cohorts, we may be seeing women delay childbearing until they are better integrated in the labour force, and consequently, it would be the women who are better integrated in the labour market who would be having children. This model is encouraged by provisions for parental leave and childcare, which are oriented to women who are employed. Certain occupations are more conducive to the second model, with women in education or nursing having more flexibility to have a child compared with those in law or engineering. In a qualitative study based on women who had graduated from university in 1985, Ranson (1998) found that those in education could take advantage of leaves, and a guaranteed return to their job, while women in law or business found that they had to be concentrating on their careers to the point that they had put off childbearing.

Out of School

The transition to the completion of formal education is difficult to measure because the future may bring a return to the classroom, but there can be no doubt that this transition is occurring later. In '100 Years of Education,' Clark (2000: 4) finds that in 1911 only about 1% of persons age 20–24 were attending school, which increased to 8% in 1961, but 48% in 1996. In the period 1976 to 2001, the proportion of persons attending school full-time at age 16–24 increased from 34.0% to 47.7% for men, and from 30.7% to 52.5% for women (Morissette 2002: 33). As an average over gender, a third were attending school full-time in 1976 but this increased to half of the age group in 2001. The greater increase for women also applies to age 25–29, which saw 2.0% attending full-time in 1976 and 7.3% in 2001, while men's rates went from 4.0% to 7.7%.

The median age at school completion increased from 18.8 years for the cohort of women born in 1941–45, to 21.8 years for the one born in 1971–75 (Ravanera et al. 1998). For men over these cohorts the median ages were rather stable, at about 22 years (Ravanera et al. 2002: 299).

There are various transitions within the education system, and it is the transition from entering high school to the completion of high school that has especially increased, with 88% of the population completing high school (Bowlby and McMullen 2002). Wanner (1999) finds over cohorts born from 1905 to 1969 that the transition from high school to post-secondary education has also increased, but the one from entering post-secondary to completion of a post-secondary degree has actually declined for men.

The transition to post-secondary continues to increase, with 62% of high school graduates going on to post-secondary education within a year, and another only 20% after a one-year delay (Tomkowicz and Bushnik 2003). International comparisons show that Canada is at the very top of OECD countries in terms of the proportion of the population at various age groups who have completed a post-secondary qualification, whether a diploma or degree. For instance, at age 25–34, half of the Canadian population has obtained such a qualification, compared with an average of around 25% for European countries (Beaujot and Kerr 2004: 249). Other comparisons show that Canada has particularly high enrolment rates at age 18–21, but by age 24 it is about in the middle of OECD countries (Fussell 2002: 21)

While longer schooling is clearly involved in the delay of early life transitions, it is noteworthy that for men the median age of school completion for the 1971–75 cohort was 21.5 years, while that of first union was more than 25 years, and first childbirth was at over 31 years (extending the trends from older cohorts shown in Ravanera et al. 2002: 299). Similarly, women of this 1971–75 cohort completed their education at a median age of 21.8 years, compared with 23 years for first union and about 28 for birth of first child (Ravanera et al. 1998: 187–9). Women's longer education may be delaying men's entry into first unions, but childbearing seems to be delayed much beyond the ages when education is completed for both genders.

In their study of 'Early Life Transitions of Canadian Youth,' Ravanera and her colleagues (2003) observe that young people with more parental resources, as measured through mothers working and living in communities with more resources, are especially likely to complete their schooling later. In contrast, children who do not live with both parents to age 15 leave school a year earlier, while they start work and leave home two years earlier.

In their analysis of the factors affecting union formation in Canada, Turcotte and Goldscheider (1998) observe the increased importance of higher educational attainment for women's entry into marriage. School enrolment was found to have become a bigger impediment to first union formation for younger cohorts.

Comparisons across countries suggest similar results, highlighting the importance of distinguishing educational attainment and school enrolment. That is, educational attainment has sometimes positive, sometimes negative, and often no net effect on women's family forma-tion, but educational enrolment impedes marriage (Sorensen 1995: 229). For men, greater educational attainment increases the likelihood of union and family formation (Corijn 2001: 11). Educational enrolment involves a high degree of dependence on parents, so that young people of both genders do not consider themselves sufficiently mature for marriage (Blossfeld 1995). An Ontario survey finds similar normative expectations that young people attending school are not ready to get married. That is, the extension of education and the narrowing of the gender gap are having profound effects on the early life course. Women's increased education is delaying union formation for both genders, but childbearing is delayed beyond what would be expected simply on the basis of educational enrolment.

Into the Labour Force

The transition into the labour force typically takes place over a number of years, as young people who are still students begin working on a part-time basis. The OECD (1997) has proposed that the starting age of the school-to-work transition can be estimated as the last age at which more than 75% of youths are only attending school. The end of the tran-sition would occur when more than half are only working. On the basis of the Labour Force Survey, excluding the summer months, Bowlby (2000: 44) estimates that this transition has started at about age 16, while the end of the transition has moved from age 21 in 1984 to age 23 in 1998. Thus, the transition now takes place over seven years, and not until age 23 is half of the cohort working without also going to school.

Among youths age 15–24, the largest category in 1984 was those who were working and not attending school (37% of the total), but by 1998 the largest category was those who were attending school but not working (40% of the total). Those both attending school and working had increased, while those neither attending school nor working had declined over this period (Bowlby 2000: 43). This confirms that fewer had completed the transition from school to work.

Besides the higher proportion attending school full-time, the trends over the period 1981 to 2001 have seen a lower proportion of non-students employed full-time, among persons under the age of 30 (Morissette 2002: 33). At age 16–24 the proportion of men non-students working full-time has declined over this period from 77.6% to 69.1%, while for women the decline is from 61.0% to 56.3%. At age 25–29 there are again declines for men, from 88.1% working full-time in 1981 to 83.8% in 2001. For this age group, women made significant gains, with from 50.9% to 66.2% working full-time. Morissette then calculates the earnings of full-year, full-time employees, finding declines over this period for both age groups of men, and stability for women.

Other studies have confirmed the disadvantage of younger men, especially in comparison with older men (Morissette 1998; Picot 1998). The proportion working, the hours worked per week, and the wages per hour, have all declined relative to older men. For women, data from the 1998 Survey of Labour and Income Dynamics suggest that the labour force advantages associated with delaying parenthood have increased for younger generations of mothers (Drolet 2002; 2003).

Tanner and Yabiku (1999) conclude that contemporary youth's transition to adulthood is delayed not as a function of their having different goals, because the goals of stable jobs remain dominant. It is the economic realities that are frustrating their achievement of these goals. In their analysis, Turcotte and Goldscheider (1998) find that working is increasingly important for entering any kind of union, since union formation increasingly requires the earning power of both partners. Thus, the labour market disadvantages of young men are reducing union formation, while young women have become more aware of the labour market disadvantages of early parenthood.

Implications of Delayed Early Life Transitions

The timing of early life transitions has implications not only for that period of life, but also for other parts of life, since the stages of the life course are clearly linked. As proposed by the Kaplan (1997) theory of the life course, later transitions can also be linked to longer life spans and lower fertility.

The life span has often been divided into three stages: a dependent childhood phase, a productive and reproductive adult stage, and a retirement stage. This third stage has been called a *troisième age*. With the lengthening of this third stage, some have proposed that we should also designate a *quatrième age* (Lachapelle and Stone 2001). Other authors have subdivided the childhood stage, adding a period of adolescence and youth. In the discussions that follow, we will consider implications for five stages of the life course: childhood at ages 0 to 14 years, when most are not working; adolescent and youth at ages 15 to 34, which includes the early life transitions under consideration; adult, at ages 35 to 59, when most are working and raising children; a troisième age, at 60 to 79; followed by a quatrième age of sometimes frail elderly who are living beyond the average life expectancy. Persons in this quatrième age are not necessarily dependent and they remain involved in caring roles. Clearly, these ages are not cut in stone, but they help focus the attention on the different dynamics over the life course and the links across stages.

Implications for Children under 15

The delay of early life transitions does not affect young children directly, since most at this age have been living at home and going to school. Indirectly, children are affected by parents who are on average older, and there is a larger age gap between generations.

The literature regarding the effects of family change on children largely concludes that children have benefited from having fewer siblings, more mature parents, more educated parents, and more two-income families, but they have been disadvantaged by the greater likelihood of experiencing the separation of their parents (Picot et al. 1998; Kerr 1992; Kerr and Beaujot 2003; Beaujot 2000: 270–4).

The advantage of more mature parents is largely seen in terms of their stronger acquired financial and human capital. Given that the delay in parenting has permitted more education, Lochhead (2000) finds increasing socioeconomic disparities between younger and older parents. Younger parents are also more likely to separate.

This has led some authors to speak of a bifurcation of models in terms of early and late childbearing. Based on census data, Lochhead (2000) finds that delayed childbearing is more pronounced among women who have university education, and there are increasing income differentials to the disadvantage of younger first-time mothers, even in two-parent families. Using data from the United States, Martin (2000) finds that delayed childbearers, who tend to have more education, are increasingly likely to raise their children in intact marriages, while early childbearers are more likely to raise children outside of marriage. Canadian data also indicate that women under 30 who used to be married are much more likely to have children than those who are single, cohabiting, or married (Ravanera 1995: 18). Consequently, Bianchi (2000) speaks of a possible bifurcation of models, with one group taking advantage of parental investment from both mothers and fathers, and another where fathers are absent and mothers do not have adequate time and resources to invest in children. Children born of mature parents are more likely to have the advantages of a mother with more human capital, along with the presence of a father in a dual-income family, which contrasts with the greater likelihood of lone parenthood for those who parent early.

In asking people about the best time to have children, a certain number say that one should not wait too long, in order to have the necessary energy and patience and to minimize the gap between parents and children. Observing that later childbearing is more likely to involve a first child or an only child, Marcil-Gratton (1988) notes that the parents are more likely to be inexperienced at taking care of children, and the child is less likely to have the advantage of an older brother or sister from whom to learn. While only children also have advantages, such as the undivided attention of parents, respondents in a qualitative survey often mention the concern of not having lived in a close interpersonal environment with someone of one's own age, which could be important to establishing marital relationships (Beaujot and Bélanger 2001).

From the point of view of young children, delayed childbearing, therefore, comes with the advantages of parents who are more mature, with more financial and human capital, but with the possible disadvantages of less sibling interaction and a larger age gap with their parents.

Implications for Adolescents and Youth, Ages 15 to 34

The ages to use for this discussion are necessarily less precise than the age groups used by demographers. The category of adolescence and youth is seeking to capture the segment of the life course during which the early life transitions are being delayed. At age 15 most children in advanced industrialized societies are living at home and going to school, and by age 35 most are working and raising children. It is tempting to use the age range 15 to 29, since most have already finished school and are working by age 25, but with the median age of first birth now 27.3 years for women and probably 30 years for men, a significant number have not completed the transition to parenthood until after age 30.

In an overview article, Arnett (2000: 469 and 479) uses the concept of 'emerging adulthood' to refer to the period of late teens to the twenties, especially ages 18 to 25. He observes that this life stage exists 'only in cultures that allow young people a prolonged period of independent role exploration.' During this period of change and exploration, young people would 'gradually arrive at more enduring choices in love, work and world views.'

The implications of delayed life transitions for adolescents and youth depend critically on the extent to which the extra time is used accumulating human and financial capital. Among persons with low skills, there is some evidence in the United States that the rotation across jobs is not building their human capital (Klerman and Karoly 1994). In earlier times, young men with limited education would largely be married parents and they would need to stay with their job. But if the instability in employment is better interpreted as 'churn' rather than the acquisition of human capital through mobility across jobs, then their time is wasted rather than being used productively. Without the pressure of marriage and parenthood, some young people seem to be spending a lot of time 'deciding' how they want to face adult life. It can be argued that delayed home leaving and late entry into full-time work means a delay in participation in society as a full citizen.

If the time is spent acquiring more education and skills, or getting established before having children, then one can well argue that there are more benefits than costs. However, this argument is based on the experience of past cohorts and thus may not apply to future ones. In particular, those who delayed among older generations were very selective, typically spending considerably more time in education. To the extent that this investment has paid off, they are likely to have benefited from their delays relative to others in their cohort.

Most studies see *advantages for individuals* who delay, relative to the remainder of their cohort. In their study of early life transitions of Canadians, Ravanera and her colleagues (1998; 2002) find that the delay in family formation is more likely to occur for persons with more opportunities. For instance, the timing of first marriage is later for women who work before marriage, for those with more education, and for those whose mother has more education.

Focusing on post-secondary school graduates, Finnie (2001) finds that their unemployment rates are significantly lower than for youth who have not obtained post-secondary degrees or diplomas, and the average earnings of young men have been steady or have only declined slightly, while the earnings of women graduates have increased for the graduating classes of 1982 to 1990. That is, the Generation X phenomenon of disadvantages in the labour market applies much less to persons who completed post-secondary degrees or diplomas.

Goldscheider and Goldscheider (1999: 209–10) also conclude that children from more affluent families are more likely to leave home to further their education; more likely to delay their career paths; and less likely to enter unstable relationships, such as cohabitation and early marriages. In contrast, parental family structures that are not intact lead to early home leaving, the early formation of relationships, and decreased investment in education (Bernhardt et al. 2003). These authors further observe that leaving home at a very young age, particularly when this does not involve attending school, has a variety of negative consequences for establishing successful career patterns and stable families. Co-residence provides greater subsidies than are provided through financial support for independent living. Bernhardt and her colleagues further summarize that leaving home early can pose problems for completing high school, establishing savings, and testing new relationships, and that it is linked to lower educational aspirations and attainment.

While individuals may profit from later transitions, the benefits may not apply to the *whole cohort*, in comparison with earlier cohorts. With the higher proportions attending school full-time, the lower proportions of non-student men working full-time, and declines in men's earnings, it is not surprising that Morissette (2002) finds deteriorating cumulative earnings to ages 26 to 35. In this study, earnings are cumulated over twelve years, for synthetic cohorts as they changed from age 15–24 to 26–35. Leaving aside the immigrants who arrived during these periods, the cumulative earnings declined over the period 1988–99 by 22.5% for men, and by 3.3% for women, compared with the 1973–84 period. The decline in cumulative earnings for men is because they stayed in school longer, non-students were less likely to work full-time, and the earnings of those working full-time, were slightly lower. For women, the longer period at school was somewhat compensated through greater proportions working full-time and the earnings of those working full-time did not decline. These changes also apply to the

United States where the financial situation of young adults has deterio-rated substantially relative to that of older adults; renters and first-time homebuyers have been especially affected (Goldscheider et al. 2001).

These results on cumulative earnings are confirmed by data on wealth acquisition. The median wealth of families where the major income recipient was Canadian-born and between the ages of 26 and 35 declined by 26.2% between 1984 and 1999 (Morissette 2002: 37). Part of this difference would be a function of the greater predominance of lone-parents as major income recipients of families. While housing prices have increased, these wealth surveys do not show a deteriora-tion in the proportion of families owning a principal residence, which has been stable at just over 50% among Canadian-born where the prin-cipal income recipient is from 26 to 35 years old. For a variety of rea-sons, some of which are a function of spending more time at school, the typical young family in the late 1990s had accumulated fewer assets than had their counterparts in the mid-1980s, and about half were home owners.

Student loans are part of the difficulty in acquiring assets. Close to half of those graduating in 1995 had student loans, with average loans of $9,600 for college graduates, $13,300 for university students with a bachelor's degree, and $21,000 for those with a professional degree (Clark 1999). Nonetheless, after five years, over half of these loans had been paid, and only 16% reported difficulty in paying back the loans (Allen et al. 2003).

In summary, while delayed transitions come with several advantages for individuals, especially permitting a greater acquisition of human capital, there are also disadvantages at the cohort level, with lower cumulative income and acquired wealth by age 35. There are also dis-advantages for individuals who take longer to pay off debts and to acquire equity. In addition, without the pressure of marriage and par-enthood, some young persons, especially those with low-level skills, may be wasting their time rather than acquiring the resources that will better prepare them for the prime productive ages.

Prime Productive Ages, 35 to 59

With low starting salaries and fewer work hours associated with child-bearing, many people are not into their prime productive ages until well after age 35. The median age of retirement has moved in the oppo-site direction, to about 62.

Calculating the cumulative earnings over twelve years, to age 36 to 45, Morissette (2002: 35) finds that the period 1988–99 saw a 10.5% loss for Canadian-born men, but a 52.3% gain for women, compared with the period 1973–84. Over a similar twelve years, those who became 46 to 55 years old saw about the same cumulative earnings in the two synthetic cohorts for men, but gains of 86.3% for women. In these age groups, women's increased participation in the labour force, and better-paying jobs, produced these large increases in their average earnings. Nonetheless, women's cumulative earnings only represented 51.9% of men's earnings for the age group 46–55 in 1999.

Compared with their median wealth in 1984, the median wealth by age of major income recipient had declined in 1999 by 11.6% for the age group 36–45 and by 4.8% at age 46–55. The proportion of families owning their principal residence remained rather stable for these two groups, at about 70%.

Part of the difficulty in making gains on wealth and home ownership may be a function of concentration on the needs of youth, who remain at school and at home for longer periods. Thus, especially in one-income families, it may be difficult for couples and lone parents in their prime productive years to put aside enough to satisfy future requirements for a longer retirement period.

Troisième Age, 60 to 79

It is especially for people in their sixties, but also for those in their seventies, that one sees how there are connections over the life course, requiring accommodations at other stages for the delay in early life transitions. When a small proportion of given cohorts were delaying their early life transitions, these selective individuals could probably use their higher human capital to catch up in financial terms by the time they reached retirement. In effect, early retirement is most common for persons who have bachelor's or graduate degrees, and for persons who work in utilities, public administration, and educational services (Kieran 2001).

At the macro-level, the period 1965 to 1985 benefited from great growth in the labour force, with the arrival of the baby boom to these ages, and women's greater participation. Now that this 'demographic bonus' has been used up, there may be a need to extend the period of 'post-reproductive productivity' into later ages to accommodate for longer lives and later transitions into the years of prime productivity.

In *Reforms for an Ageing Society*, the OECD (2000) observes a dramatic fall in the number of expected years of life spent in employment, along with a rise in the number of years in school and in retirement. Since the 1960s, the percentage of the population at work has been growing: there are fewer children, the baby boom is in the labour force, and women's participation has increased. For Canada the percentage of the population employed is expected to continue increasing until 2010, but then to decline if there is a continuation of present trends in participation by age. The continuation of current trends to the year 2030 would mean that Canadians would spend only 44% of their lives employed, compared with the men having spent 74% of their lives employed under 1960 conditions (OECD 2000: 141; Hicks 2003a).

This OECD (2000) document argues, in particular, for changes that would promote the employment of older workers. They suggest reforms to public pension systems, taxation systems, and social transfer programs to remove incentives to early retirement. For pensions themselves, the document proposes a better mix with more private plans, phased reductions in public pension benefits, and hikes in contribution rates. International comparisons suggest that early retirement is at least partly due to incentives built into retirement policies (Gruber and Wise 1997). That is, retirement is earlier when the minimum age for entitlement to pension benefits is lower, when the value of pensions is higher, when there are fewer pension benefits from additional years of work, and when disability pensions are available below the normal retirement age.

At the same time there is much variability in people's health and potential in their sixties and seventies. Some are able to maintain a high level of productivity, others suffer from lowered potential, chronic conditions, and disability. While some can continue at the same pace of productivity, many should be carrying fewer responsibilities. Instead of encouraging retirement, there may be ways to encourage a change in occupation. Instead of being teachers, professors, or daycare workers, could persons who are past their prime ages of productivity not be assistants? Rather than being managers, could they not be drivers and administrative assistants? For others, it may be possible to reduce hours at work, encouraging more time spent volunteering or caring for family members.

That is, in an economy based on high skills, post-reproductive productivity could be rather different from productivity in the prime ages, and it could be devoted more to caring, both paid and unpaid, in the family and beyond the family. This would partly relieve young parents who would be better able to balance their family and work lives. It might even encourage more people to become parents, knowing that there is more support, both formal and informal.

Quatrième Age, 80 Plus

The demarcation between the third and fourth ages cannot be made precisely, since it depends much on health. Not only do we live longer, but part of this longer life involves more years of poor health. At the same time, a shorter productive life may mean less accumulated earnings.

Martel and Bélanger (1999) find that health-adjusted life expectancy has increased over the period 1986–96. They estimate that at age 65 the average person has a dependence-free life expectancy of 13 years, that is, to age 78. Lachapelle and Stone (2001) propose that the fourth age be defined through activity limitations, more or less serious dependency, and loss of the state of good health. They propose that this threshold has changed from an average age of 74 years in 1951 to 78 years in 1996. Using the demarcation of 80 years would mean people living longer than the average life expectancy. One could use age 72 where 75% of the cohort is still living.

Using the measure based on health, Lachapelle and Stone (2001) estimate that 2% of the Canadian population was in this fourth age in 1951, compared with 2.7% in 2001, but this will rise to 6% in 2051. The proportion of the population age 80 and over has increased from 1% in 1951 to 3% in 2001, but it will further increase to over 8% in 2051.

Rather than calculating this stage through years since birth, it might be measured from the other end of life. There comes a time when life needs to be calculated not from the beginning, but from the end, as people do when they are planning for retirement. Disability and chronic conditions call for less involvement in production, but persons at these ages are not necessarily dependent. Some remain able to care for others, in their family and beyond. The purpose should be to downplay ideas like 'freedom 55' or retirement at age 65 and to establish more flexibility over the life course.

Conclusion

The delay in early life course transitions cannot be separated from the rest of the life course, which means that there are significant implications for individuals and societies. As with other changes that are central to life, there are both positives and negatives, and significant adjustments are necessary.

In looking forward to the year 2100 as editor of *La démographie québécoise: enjeux du XXIe siècle*, Piché proposes that there will be at least as much change as we have seen in the past 100 years (Piché and Le Bourdais 2003). He proposes that technology may make pregnancies common at age 60. In his case, he says that it would have been good to have a first child at age 45, given career priorities and all the work that needed to be done when he was a young professional. While advances in technology allowing further delays in childbearing can certainly be envisaged, might one also envisage a world that is less centred on work, and where family has more priority? Rather than adjusting reproduction to suit the needs of production, might we not also make adjustments to benefit reproduction? For instance, is it always more important to maximize the number of people working, at the expense of family time and leisure?

A commentator on my *Earning and Caring in Canadian Families* has proposed that I should switch the title to say 'caring and earning' forcing more thinking about how production should be made to accommodate reproduction, rather than always giving priority to economic production (Bernier 2001). When asked to talk about their life goals, most people give high priority to their jobs and economic well-being, but they also attach high priority to family questions. Most would want to have their children in their twenties and thirties, rather than in their forties.

In spite of the generalized interests to have children, fertility is down to some 1.5 births per woman, and childbearing is occurring at older ages. These are core features of the second demographic transition, which includes new understandings regarding family relationships, with more focus on self-centred fulfilment and greater flexibility in the entry and exit from unions. Given the need for both men and women to be economically independent, it makes sense that unions and childbearing are delayed as education is completed and as work lives are established. Given the economic uncertainty and the need for high skills, it also makes sense that people are longer in education and later in starting their first full-time employment. The economic uncertainties faced by men, partly because they are competing with equally educated women, have brought delays in union formation. In some regards, women's greater economic participation has compensated, with rates of home ownership similar to what they were in the past. But the uncertainties in men's work lives, and the stronger labour force participation of women, have made it difficult to fit children into busy lives, thus bringing delays in reproduction and higher proportions of people without children, in spite of the high values typically placed on having children. In particular, low fertility is partly due to delays in childbearing, as some people miss the opportunity to have children in a narrow window from the late twenties to early thirties, or as fecundity becomes reduced with age.

In many regards, the implications of these delays are positive. By leaving home later, children are receiving more transfers from their parents; by staying in education longer, youth is better prepared for a world where the labour force is growing much more slowly and we need to depend on quality of workers. Two-worker families reduce the dependence of women on men and reduce the exposure of women and children to the risks associated with family instability.

At the individual level, the most negative implication is that people will not have saved enough during a shorter work life, partly because they entered full-time work later, partly because children have spent more time in education and have been slow at establishing their financial independence and leaving home. The accommodations here are obvious, to work longer while one is still healthy and productive, turning at least part of what we have called the troisième age (60–79) into a longer period of post-reproductive productivity.

The stronger negatives are at the societal level, because delayed early life transitions bring lower fertility and population aging. Accommodations to population aging are more complex, including promoting more economic productivity at older ages, partly by reducing the benefits of retirement without leaving stranded those who are unable to work for health or other reasons. Population aging affects a number of policy questions ranging from pensions and other transfers to education and labour market issues. Hicks (2003b) argues, in particular, for the introduction of greater life course flexibility in our systems of education and work. There may also be a need to reduce the incentives for early retirement and to increase work opportunities for older workers. Other structural adjustments could benefit young families and reduce the barriers to childbearing. That is, we need to find ways for production to accommodate reproduction.

There are also potential policies that would apply particularly to people at ages where they are making these early life course transitions. Greater societal investments in post-secondary education would allow young people to leave home sooner and to finish their education more efficiently without the distraction of part-time jobs. Greater investments in the school-to-work transition, especially for the benefit of those who leave school early, would reduce the uncertainties of the initial years on the labour market. Stronger investments in young families, including subsidies for parental leaves, tax benefits, reduced work hours, and childcare, would enable more people in this stage of life to achieve their work and family goals.

Subsidies for young families would correspond to the unique ways in which the human life course has evolved, with a long life expectancy, and long period of youth dependency that is subsidized by a long period of post-reproductive productivity. Sometimes this productivity in the troisième age can occur through direct care of grandchildren, as was the historical case, at other times it can occur through extending the regular work life, but at still other times it can occur through volunteer work or new careers of reduced responsibility.

These are difficult questions, in part, because an aging society tends to think especially of ways in which the lives of older people can be improved, and we tend to ignore the needs of the young who are less numerous and have limited political voice. For instance, in the countries that have greater employment protection, which benefits workers who have more seniority, there tend to be higher relative levels of youth unemployment (Breen and Buchmann 2002). As the demographic bonus gets spent, it is important to recognize that investments in the early stages of the life course provide the best basis for long-term security.

NOTE

This is a revised version of a chapter published under the same title by the Vanier Institute of the Family, in the series on Contemporary Family Trends. The author also wishes to indicate appreciation for the comments and suggestions made by Jim Côté, Alain Gagnon, Anne Gauthier, Robert Glossop, Wolfgang Lehmann, Kevin McQuillan, Livia Olah, Walter Omariba, Zenaida Ravanera, Daniel Sahleyesus, Eric Tenkorang, Tom Wonnacott and Henry Yeboah.

REFERENCES

Allen, Mary, Shelley Harris, and George Butlin, 2003. *Finding Their Way: A Profile of Young Canadian Graduates*. Ottawa: Statistics Canada, cat. no. 81-595-MIE2003003.

Arnett, Jeffrey. 2000. 'Emerging Adulthood: A Theory of Development from the Late Teens through the Twenties.' *American Psychologist* 55(5): 469–80.

Beaujot, Roderic. 2000. *Earning and Caring in Canadian Families*. Peterborough, ON: Broadview Press.

Beaujot, Roderic, and Alain Bélanger. 2001. 'Perspective on Below Replacement Fertility in Canada: Trends, Desires, Accommodations.' Paper presented at the International Union for the Scientific Study of Population, Working Group on Low Fertility Meeting, Tokyo, 21–3 March. Available at: http://www.ssc.uwo.ca/sociology/popstudies/dp/dp01-6.pdf.

Beaujot, Roderic, and Don Kerr. 2004. *Population Change in Canada*. Toronto: Oxford University Press.

Beaujot, Roderic, and Jianye Liu. 2005. 'Models of Time use in Paid and Unpaid Work.' *Journal of Family Issues* 26(7): 924–46.

Becker, Gary. 1981. *A Treatise on the Family*. Cambridge, MA: Harvard University Press.

– 1991. *A Treatise on the Family* (enlarged ed.). Cambridge, MA: Harvard University Press.

Bélanger, Alain, and Pierre Turcotte. 1999. 'L'influence des caractéristiques socio-démographiques sur le début de la vie conjugale des Québécoises.' *Cahiers québécois de démographie* 28(1–2): 173–97.

Bernhardt, Eva, Michael Gahler, and Frances Goldscheider. 2003. 'The Impact of Childhood Family Structure and Conflicts on Routes out of the Parental Home in Sweden.' Manuscript.

Bernier, Christiane, 2002. 'Comment on *Earning and Caring in Canadian Families*.' Paper presented at the meetings of the Canadian Sociology and Anthropology Association, Toronto, 29 May–1 June.

Bianchi, Suzanne. 2000. 'Maternal Employment and Time with Children: Dramatic Change or Surprising Continuity? *Demography* 37(4): 401–14.

Billari, Francesco, Dimiter Philipov, and Pau Baizan. 2001. 'Leaving Home in Europe: The Experience of Cohorts Born around 1960.' *International Journal of Population Geography* 7(5): 339–56.

Blossfeld, Hans-Peter, ed. 1995. *The New Role of Women: Family Formation in Modern Societies*. Boulder, CO: Westview.

Bowlby, Geoff. 2000. 'The School-to-Work Transition.' *Perspectives on Labour and Income* 12(1): 43–8.

Bowlby, Jeffrey, and Kathryn McMullen. 2002. *At a Crossreads: First Results for the 18–20-Year-Old Cohort of the Youth in Transition Survey*. Ottawa: Statistics Canada, cat. no. 81-591-XIE.

Boyd, Monica, and Doug Norris. 1995. 'Leaving the Nest? Impact of Family Structure.' *Canadian Social Trends* 38: 14–17.

- 1999. 'The Crowded Nest: Young Adults at Home.' *Canadian Social Trends* 52: 2–5.
Boyd, Monica, and Edward Pryor. 1989. 'The Cluttered Nest: The Living Arrangements of Young Canadian Adults.' *Canadian Journal of Sociology* 14(4): 46–79.
Breen, Richard, and Marlis Buchmann. 2002. 'Institutional Variation and the Position of Young People: A Comparative Perspective.' In Alan Heston (ed.), *Early Adulthood in Cross-National Perspective*, 288–305. Annals of the American Academy of Political and Social Science. Thousand Oaks, CA: Sage.
Clark, Warren. 1999. 'Paying Off Student Loans.' *Canadian Social Trends* 51: 24–8.
- 2000. '100 Years of Education.' *Canadian Social Trends* 59: 3–7.
Corijn, Martine. 2001. 'Transition to Adulthood: Socio-Demographic Factors.' In M. Corijn and E. Klijzing (eds.). *Transition to Adulthood in Europe*, 1–25. Dordrecht: Kluwer.
Drolet, Marie. 2002. *Wives, Mothers and Wages: Does Timing Matter?* Ottawa: Statistics Canada, cat. no. 11F0019, no. 186.
- 2003. 'Motherhood and Paycheques.' *Canadian Social Trends* 68: 19–21.
Finnie, Ross. 2001. 'Employment and Earnings of Postsecondary Graduates.' *Perspectives on Labour and Income* 13(3): 34–45.
Fussell, Elizabeth. 2002. 'The Transition to Adulthood in Aging Societies.' In Alan Heston (ed.), *Early Adulthood in Cross-National Perspective*, 16–39. Annals of the American Academy of Political and Social Science. Thousand Oaks, CA: Sage.
Gauthier, Anne, and Frank Furstenberg. 2002. 'The Transition to Adulthood: A Time Use Perspective.' In Alan Heston (ed.), *Early Adulthood in Cross-National Perspective*, 153–71. The Annals of the American Academy of Political and Social Science. Thousand Oaks, CA: Sage.
Goldscheider, Frances, and Calvin Goldscheider. 1993. *Leaving Home before Marriage: Ethnicity, Familism, and Generational Relationships*. Madison: University of Wisconsin Press.
- 1998. 'Effects of Childhood Family Structures on Leaving and Returning Home.' *Journal of Marriage and the Family* 60(3): 745–56.
- 1999. *The Changing Transition to Adulthood: Leaving and Returning Home*. Thousand Oaks, CA: Sage.
Goldscheider, Frances, A. Thornton, and L. Yang. 2001. 'Helping Out the Kids: Expectations about Parental Support in Young Adulthood.' *Journal of Marriage and the Family* 63(3): 727–40.
Goldscheider, Frances, and Linda J. Waite. 1986. 'Sex Differences in the Entry into Marriage.' *American Journal of Sociology* 92(1): 91–109.

– 1991. *New Families, No Families?* Berkeley: University of California Press.

Gruber, J., and D. Wise. 1997. *Social Security Programs and Retirement around the World.* Working Paper 6134. Cambridge, MA: National Bureau of Economic Research.

Hall, David. 2002. 'Risk Society and the Second Demographic Transition.' *Canadian Studies in Population* 29(2): 173–93.

Hicks, Peter. 2003a. 'The Policy Implications of Aging.' *Horizons* 6(2): 12–16.

– 2003b. 'New Policy Research on Population Aging and Life-Course Flexibility.' *Horizons* 6(2): 3–6.

Iacovou, Maria. 2002. 'Regional Differences in the Transition to Adulthood.' In Alan Heston (ed.), *Early Adulthood in Cross-National Perspective,* 40–69. Annals of the American Academy of Political and Social Science. Thousand Oaks, CA: Sage.

Kaplan, Hillard. 1997. 'The Evolution of the Human Life Course.' In K. Wachter and C. Finch (eds.), *Betweem Zeus and the Salmon: The Biodemography of Longevity,* 175–211. Washington, DC: National Acadamy Press.

Kerr, Don. 1992. 'Life-Cycle Demographic Effects and Economic Well-Being of Children.' Doctoral dissertation, University of Western Ontario, London, Ontario.

Kerr, Don and Roderic Beaujot. 2003. 'Child Poverty and Family Structure in Canada, 1987–1997.' *Journal of Comparative Family Studies* 34(3): 321–35.

Kieran, Partrick. 2001. 'Early Retirement Trends.' *Perspectives on Labour and Income.* 13(4): 7–13.

Klerman, Jacob, and Lynn Karoly. 1994. 'Young Men and the Transition to Stable Employment.' *Monthly Labor Review* 117(8): 31–48.

Lachapelle, Réjean, and Leroy Stone. 2001. 'Consequences of the Aging Population: Expanding the Notion of Age.' Paper presented at the meetings of the Federation of Canadian Demographers, Ottawa, 14–15 Dec.

Lapierre-Adamcyk, Evelyne. 1990. 'Faire face au changement démographique: la nécessaire participation des femmes.' In R. Beaujot (ed.), *Faire face au changement démographique,* 12–14. Ottawa: Royal Society of Canada.

Lapierre-Adamcyk, Eveline, Céline Le Bourdais and Karen Lehrhaupt. 1995. 'Le départ du foyer parental des jeunes Canadiens nés entre 1921 et 1960.' *Population* 50(4–5): 1111–35.

Lochhead, Clarence. 2000. 'The Trend toward Delayed First Childbirth: Health and Social Implications.' *ISUMA: Canadian Journal of Policy Research* (Autumn) (2): 41–4.

Marcil-Gratton, Nicole. 1988. *Les modes de vie nouveaux des adultes et leur impact sur les enfants au Canada.* Report for the Review of Demography. Ottawa: Health and Welfare Canada.

Martel, Laurent, and Alain Bélanger. 1999. 'An Analysis of the Change in Dependence-Free Life Expectancy in Canada between 1986 and 1996.' In A. Bélanger (ed.), *Report on the Demographic Situation in Canada 1998–1999*. 164–86. Ottawa: Statistics Canada, cat. no. 91–209.

Martin, S.P. 2000. 'Diverging Fertility among U.S. Women Who Delay Childbearing Past Age 30.' *Demography* 37(4): 523–33.

Milan, Anne. 2003. 'Would You Live Common-Law?' *Canadian Social Trends* 70: 2–6.

Mongeau, Jael, Ghyslaine Neill, and Céline Le Bourdais. 2001. 'Effet de la précarité économique sur la formation d'une première union au Canada.' *Cahiers québécois de démographie* 30(1): 3–28.

Morissette, René. 1998. 'The Declining Labour Market Status of Young Men.' In M. Corak, (ed.), *Labour Markets, Social Institutions and the Future of Canada's Children*. 31–50 Ottawa: Statistics Canada, cat. no. 89–553.

– 2002. 'Cumulative Earnings among Young Workers.' *Perspectives on Labour and Income* 14(4): 33–40.

Oppenheimer, Valerie. 1988. 'A Theory of Marriage Timing: Assortative Mating under Varying Degrees of Uncertainty.' *American Journal of Sociology* 94(3): 563–591.

– 1997. 'Women's Employment and the Gain to Marriage: The Specialization and Trading Model.' *Annual Review of Sociology* 23: 431–53.

Organization for Economic Coyoperation and Development. 1997. *Education at a Glance 1996*. Paris: OECD.

– 2000. *Reforms for an Ageing Society*. Paris: OECD.

Palomba, Rossella. 2001. 'Postponement of Family Formation in Italy, within the Southern European Context.' Paper presented at the International Union for the Scientific Study of Population, Working Group on Low Fertility meeting, Tokyo, 21–3 March.

Piché, Victor, and Céline Le Bourdais. 2003. *La démographie québécoise: enjeux du XXIe siècle*. Montreal: Presses de l'Université de Montréal.

Picot, Garnett. 1998. 'What Is Happening to Earnings Inequality and Youth Wages in the 1990s?' *Canadian Economic Observer* 11(9): 3.1–3.18.

Picot, Garnett, John Myles, and Wendy Pyper. 1998. 'Markets, Families and Social Transfers: Trends in LowyIncome among the Young and Old, 1973–95.' In M. Corak (ed.), *Labour Markets, Social Institutions and the Future of Canada's Children*. 11–30. Ottawa: Statistics Canada, cat. no. 89–553.

Ranson, Gillian. 1998. 'Education, Work and Family Decision Making: Finding the Right Time to Have a Baby.' *Canadian Review of Sociology and Anthropology* 35(4): 517–33.

Ravanera, Zenaida. 1995. 'A Portrait of the Family Life of Young Adults.' In R.

Beaujot, E.M. Gee, F. Rajulton, and Z. Ravanera (eds.), *Family over the Life Course*, 7–35. Ottawa: Statistics Canada, cat. no. 91–543.

Ravanera, Zenaida, and Fernando Rajulton. 2000. 'Variations in Length of Male Parenting.' *Canadian Studies in Population* 27(1): 63–84.

Ravanera, Zenaida, Fernando Rajulton and Thomas Burch. 1998. 'Early Life Transitions of Canadian Women: A Cohort Analysis of Timing, Sequences and Variations.' *European Journal of Population* 14(2): 179–204.

– 2003. 'Early Life Transitions of Canadian Youth: Effects of Family Transformation and Community Characteristics.' *Canadian Studies in Population* 30(2): 327–54.

Ravanera, Zenaida, Rajulton Fernando, Thomas Burch, and Céline Le Bourdais. 2002. 'The Early Life Courses of Canadian Men: Analysis of Timing and Sequences of Events.' *Canadian Studies in Population* 29(2): 293–312.

Reher, David S. 1998. 'Family Ties in Western Europe: Persistent Contrasts.' *Population and Development Review* 24(2): 203–34.

Rindfuss, Ronald, S. Philip Morgan, and Kate Offutt. 1996. 'Education and the Changing Age Pattern of American Fertility: 1963–1989.' *Demography* 33(3): 277–90.

Rindfuss, Ronald, S. Philip Morgan, and Gray Swicegood. 1988. *First Births in America: Changes in the Timing of Parenthood*. Berkeley: University of California Press.

Smith, Michael.1999. 'Insecurity in the Labour Market: The Case of Canada since the Second World War.' *Canadian Journal of Sociology* 24(2): 193–224.

Sorensen, Annemette. 1995. 'Women's Education and the Costs and Benefits of Marriage.' In H.-P. Blossfeld (ed.), *The New Role of Women: Family Formation in Modern Societies*, 229–35. Boulder, CO: Westview Press.

Statistics Canada. 2002a. *Profile of Canadian Families and Households: Diversification Continues*. Ottawa: Statistic Canada, cat. no. 96F0030-XIE-2002003.

– 2002b. *Changing Conjugal Life in Canada*. Ottawa: Statistics Canada, cat. no. 89-576, XIE.

– 2003a. *Births, 2001*. Ottawa: Statistics Canada, cat. no. 84F0210, XPB.

– 2003b. *Marriages, 2001*. Ottawa: Statistics Canada, cat. no. 84F0212, XPB.

Sweeney, Megan. 1997. *Women, Men and Changing Families: The Shifting Economic Foundations of Marriage*. Working Paper No. 97–14. Madison: University of Wisconsin-Madison, Center for Demography and Ecology.

Tanner, Jennifer, and Scott Yabiku. 1999. 'Conclusion: The Economics of Young Adulthood – One Future or Two.' In A. Booth, A. Crouter, and M. Shanahan (eds.), *Transitions to Adulthood in a Changing Economy: No Work, No Family, No Future?* 254–68. Westport: Praeger.

Tomkowicz, Joanna, and Tracey Bushnik. 2003. *Who Goes to PostySecondary*

Education and When: Pathways Chosen by 20 YearyOlds. Ottawa: Statistics Canada, cat. no. 81-595-MIE2003006.

Turcotte, Pierre, and Frances Goldscheider. 1998. 'The Evolution of Factors Influencing First Union Formation in Canada.' *Canadian Studies in Population* 25(2): 145–74.

Wanner, Richard. 1999. 'Expansion and Ascription: Trends in Educational Opportunities in Canada, 1920–1994.' *Canadian Review of Sociology and Anthropology* 36(3): 409–42.

White, Lynn. 1999. 'Sure, I'd Like to Get Married ... Someday.' In A. Booth, A. Crouter, and M. Shanahan (eds.), *Transitions to Adulthood in a Changing Economy: No Work, No Family, No Future?* 56–65. Westport: Praeger Publishers.

Wu, Zheng. 1999. 'Premarital Cohabitation and the Timing of First Marriage.' *Canadian Review of Sociology and Anthropology* 36(1): 109–27.

PART TWO

Family Transformation and Investment in Children

6 The Evolving Family Living Arrangements of Canada's Children: Consequences for Child Poverty and Child Outcomes

DON KERR

Children can draw parents into closer contact with others in their neighborhood, at school, and in the community (Scheon et al. 1997; Beaujot and Ravanera 2001). With a common interest in providing for educational and recreational activities for their children, family life and the raising of children might very well be understood as one means, among many others, to potentially increase the degree of social integration in a community.

Yet just as children are a source of social integration for adults, families can be conceived of as fundamental to the integration of children. In the first decade of life, the family serves as a primary agent of socialization to only gradually be replaced by peers, neighbours, and schools. For this reason considerable effort has been directed into understanding how family processes shape children's well-being and outcomes. Several family changes over recent decades have been particularly beneficial in this regard, whereas others have been detrimental.

This chapter focuses on family changes that bring a new kind of insecurity and greater instability in marital and parental relationships. The following section reviews some theoretical arguments and empirical research on the interrelationships between family change, income poverty, and child outcomes. The next section focuses more specifically on the relevance of familial change to the recent trends in the incidence of child poverty in Canada. This is followed by an examination of child outcomes using the first wave of Canada's National Longitudinal Survey of Children and Youth (NLSCY; Statistics Canada 1997). The two concluding sections discuss the potential for future research of subsequent waves of the NLSCY and summarize important insights about family changes and their relation to children's outcomes.

Family Change and Child Outcomes

Young children are completely dependent upon others for their well-being. The ability to cope with economic uncertainty and/or family change varies by age, with childhood clearly a vulnerable stage of the life cycle. Correspondingly, the well-being of children is often jeopardized by the difficulties experienced by the adults in their lives. In recognizing this fact, it is useful to consider the impact of familial change on various dimensions of child well-being, including child behavioural, psychological, and cognitive outcomes.

As the incidence of lone parenthood has risen, so too has the proportion of children living in stepfamilies. This has served to introduce considerable diversity in family patterns, both in terms of family types and resources available from parents. According to data from the NLSCY, about one in four Canadian children (age 0–11 years) are not living with both biological parents, with about one in six living in a lone-parent family and one in twelve living in a stepfamily (Statistics Canada 1998). This has important repercussions with regard to the amount of financial, human, and social capital that comes to children from their parents (Beaujot 2000; Picot and Myles 1996; Ross, Scott, and Kelly 1996; Dooley 1991).

In particular, large proportions of fathers are not living with their children and are less involved with daily childcare. As emphasized by Lefebvre and Merrigan (1998), while the majority of children across family types appear to be doing relatively well, the children most at risk are those who are in poor families and those living in non-intact homes. As economic hardship is highly associated with family type, it becomes difficult to delineate the relative impact of each separately – not to mention several other basic determinants of children's well-being.

In empirically examining how family life can shape child outcomes, prior studies differ in terms of emphasis, from research studies that pay a great deal of attention to family structure through to those that suggest that it has a very dubious status as a risk factor (Avison and Wade 2002). Similarly, researchers differ in terms of their emphasis on income poverty, as many other non-economic risk factors are also associated with childhood difficulties. Beyond both family structure and income poverty, other researchers have attempted to more fully spell out some of the 'family process' variables involved – such as the quality of interpersonal relationships within the home (Lansford et al. 2001; Benson et al. 1994). In this context, it is useful to briefly consider some of the reasons for the above differences in emphasis, beginning with the impact of income poverty on children's well-being.

Income Poverty

A wide assortment of studies have pointed to the impact of material deprivation on both internalizing and externalizing problems of young children (Hanson, McLanahan, and Thomson 1997) and on their academic success and cognitive development (Duncan et al. 1998). Income poverty is expected to contribute to childhood difficulties, to the extent that parents are unable to provide for the most fundamental requirements of healthy childhood development, including the basic nutritional and health requirements of the young, a safe neighbourhood and family environment, and adequate recreational and educational facilities (Mayer 1997; Brooks-Gunn et al. 1997; Massey 1996).

Low income not only implies a higher likelihood of inadequate housing and difficult living conditions, but in many cases a home environment that constrains somewhat the normal psychological and/or intellectual development of the young. For example, difficult economic circumstances can have a direct impact on the potential cognitive development of children, as low income parents are less able to 'purchase' the many products and services that assist the young in their learning, including books, magazines, computers, and travel (Guo and Harris 2000). Similarly, low income families are less able to afford the many recreational activities that are important for the physical, emotional, and intellectual development of children, which middle- and high income groups often take for granted.

In recent research on child outcomes, Carlson and Corcoran (2001) conclude that both behavioural and cognitive outcomes of American children (age 7–10) are particularly sensitive to persistent income poverty to a greater extent than family structure variables often cited in the literature. This conclusion is found to persist even after introducing controls on family functioning and parenting style, the fundamental 'family process' variables frequently raised in the explanation of child outcomes. In contrast, when summarizing the results from a comprehensive volume of studies on income poverty and child outcomes, Duncan and Brooks-Gunn (1997) conclude that family income matters, yet perhaps in a narrower manner than widely believed. In fact, much of the research in this area has been somewhat inconsistent in delineating the relative impact of low income on child outcomes, with researchers often deriving what are essentially contradictory conclusions.

The difficulties that surround much of this research at least partially relate to problems in operationalizing the multidimensional concept of 'poverty,' which is obviously only partly measured through household or family income. What is clear is that the experience of most poor Canadians is quite different from that of the middle class, often experiencing the social stigma associated with unemployment, potentially facing racial and/or ethnic discrimination, not to mention poor health and a higher likelihood of being disabled. Income alone cannot possibly capture fully what is meant by the broader sociological concepts of social class, stratification, and socioeconomic disadvantage. As Hauser and Sweeney (1997: 554) acknowledge 'overly economistic thinking may have diverted researchers from other major sources, dimensions, and conseqeunces of social inequality.'

Family Structure

A basic family structure model stresses the primary importance of family structure for child outcomes (Biblarz and Gottainer 2000). Whether or not a child is raised by two biological parents is considered a crucial determinant of children's well-being. It has been suggested that the well-being of the children is moderated to the extent that both parents can continue to be involved in a child's life after divorce or separation (Amato and Booth 1997). The increased frequency of lone parenthood has had its impact on the well-being of children, as non-custodial parents frequently lose regular contact with their children (Beaujot 2000; Marcil-Gratton 1993; Peron et al. 1999).

Children raised in lone-parent families obviously receive, on average, less parental supervision, an observation which is especially true with fathers. To the extent that fathers discontinue the investment of human and social capital in their children, this loss of regular contact and support is expected to be a net negative for children, except in cases where the absent parent would have been harmful to the child. As the argument goes, absence of two parents can lead intergenerational relations to become almost peer-like in form, consequently, children are more likely to miss important yet often subtle lessons on the nature of authority and interpersonal relations (Biblarz and Gottainer 2000). The absence of one parent is frequently understood as not only leading to lower levels of parental involvement, but even further, a higher likelihood of parental neglect (Thomson, Hanson, and McLanahan 1994).

While remarriage often leads to a significant improvement in the financial situation of children, it does not always lead to a significant gain in terms of parental supervision. Stepparents potentially contribute to children both in terms of their time and financial resources; however, it has also been documented that non-biological parents tend to be less involved with stepchildren than is the case with biological parents, and in fact, potentially disrupt relations with the absent parent (Amato 1998). In some cases, the concept of stepparent may be too strong, since the adult is seen as the parent's partner rather than a parent (McLanahan 2000). Children raised in stepparent families appear to do just about as well (or as poorly) as children raised in single-parent families, an observation that is true in spite of the fact that the economic situation of stepfamilies tends to be better, on average, than the economic situation of lone-parent families. This finding is certainly consistent with a line of argument that income alone is often overstated as a causal factor responsible for negative child outcomes.

This research on the impact of family structure might be reworked in terms of the insight of Coleman (1988), who observed that child outcomes not only depend on the financial capital available to families, but also on the transfer of human and social capital to children. The financial capital available to children is largely a function of the income of parents, and transfers may be disrupted through parental separation. When one of the parents is not living with the child, there is the potential of smaller transfer of human capital, that is, the absent parent's education and experience may be less useful to the child. It is similar for social capital, that is, the contacts and social relations that children receive from parents may be affected by family type. Amato (1998) emphasizes that fathers are potentially important to meeting the economic and emotional needs of children. Unless one or both parents are a net negative for the child, children in intact families can most readily benefit from such transfers. In non-intact families, non-resident fathers can still provide these various forms of capital, but the conditions are often less than favourable. Children benefit less from the father's human capital because they receive a lower investment in parental time (Bumpass 1994). Separated parents have particular difficulties generating co-parenting social capital. Stepparents would have a similar problem, possibly because the child does not 'buy into' the co-parenting social capital in the reconstituted relationship (Amato

1998). Amato observes that stepparents, in particular, operate through the biological parent, and they are often no longer involved once they no longer live with the biological parent.

Family Processes

The home environment of children, in terms of the quality of interpersonal relations, obviously plays an important role in the healthy emotional and intellectual development of children, regardless of family structure and economic status (Avison 1999; Lansford et al. 2001). Problems in terms of interpersonal relations (both between generations, siblings, and/or spouses) can impinge upon the ability of parents to be effective in meeting the needs of their children. Regardless of family circumstances, children in high-conflict families experience more adjustment problems than do children in low-conflict families, as conflict is often correlated with a less than adequate level of emotional support and less responsive and/or more punitive parenting styles, among other potential problems (Conger et al. 1990; 1997; McLoyd and Wilson 1991; Dodge Pettit and Bates 1994; Guo and Harris 2000).

The effect of conflict, independent of both family structure and economic circumstances, is expected to be minimized to the extent that parents manage to somehow shield their children from the worst interpersonal conflict. A growing proportion of Canadian children are witnessing the separation and/or divorce of their parents, although the relative success of parents in shielding their children from any hostility or distrust is far from clear. Parents obviously differ in terms of their success in shielding children from interpersonal conflict, with children witnessing violence within the home or suffering child abuse, in extreme cases. In this regard and under some circumstances, divorce can be considered advantageous to children's well-being. As emphasized by Amato and Booth (1997: 238) 'the worst situation for children to be in is either a high-conflict marriage that does not end in divorce or a low-conflict marriage that does end in divorce.' A history of mutually hostile marital patterns in families with children often predicts childhood difficulties that can be independent of either current income status or family structure (Katz and Gottman 1993; Wallerstein 1991). In this context, it is not so much whether a child lives with both biological parents or in a lone-parent or stepfamily that is considered as crucial, but it is the quality of interpersonal relationships that counts in shaping child outcomes.

Clearly, the difficulties due to economic disadvantage can serve to disrupt family life and increase the psychological distress of both parents and children. Similarly, the difficulties of marital conflict, divorce, and the absence of a parent can increase a child's psychological distress. To further complicate matters, low income status is correlated with higher levels of family tension, conflict, and parental depression, factors associated with negative child outcomes (McLoyd 1990; Lipman et al. 1998). The difficulty rests in efforts to delineate the relative impact of these different factors on the lives of children.

It is, consequently, important to consider the impact of both the parents' marital relationship as well as the quality of child-parent relationships (Davies and Cumming 1994; Grych and Fincham 1993). For example, conflict within the home has repeatedly been shown to have a negative impact on young children. Children may simply suffer from the conflict, but they may also model problematic interpersonal styles or make self-attributions as to the cause of family conflict. As a determinant of psychological and behavioural problems, the quality of both marital and child-parent relationships have also been shown to interact in an important manner with family types (Rogers 1996; Hanson, McLanahan, and Thomson 1997). While marital conflict is associated with childhood difficulties in both intact and stepfamilies, its impact appears to be less important in stepfamilies. As Coleman and Ganong (1987) have argued, because children may be less attached to stepparents and less committed to new relationships, they may be less negatively affected by resultant conflict.

Income Poverty in Canada

Recent Trends in Child Poverty

There are several obstacles to accurately documenting recent trends in child poverty. For example, because of the many constraints in measurement that are typically encountered when working with large-scale national surveys, most research studies on national poverty trends in Canada are limited to working with some form of an income-based measure of poverty. Income-based measures have many well-known limitations, most of which have been discussed in detail elsewhere (Ruggles 1990; Wolfson and Evans 1989; Cotton et al. 1999). For example, most income-based measures exclude information on property or wealth, just as they exclude various sources of potential income and services not easily captured through survey research. They tend to systematically underreport or exclude various types of in-kind public assistance, the sharing of resources and services across households and generations, the impact of exchanges outside the formal economy, and the bartering of goods and services, among other potential sources of non-declared income.

Other measurement difficulties relate to the income threshold that is chosen to represent a 'minimal standard of living' or 'poverty,' especially when considering income trends over time. For example, one of the most commonly encountered low income cut-offs (LICOs) has been the somewhat arbitrary '50% of median family income' – with adjustments for family size and composition (Canadian Council for Social Development 2000). As a strictly 'relative' measure of income poverty, this indicator is sensitive to shifts over time in the distribution of income but not to shifts in average income levels (Wolfson and Evans 1989; Sharif and Phipps 1994). As an alternative, it is possible to work with one set of LICOs solely adjusted to account for changes in the cost of living over time. This procedure provides for some indication as to whether there have been absolute gains or losses for those towards the bottom of the income scale – regardless of what happens overall in terms of income inequality.

Working with this latter approach, figure 6.1 shows the incidence of low income in Canada for the period 1980–2000 based on Statistics Canada's 1992 base pretax LICOs. While Statistics Canada has never claimed to measure poverty through its LICOs (given the aforementioned difficulties), nonetheless, these data provide a reasonable indication of recent trends in terms of the proportion of Canadians experiencing 'straitened circumstances.' These LICOs continue to be among the most widely cited 'poverty lines' in the media and popular discussions of social policy, for example, the 2001 census relied upon these same low income cut-offs in its official release on the income distribution of Canada's population (Statistics Canada 2003a; 2003b). After adjusting this time series using the consumer price index, this figure demonstrates that (1) low income rates have varied considerably over time, following the ups and downs of the Canadian economy and labour market; (2) family type is particularly important in documenting the incidence of low income, with female lone-parent families particularly disadvantaged; and (3) despite considerable fluctuation, the incidence of child poverty in Canada is slightly higher at the end of this twenty-year period than at the beginning (at 16.5% in 2000 as opposed to 15.7% in 1980).

Figure 6.1 Low income rates (%) for Canadian families, 1980–2000.

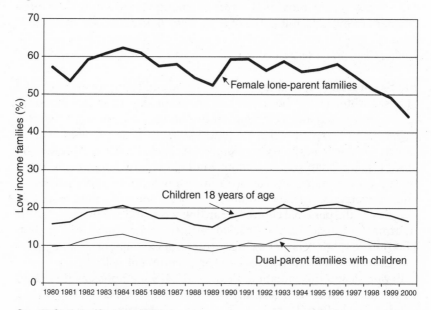

Source: Statistics Canada, (2003a).

Over the last two decades of the twentieth century, the problem of child poverty in Canada appears to have neither dramatically worsened nor substantially improved. Two of the more notable events to characterize the Canadian economy over this period were the recessions of the early 1980s (about 1982–83) and the early 1990s (about 1991–93). True of both dual-parent families with children and lone-parent families, the incidence of low income rose in both the recessions of the early 1980s and early 1990s, and fell again with the subsequent economic recoveries. Underlying these trends in family income have been some important longer term changes in North America's labour market, including an expansion of employment opportunities in the service sector in Canada (Torjman and Battle 1999). Many of these new jobs have been described as more likely to be part-time, temporary, low-paid, without job security, and often with irregular hours (Ternowetsky and Riches 1990). As a concurrent trend, female labour force participation increased considerably throughout the 1980s, particularly among women with children. This has served to increase or at least stabilize family income by increasing the number of earners per family in a context where individual earnings among young adults were often stagnant or even declining (Picot et al. 1998; Baker 2001; Beaujot 2000).

Family Change and Income Poverty

In a recent review of sociological research on child poverty in the United States, Lichter (1997) observes that much of this literature has been highly politicized and polarized. In the American context, part of this debate can be explained by the hard reality that the problem of child poverty is particularly severe (Rainwater 1995; Battle and Muszynski 1995; Osberg 2000). Yet in a more fundamental manner, much of the debate can be understood as a result of 'monocausal explanations' of child poverty. As Lichter summarizes, behavioural explanations that emphasize the personal choices regarding work and family life (e.g., the detrimental impact on non-marital fertility, divorce, and lone parenthood) have often been set against structural explanations that emphasize the role of labour markets and/or government policy.

In appraising this situation, Picot et al. (1998) emphasize three fundamental institutions in shaping the economic well-being of Canadian children, including (1) the market, especially the labour market; (2) the state, with direct transfers of both services and payments; and (3) the family, in explaining how Canadians earn and pool resources. Without downplaying the importance of structural explanations that emphasize the role of labour markets and/or government policy, it is possible to highlight several family changes that obviously hold implications for the economic well-being and societal integration of Canadian children. While obviously changes in labour market conditions are particularly salient in this context, this is not to suggest that shifts in living arrangements and family structure are irrelevant. The incidence of low income among children in 2000 is surprisingly close to what it was fully two decades earlier, and clearly a series of offsetting changes are responsible for this situation.

Over recent decades various changes in family life have had an impact on the incidence of child poverty in Canada. Among the most important demographic changes to have a net beneficial impact has been the well-documented decline in fertility that followed the baby boom (Romaniuc 1984). A decrease in the number of children per family has direct economic ramifications, since it is associated with fewer dependent youth per household and, thus, a decline in the number of claimants on family income (Dooley 1989; Brouillette et al. 1990). We have also witnessed an upward shift in the age pattern of fertility (Ram 1990; Beaujot et al. 1995; Bélanger 1999). This is associated with a lower level of child poverty, as adults delay having children until later in their reproductive years when economic resources are generally greater (Oppenheimer 1988; Grindstaff et al. 1989).

While fertility has declined, non-marital fertility as a proportion of all births has steadily risen. For example, whereas only about 14% of all births were to unmarried mothers in 1981, this proportion approached 40% as we moved into the twenty-first century (Beaujot 2000). This growth in the relative number of non-marital births is not the by-product of an increased incidence of births to single women but of the growing popularity of common law unions in Canada. For a growing number of Canadians, common law unions are considered a preferred option to legal marriage, even in the event of children. While the fertility rate for common law partners continues to be lower than among married couples (Dumas and Bélanger 1997), this growing popularity of common law unions directly explains the above-mentioned trend in non-marital fertility.

According to the 2001 census, the proportion of all couples living common law was 16.4%, which is much higher than the 1981 figure of 6.4%. Among younger cohorts this change is far more dramatic, for example, well over one-half of first unions entered into since 1985 were common law unions rather than marriages (Dumas and Bélanger 1997). This fundamental change in nuptiality has important ramifications for children, as common law unions are far less stable than legal marriages – even when they include children (Marcil-Gratton 1993; Marcil-Gratton and Le Bourdais 1999). Correspondingly, recent years have witnessed trends towards higher rates of union dissolution (whether legal marriages or cohabiting unions).

As with births to single parents, there is ample evidence to suggest considerable economic hardship for both women and children as a by-product of separation and/or divorce (Ross and Shillington 1989; Dooley 1991; Rashid 1994). While the long-term economic repercussions of union dissolution are generally not as difficult as those faced by single women who have births without a partner, in general, children experience considerable economic hardship as a result of their parents' inability to continue their relationship (McQuillan 1992). As a consequence of both lower proportions of married people and higher rates of union dissolution, the proportion of all families headed by a single parent has increased. According to the 2001 census, about one in four (24.7%) families with children (under age 25 and living at home) in Canada involve a lone parent, compared with 16.6% in 1981. Furthermore, over recent decades, the average age of lone parents has declined, as fewer involve widowhood and a greater proportion are the result of union dissolution and marital breakdown (Peron et al. 1999).

Table 6.1 presents data that are consistent with the aforementioned trends on the distribution of children, by family type, number of children per family, and age of parents (that is, mother's age in all but male lone-parent families) for the years 1981, 1989, and 1997. Also included in Table 6.1 is the same distribution but focusing solely on children classified as income poor. For all Canadian children, table 6.1 demonstrates a continuing decline in the proportion of Canadian children living with two parents, a continuing decline in the number of siblings per family, and a clear shift towards older ages in parenting. Since childbearing at older ages is generally associated with a higher income, and few children means fewer claimants on family income, these changes have at least partially offset the negative impact of increased lone parenthood on the economic well-being of the young (Oppenheimer 1988; Grindstaff et al. 1989; Dooley 1991; Kerr and Bélanger 2001),

In considering this same distribution for only those children classified as income poor, not surprisingly, the distribution of children shifts, as certain types of families are far more likely to be classified as poor (table 6.1). For example, whereas 13.7% of all children reportedly lived in female lone-parent families in 1997, of children falling below the official LICOs 41% did so. Similarly, whereas only 3.4% of all children in 1997 reportedly lived in a family with a mother under the age of 25, almost one in ten children (9.7%) falling below the offical LICOs did so. Over the 1981–97 period, change that characterized all children – an increased proportion living in lone parent families, an increased proportion living with older parents, a decline in the average number of children per family – also characterized children classified as income poor.

Canada has witnessed at least four consecutive years of declining income poverty among children in the year 1997 to 2003 (Statistics Canada 2003a; 2003b). This trend has been described as predominantly the result of rising market income, although a slight increase in the level of government transfer payments to low income families has also had a modest impact. It is within this broader context that the interrelationship between family change and economic well-being must be considered. A trend that continues through to the present is an ongoing

TABLE 6.1 Distribution of Children (%) and Children Classified as Income Poor, by
Selected Variables, 1981–1997

	1981	1989	1997
	All children		
Family type			
Married couple	89.6	87.7	83.9
Female lone parent	9.0	11.0	13.7
Male lone parent	1.5	1.3	2.4
	100.0	100.0	100.0
Age of mother/male lone parent (years)			
<25	6.5	4.1	3.4
25–29	16.6	15.3	10.4
30–34	24.6	26.4	22.6
35–39	23.3	26.0	28.5
≥40	29.0	28.2	35.0
	100.0	100.0	100.0
Children under 18 (n)			
1	21.6	22.5	23.9
2	42.6	46.3	45.0
3	23.5	21.9	22.5
≥4	12.2	9.3	8.6
	100.0	100.0	100.0
	Children classified as income poor		
Family type			
Married couple	66.2	56.8	56.2
Female lone parent	31.9	41.4	41.0
Male lone parent	1.9	1.8	2.8
	100.0	100.0	100.0
Age of mother/male lone parent (years)			
<25	12.1	10.3	9.7
25–29	19.0	20.9	15.4
30–34	24.6	28.0	25.1
35–39	19.4	21.4	24.6
≥40	24.8	19.4	25.2
	100.0	100.0	100.0
Children under 18 (n)			
1	17.9	21.2	23.1
2	35.2	42.2	40.2
3	27.9	21.7	24.0
≥4	19.0	14.9	12.6
	100.0	100.0	100.0

Source: Kerr and Beajot (2003b).

increase in the prevalence of lone-parent families, which shows little sign of slowing. With regard to the future fertility behaviour of Canadians, many demographers doubt that Canada's total fertility rate will fall much further from its historic low of only 1.49 births in 2000. With respect to the timing of childbearing, we are obviously approaching an upper limit in terms of the age at which Canadian women can start their families. Overall, it is likely that the impact of familial change into the future will be dominated by a continued growth in the number of lone-parent families, without the offsetting impact of further fertility decline or further delays in the timing of childbearing.

Child Outcomes by Family Type

To what extent do child outcomes vary by family type in Canada? The National Longitudinal Survey of Children and Youth (NLSCY), currently being conducted by Statistics Canada and Human Resources and Development, provides us with some empirical data on this issue. The NLSCY was designed to measure children's development and well-being, with the long-term goal of developing a national database on the life course of Canadian children from infancy into young adulthood. This survey provides for a series of age-appropriate indicators of behavioural and psychological difficulties, allowing for empirical research on child outcomes for a sizeable sample of Canadian children. This survey builds on previous Canadian research on psychosocial health (Tremblay et al. 1991; Offord et al. 1987; 1992) by including a series of items meant to measure the multiple components of healthy child development.

Table 6.2 provides several indicators on children's well-being from a sample of 10,599 children (age 4–11) in intact families, 1,981 children living in lone-parent families, and 1,467 in stepfamilies. With detailed information on a variety of child and family background characteristics, a series of indicators were developed, including scales meant to measure hyperactivity (inattention, impulsive behaviour, and symptomatic motor activity), emotional disorder (feelings of anxiety and depression), physical aggression (physical violence against other persons), indirect aggression (verbal aggression and cruelty to others), and property offence (vandalism, theft). In addition, table 6.2 indicates how these different family types vary in terms of the incidence of income poverty, parental age and education, labour force participation, number of children per family, and family functioning (i.e., a scale meant to measure the degree of constructive and supportive relations between family

TABLE 6.2 Child Outcomes and Selected Variables, by (means and standard deviations) Family Type, 1994

	Intact families		Stepfamilies		Female lone parent	
	Mean	SD	Mean	SD	Mean	SD
Child outcomes						
Hyperactivity	4.29	3.48	5.37*	3.71	5.52*	3.85
Emotional disorder	2.38	2.44	2.87*	2.78	3.37*	3.02
Aggressive behaviour	1.27	1.75	1.45*	1.04	1.87*	2.34
Indirect aggression	1.08	1.60	1.44*	1.78	1.67*	2.12
Property offence	0.72	1.08	1.07*	1.28	1.24*	1.64
Family/demographic behaviour						
Incidence of low income	0.14	0.35	0.23*	0.42	0.67*	0.47
Family functioning	17.10	2.27	16.90*	2.31	16.60*	2.52
No. of children	2.43	0.82	2.43	0.97	2.11*	0.92
Average hours worked (n)	22.30	18.19	23.70	18.58	19.60*	18.89
Less than high school	0.14	0.35	0.22*	0.41	0.23*	0.42
Age <35 years	0.37	0.48	0.61*	0.49	0.52*	0.50
N	10,599		1,981		1,467	

Source: Kerr and Beaujot (2003a).
*Indicates significant difference relative to intact families, $p < .05$.

members). This information was largely gathered from the parent (typically the mother) classified as most knowledgeable about the selected child. Since male lone parenting is not common among these children's families (at less than 1.5% of families), children living in this type of family are excluded.

Using intact families as a reference, those living in female lone-parent and stepparent families appear to be relatively disadvantaged across all of the additive scales measuring child outcomes. Children living in stepfamily households exhibit greater difficulties (higher scores) relative to intact family households, although the relative disadvantages are larger for children living with a lone parent. Children in female lone-parent and stepfamily households are more likely to be exhibiting signs of hyperactivity, emotional distress, and anxiety, as well as signs of direct and indirect aggression. On average, children in female lone-parent families scored about 0.4 of a standard deviation (SD) unit higher across these child outcome scales (relative to those in intact families), whereas children in stepfamilies scored 0.23 SD units higher.

These differences are significant and need to be acknowledged, as a growing proportion of Canadian children are being raised in non-intact families, although, as seen in the distribution of scores, the majority of children show relatively little or no sign of childhood difficulties regardless of family type.

With regard to the incidence of low income, table 6.2 is consistent with the literature previously cited, as young children in female lone-parent families are much more likely to be experiencing low income than are those in intact families (at 67% relative to 14% low income). Although children in stepfamilies also experience a higher incidence of low income (at 23%), in terms of the financial resources available to children, they clearly have more in common with intact families than with female lone-parent families. Table 6.2 includes information on 'family functioning,' although only very slight differences (again, statistically significant) are reported across family types. Female lone-parent families are slightly disadvantaged on family functioning (lower score), with stepfamilies falling somewhere between the other two family types. In terms of number of children per family and number of hours worked (by the parent most knowledgeable), there are non-significant mean differences between stepfamily and intact families; and the lone-parent families are somewhat distinct with fewer children and fewer hours worked in paid employment. The age and education of the parents indicate that stepfamilies have more in common with female lone-parent families than with intact families; like lone parents, a higher proportion of stepparents are under 35 and have not graduated from high school.

These statistics are consistent with recent American research that suggests an increased bifurcation of resources made available to children, with families delineated in terms of early and late childbearing (Bianchi 2000). For example, Martin (2000) emphasizes that delayed childbearers, who also tend to have more education, are increasingly likely to raise their children in intact marriages, while early childbearers are more likely to raise children outside of marriage. Homogamy would suggest that fathers in non-intact families would also tend to be younger and less educated. Based on data from the United States and Sweden, Goldscheider et al. (1996) find that stepfathers tend to be quite different from men living with their biological children: they are more likely to have less education and lower incomes and to be younger. In considering these differences across family types, clearly a portion of what is observed in table 6.2 in terms of child outcomes can be explained in terms of associated human and financial capital.

Social Causation versus Social Selection

As the results discussed above are based solely on cross-sectional data of the NLSCY, not much could be said about the causal factors at play in the interrelationship between family change, income poverty, and children's well-being. For example, consider the aforementioned relationship between family type and child outcomes, as was indicated via the mean ratings on child outcomes in table 6.2. Do these differences reflect the effect of family structure, or alternatively, are they due to other difficulties experienced by children even before the formation of current family type (e.g., a history of parental conflict or mental illness that led to the establishment of a non-intact family in the first place). Once several waves from the NLSCY become available it will be possible to examine this issue in greater detail.

While being limited to only the first and second waves of the NLSCY, O'Connor and Jenkins (2000) have moved in this direction, by systematically examining the characteristics of children and their families prior to and after the event of separation and/or divorce. In working with the first two waves, they provide early evidence as to a 'selection effect' in explaining child outcomes, that is, two-parent families that eventually become one-parent families appear to be quite distinct or selective relative to all other two-parent families – with repercussions for the children. This position is supported empirically by the finding that problematic adjustment already exists among children in Wave 1 of the NLSCY, prior to the event of separation and/or divorce, as recorded through Wave 2 of the survey. In other words, many of those factors found to predict separation in the first place are also found to predict child maladjustment (most notably, parental depression and conflict within the home).

In parallel research on the interrelationship between family structure, marital status, and health outcomes, Avison (1999) reviews these two alternate positions, while acknowledging the relative merits of both. Although Avison was specifically interested in the relationship between marital status and mental health among adults, a parallel argument clearly follows when shifting emphasis to family structure and child outcomes. The social causation hypothesis implies that being raised in a single-parent or stepfamily is in and of itself a disadvantage for children (consistent with the aforementioned argument that children in non-intact families benefit less from the ongoing transfers from both biological parents). The social selection hypothesis leads logically

to the argument that membership in such a family is merely an epiphe-
nomenon of more basic risk factors tied to the parents or community in
which the family lives. In other words, family structure itself can be
understood as a social consequence of prior experience as well as a
social determinant of subsequent psychosocial outcomes. As sociologists continue to follow individuals and families over their life course,
there seems to be a greater acknowledgment that both social selection
and social causation processes interplay in the explanation of individual health and behavioural outcomes. In the Canadian context, it is
necessary to await data over a longer period in order to derive further
insight from the NLSCY into developmental processes among young
Canadians.

Conclusion

The lack of progress in terms of child poverty over recent decades suggests ongoing difficulties for children, their families, and the communities in which they live. Whereas some gains were made during the late
1990s in terms of both market income and government transfers, the
overall level of child poverty in Canada is comparable in 2000 to the
level observed in 1980. Simultaneously, there is evidence of increased
income inequality across families over recent years, as upper income
Canadians have benefited the most from the recent period of economic
growth (Statistics Canada 2002).

One factor that has contributed to this persistently high level of child
poverty has been a continued growth in the number of lone-parent families, a trend that continues unabated into the twenty-first century. In
addition, a growing proportion of Canadian children are living in stepfamilies, a family type also noted for its higher than average level of
income poverty. Recent Canadian statistics are consistent with American data in demonstrating how we have witnessed an increased bifurcation of resources made available to children, with families delineated
in terms of the timing of fertility and whether they stay 'intact.' Delayed
childbearers, who also tend to have higher education, are much more
likely to be raising their children in intact marriages. Early childbearers
are more likely to raise their children outside of marriage, as lone parents or in reconstituted families. The consequences of these changes are
unclear, although it is well documented that children living in lone-parent families and stepfamilies are not only experiencing higher levels of
income poverty, but also, on average, appear to have greater behav-

ioural and psychological difficulties. While the advantages of living in an intact family should not be exaggerated, a comparison of mean ratings across family types on a wide variety of child outcome scales does suggest significant differences. As several multivariate analyses have demonstrated, family structure continues to have a significant effect on child outcomes, even after controlling for family income and other socioeconomic variables.

Various factors have been put forth in explanation, including the fact that the children in non-intact families tend to receive smaller transfers from at least one biological parent, both in terms of income support and the human and social capital. As it is typically the father who is the non-custodial parent, non-resident fathers can still provide for these children, although often the conditions for this are less than favourable. In terms of the ongoing debate between social causation and social selection, the social causation argument suggests that it is being raised in a non-intact family, in and of itself, that tends to be the problem whereas the social selection argument suggests that family structure may, in fact, be largely irrelevant in light of more basic risks factors to children. Even prior to the establishment of a lone-parent or stepfamily household, problematic adjustment may already be apparent, for example, among the children of a high-conflict marriage or among those who suffer under an abusive parent. The methodological challenge in this context is in disentangling the relative importance of social selection and social causation in explaining child outcomes, a task that is particularly difficult with only a few waves from the NLSCY.

REFERENCES

Amato, P. 1998. 'More Than Money? Men's Contribution to Their Children's Lives.' In A. Booth and A. Crouter (eds.), *Men in Families: When Do They Get Involved? What Difference Does It Make?* 241–78. Mahway, NJ: Lawrence Erlbaum.
– and A. Booth. 1997. *A Generation at Risk: Growing Up in an Era of Family Upheaval.* Cambridge, MA: Harvard University Press.
Avison, W. 1999. 'Family Structure and Processes.' In A.V. Horwitz and T.L. Scheid (eds.), *A Handbook for the Study of Mental Health*, 228–40. New York: Cambridge University Press.
Avison, W., and T. Wade. 2002. 'The Kids Are Alright: The Dubious Status of

Single Parenthood as a Risk Factor for Children's Mental Health.' Paper presented at the Eighth International Conference on Social Stress Research, Portsmouth, NH, 20–2 April.

Baker, M. 2001. *Families: Changing Trends in Canada.* Toronto: McGraw-Hill Ryerson.

Battle, K., and L. Muszynski. 1995. *One Way to Fight Child Poverty.* Ottawa: Caledon Institute of Social Policy.

Beaujot, R. 2000. *Earning and Caring in Canadian Families.* Peterborough, ON: Broadview.

Beaujot, R., E. Gee, F. Rajulton, and Z. Ravanera. 1995. *Family Over the Life Course.* Ottawa: Statistics Canada.

Beaujot, R., and Z. Ravanera. 2001. *An Interpretation of Family Change, with Implications for Social Cohesion.* Discussion Paper No. 01-1. London, ON: Population Studies Centre, University of Western Ontario.

Beaujot R., E. Gee, F. Rajulton, and Z. Ravanera. 1995. *Family over the Life Course.* Ottawa: Statistics Canada, cat. no. 91-543.

Bélanger, A. 1999. *Report on the Demographic Situation in Canada 1998.* Current Demographic Analysis. Ottawa: Statistics Canada. cat. no. 91-209-XPE.

Benson, P., A. Sharma, and E. Roehlkepartain. 1994. *Growing Up Adopted: A Portrait of Adolescents and Their Families.* Minneapolis, MN: Search Institute.

Bianchi, S. 2000. 'Maternal Employment and Time with Children: Dramatic Change or Surprising Continuity?' *Demography* 37(4): 401–14.

Biblarz, T.J. and G. Gottainer. 2000. 'Family Structure and Children's Success: A Comparison of Widowed and Divorced Single-Mother Families.' *Journal of Marriage and the Family* 62(2): 533–48.

Brooks-Gunn, J., G. Duncan, and J. Aber. 1997. *Neighborhood Poverty.* New York: Russell Sage Foundation.

Brouillette, L. C. Felteau, P. Lefebvre, and A. Pelltier. 1990. 'L'evolution de la situation économique des familles avec enfants au Canada et au Québec depuis 15 ans.' *Cahiers Québecois de Démographie* 19(2): 241–71.

Bumpass, L. 1994. 'L'enfant et les transformation d'une milieu familial aux États Unis.' *Cahiers québécois de démographie* 23(1): 27–52.

Canadian Council for Social Development. 2000. *Progress of Canada's Children: 1999/2000.* Ottawa: CCSD.

Carlson, M., and M. Corcoran. 2001. 'Family Structure and Children's Behavioral and Cognitive Outcomes.' *Journal of Marriage and Family* 63(3): 779–92.

Coleman, J. 1988. 'Social Capital in the Creation of Human Capital.' *American Journal of Sociology* 94 (Supplement): S95–S120.

Coleman, J., and L. Ganong. 1987. 'Marital Conflict in Stepfamilies: Effects on Children.' *Youth and Society* 19(2): 151–172.

Conger, K., R. Conger, and L. Scaramella. 1997. 'Parents, Siblings, Psychological Control, and Adolescent Adjustment.' *Journal of Adolescent Research* 12(1): 113–38.

Conger, R., G. Elder, F. Lorenz, K. Conger, R. Simons, L. Whitbeck, S. Huck, and J. Melby. 'Linking Economic Hardship to Marital Quality and Instability.' *Journal of Marriage and the Family* 52(3): 643–56.

Cotton, C., M. Webber, and Y. Saint-Pierre. 1999. *Should Low Income Cutoffs be Updated?* Ottawa: Statistics Canada, cat. no. 75F002-MIE-99009.

Davies, P., and E. Cumming. 1994. 'Marital Conflict and Child Adjustment: An Emotional Security Hypothesis.' *Psychological Bulletin* 116(3): 387–411.

Dodge, K., G. Pettit, and J. Bates. 1994. 'Socialization Mediators of the Relationship between Socio-Economic Status and Child Conduct Problems.' *Child Development* 65(2): 649–65.

Dooley, M. 1989. *An Analysis of Changes in Family Income and Family Structure in Canada between 1973 and 1986 with an Emphasis on Poverty among Children.* QSFP Research Report No. 238. Hamilton: McMaster University.

– 1991. 'The Demography of Child Poverty in Canada: 1973–1986.' *Canadian Studies in Population* 18(1): 53–74.

Dumas, J., and A. Bélanger, 1997. *Report on the Demographic Situation in Canada 1996.* Current Demographic Analysis. Ottawa: Statistics Canada, cat. no. 91-209-XPE.

Duncan, G., and J. Brooks-Gunn. (Eds.). 1997. *The Consequences of Growing Up Poor.* New York: Russell Sage Foundation.

Duncan, G.J., W. Yeug, J. Brooks-Gunn, and J. Smith. 1998. 'How Much Does Childhood Poverty Affect the Life Chances of Children?' *American Sociological Review* 63(3): 406–23.

Goldscheider, F., E. Bernhardt, and G. Kaufman. 1996. *Complex Paternal Roles in the United States and Sweden: Biological, Step- and Informal Fatherhood.* PSTC Working Paper No. 96–06. Brown University:

Grindstaff, C., T.R. Balakrishnan, and P. Maxim. 1989. 'Life Course Alternatives: Factors Associated with Differential Timing Patterns in Fertility among Women Recently Completing Childbearing, Canada 1981.' *Canadian Journal of Sociology* 14(4): 443–60. Population Studies & Training Center (PSTC)

Grych, J. and F. Fincham. 1993. 'Children's Appraisals of Marital Conflict: Initial Investigations of the Cognitive-Contextual Framework.' *Child Development* 64(1): 215–30.

Guo, G., and K. Harris. 2000. 'The Mechanisms Mediating the Effects of Poverty on Children's Intellectual Development.' *Demography* 37(4): 431–47.

Hanson, T., S. McLanahan, and E. Thomson. 1997. 'Economic Resources, Parental Practices and Children's Well-Being.' In G.J. Duncan and J. Brooks-Gunn (eds.), *Consequences of Growing Up Poor*, 190–238. New York: Russell Sage Foundation.

Hauser, R., and M. Sweeney. 1997. 'Does Poverty in Adolescence Affect the Life Chances of High School Graduates?' In G. Duncan and J. Brooks-Gunn (eds.), *The Consequences of Growing Up Poor*, 541–95. New York: Russell Sage Foundation.

Katz, L., and J. Gottman. 1993. 'Patterns of Marital Conflict Predict Children's Internalizing and Externalizing Behaviors.' *Developmental Psychology* 29(6): 940–50.

Kerr, D., and A. Bélanger. 2001. 'Family Demographic Change and the Economic Well-Being of Preschool Age Children in Canada, 1981–1997.' In *Report on the Demographic Situation in Canada*, 153–68. Current Demographic Analysis. Ottawa: Statistics Canada, cat. no. 91-209-XPE.

Kerr, D., and R. Beaujot. 2003a. 'Family Relations, Low Income and Child Outcomes: A Comparison of Canadian Children in Intact, Step and Lone-Parent Families.' *International Journal of Comparative Sociology* 43(1): 134–52.

– 2003b. Child Poverty and Family Structure in Canada, 1981–1997. *Journal of Comparative Family Studies* 34(3): 321–35.

Lansford, J., R. Ceballo, A. Abbey, and A. Stewart. 2001. 'Does Family Structure Matter? A Comparison of Adoptive, Two-Parent Biological, Single-Mother, Stepfather and Stepmother Households.' *Journal of Marriage and Family* 63(3): 840–51.

Lefebvre, P., and P. Merrigan. 1998. *Working Mothers and Their Children*. Ottawa: Human Resources Development Canada.

Lichter, D. 1997. 'Poverty and Inequality among Children.' *Annual Review of Sociology* 23: 121–45.

Lipman, E., M. Boyle, M. Dooley, and D. Offord. 1998. *Children and Lone-Mother Families: An Investigation of Factors Influencing Child Well-Being*. Ottawa: Human Resources Development Canada.

Marcil-Gratton, N. 1993. 'Growing Up with a Single Parent: A Transitional Experience? Some Demographic Measurements from the Children's Point of View.' In J. Hudson and Galaway (eds.), *Single Parent Families, Perspectives on Research and Policy*, 73–90. Toronto: Thompson.

Marcil-Gratton, N., and C. Le Bourdais. 1999. *Custody, Access and Child Support: Findings from the National Longitudinal Survey of Children and Youth*. Research Report Child Support Team CSR-1999-3E. Ottawa: Department of Justice.

Martin, S. 2000. 'Diverging Fertility among U.S. Women Who Delay Childbearing Past Age 30.' *Demography* 37(4): 523–33.

Massey, D. 1996. 'The Age of Extremes: Concentrated Affluence and Poverty in the Twenty-First Century.' *Demography* 33(4): 395–412.

Mayer, S. 1997. *What Money Can't Buy: Family Income and Children's Life Chances.* Cambridge, MA: Harvard University Press.

McLanahan, S. 2000. 'The Future of the Family: Fragile Families in the 21st Century.' Paper presented at the 2000 Population Association of America meetings, Los Angeles, 23–5 March.

McLoyd, V. 1990. 'The Impact of Economic Hardship on Black Families and Children: Psychological Distress, Parenting and Socioemotional Development.' *Child Development* 61(2): 311–46.

– and L. Wilson. 1991. 'The Strain of Living Poor: Parenting, Social Support and Child Mental Health.' In E.J. Huston (ed.), *Children in Poverty: Child Development and Public Policy,* 105–35. New York: Cambridge University Press.

McQuillan, K. 1992. 'Falling Behind: The Income of Lone Mother Families, 1970–1985.' *Canadian Review of Sociology and Anthropology* 29(4): 51–23.

O'Connor, T., and J. Jenkins. 2000. *Marital Transitions and Children's Adjustment.* Ottawa: Applied Research Branch Strategic Policy, Human Resources Development Canada.

Offord, D., M. Boyle, and B. Jones. 1987. 'Psychiatric Disorder and Poor School Performance Among Welfare Children in Ontario.' *Canadian Journal of Psychiatry* 32(6): 518–25.

Offord, D., M. Boyle, Y. Racine, and J. Flemming. 1992. 'Outcome, Prognosis and Risk in Longitudinal Follow-Up Study.' *Journal of the American Academy of Child and Adolescent Psychiatry* 31(6): 915–23.

Oppenheimer, V. 1988. *Work and the Family: A Study in Social Demography.* New York: Academic Press.

Osberg, L. 2000. 'Poverty in Canada and the USA: Measurement, Trends and Implications.' *Canadian Journal of Economics* 33(4): 847–77.

Peron, Y., H. Desrosiers, J. Juby, E. Lapierre-Adamcyck, C. Le Bourdais, N. Marcil-Gratton, and J. Mongreau. 1999. *Canadian Families at the Approach of the Year 2000.* Ottawa: Statistics Canada, cat. no. 96-321-MPE.

Picot, G., and J. Myles. 1996. 'Social Transfers and Changes in Family Structure and Low Income among Children.' *Canadian Public Policy* 22(3): 244–67.

Picot, G., J. Myles, and W. Pyper. 1998. 'Markets, Families and Social Transfers: Trends in Low Income among the Young and Old, 1973–1995.' In M. Corak (ed.), *Labour Markets, Social Institutions and the Future of Canada's Children,* 13–34. Ottawa: Statistics Canada, cat. no. 89-553-XPB.

Rainwater, L. 1995 'Poverty and the Income Package of Working Parents: The United States in Comparative Perspective.' *Children and Youth Services Review* 17(1): 11–41.

Ram, B. 1990. *New Trends in the Family.* Ottawa: Statistics Canada, cat. no. 91-535.

Rashid, A. 1994. *Family Income in Canada*. Ottawa: Statistics Canada, cat. no. 96-318.

Rogers, S. 1996. 'Marital Quality Mothers' Parenting and Children's Outcomes: A Comparison of Mother/Father and Mother/Stepfather Families.' *Sociological Focus* 29: 325–40.

Romaniuc, A. 1984. *Fertility in Canada: From Baby Boom to Baby-Bust*. Ottawa: Statistics Canada.

Ross, D., P. Scott, and M. Kelly. 1996. 'Overview: Children in Canada in the 1990s.' In *Growing Up in Canada*. Ottawa: Statistics Canada, cat. no. 89-550 pages 15–45.

Ross, D., and R. Shillington. 1989. *The Canadian Fact Book on Poverty, 1989*. Ottawa: Canadian Council on Social Development.

Ruggles, P. 1990. *Drawing the Line*. Washington, DC: Urban Institute.

Scheon, R., Y. Kim, C. Nathanson, J. Fields, and N. Astone. 1997. 'Why Do Americans Want Children?' *Population and Development Review* 23(2): 333–58.

Sharif, N., and S. Phipps. 1994. 'The Challenge of Child Poverty: Which Policies Might Help?' *Canadian Business Economics* 2(3): 17–30.

Statistics Canada. 1997 *National Longitudinal Survey of Children and Youth* (NLSCY) 1994–1995: Users Guide. Ottawa: Statistics Canada.

– 1998. 'National Longitudinal Survey of Children and Youth.' *The Daily*, 2 June 1998.

– 2002. *Income Trends in Canada, 1980–2000*. CD-ROM. Ottawa: Statistics Canada, cat. no. 75-202-XIE.

– 2003a. *Income Trends in Canada, 1980–2001*. Ottawa: Statistics Canada, cat. no. 13F0022-XCB.

– 2003b. *Income of Canadian Families, 2001*. Census Analysis Series. Ottawa: Statistics Canada, cat. no. 96F0030, XIE2001014

Ternowetsky, G., and G. Riches. 1990. *Unemployment and Welfare: Social Policy and the Work of Social Work*. Toronto: Garamond.

Thomson, E., T. Hanson, and S. McLanahan. 1994. 'Family-Structure and Child Well-Being: Economic Resources vs. Parental Behaviors' *Social Forces*. 73(1): 221–42.

Torjman, S., and K. Battle. 1999. *Good Work: Getting It and Keeping It*. Ottawa: Caledon Institute of Social Policy.

Tremblay, R., F. Vitaro, L. Bertrand, M. LeBlanc, H. Beauchesne, H. Boileau, and L. David. 'Parent and Child Training to Prevent Early Onset of Delinquenccy: The Montreal Longitudinal Experimental Study.' In J. McCord and R. Tremblay (eds.), *Preventing Antisocial Behavior: Interventions from Birth Through Adolescence*, 117–38. New York: Guilford.

Wallerstein, J. 1991. 'The Long-Term Effects of Divorce on Children: A Review.' *Journal of the American Academy of Child and Adolescent Psychiatry* 30: 349–60.

Wolfson, M., and J. Evans. 1989. *Statistics Canada's Low Income Cutoffs: Methodological Concerns and Possibilities*. Ottawa: Statistics Canada, Analytical Studies Branch.

7 The Impact of Family Context on Adolescent Emotional Health during the Transition to High School

KAREN MAC CON

Substantial evidence from middle school research indicates that transition-related changes experienced during the move to a new school contribute to how students adapt and, thus, to their emotional adjustment and academic success (Bronfenbrenner and Morris 1998; Hirsch and Dubois 1992). Few studies focus on the adolescent adjustment to high school, and even fewer include in their analyses the influence of family characteristics on adolescent emotional health during a school transition. By using the developmental systems perspective as our theoretical foundation (Lerner 1985; 2002; Bronfenbrenner and Morris 1998), this chapter will examine the influence of family structure as well as individual characteristics on individual developmental trajectories. In addition, it will assess the significance of family functioning and parenting styles on adolescent emotional health. Research focusing on the developmental contexts of adolescents is important as it can serve to identify factors that can assist young people in making successful academic transitions.

The Family Context and School Transition

The two most important developmental socializing agents are the family and the school. The family is an integrative and dynamic unit that can provide the foundation for one's core values and belief systems (Haralambos and Holborn 2000). Families that function in a healthy manner are closely knit, provide mutual aid, and engender great trust among their members. These, as well as other contributing factors, prepare families to cope with and adapt to stressful life events and transitions.

Joining a more heterogeneous community of students is an experience often faced by adolescents on entering high school. High school student populations comprise adolescents from families that differ in levels of functioning, structure, and experiences. Since family cohesion is defined as the 'emotional bonding that family members have toward one another' (Olson et al. 198, 370), we argue that adolescents who live in families that function well experience a more supportive 'launching pad' into their first year of high school. Moreover, because these adolescents have been raised by cohesive families they are less likely to experience emotional problems during their transition year, thus, increasing the likelihood of a successful transition.

The NLSCY's global assessment scale of family functioning is used in this study as a measure of family cohesion. The items relating to family functioning were developed by researchers at the Chedoke-McMaster Hospital of McMaster University (Special Surveys Division 1996). The derived scale is a multidimensional construct designed to measure various aspects of family functioning (e.g., problem solving, communications, roles, affective involvement, affective responsiveness, and behaviour control). How an adolescent's family unit functions is an important predictor of adolescent psychopathology (Ohannessian et al. 1995; Kashani et al. 1987). As well, some recent studies suggest that family functioning is related to several child psychological outcomes, although no study has investigated this relationship from a longitudinal perspective (McFarlane et al. 1995; Byrne et al. 1992; Racine and Boyle, 2002). For example, Boyle (2002) used data for children ages 6 to 11 years from the first cycle of the NLSCY, and reported that children living in dysfunctional families were approximately 40% more likely to display developmental problems than those living in average functioning families, and that these problems become more pronounced as children get older.

While no studies to date have examined how variations in family context may affect adolescent emotional health during school transitions, a number have found strong evidence of associations between family structure and various measures of early adolescent development (Clark et al. 1993; Entwisle and Alexander 1995; Lipman et al. 1996). In general, studies have found children of divorced parents to have more problems than those of one-parent families (e.g., never married, widowed), who in turn, have more problems than children in two-parent families (Landy and Tam 1998; Lipman et al. 1996). Among the negative consequences that have been linked with divorce and/or single parenthood are lower measures of academic achievement and increased levels of emotional and behavioural problems (Dawson 1991).

Other studies have examined parent-child interaction with reference to the economic circumstances of the family (Offord and Lipman 1996; Zyblock 1996; Tremblay et al. 1996). Overall, these have found that young children from lower socioeconomic backgrounds have the highest physical and indirect aggression scores, though Craig et al. (2002) uncovered only a weak association between family socioeconomic status (SES) and indirect aggression, hyperactivity, and conduct disorders, and no association with physical aggression, hyperactivity, and emotional problems in a national sample of 10- and 11-year-olds. Other researchers have found relationships that are small in magnitude or statistically insignificant between current household income and children's well-being (Dooley et al. 1998). However, there are no studies that examine the impact of family SES on the emotional well-being of young adolescents.

In addition, a small amount of recent research suggests that high school students who grow up in families characterized by different parenting styles show differential patterns of school performance (Steinberg et al. 1995; Dornbusch et al. 1987). The best-known and most utilized parenting typology is the Baumrind (1990) classification scheme, which includes authoritarian, authoritative, and permissive parenting styles. Briefly, *authoritative* parents demand age-appropriate mature behaviour from their children, simultaneously fostering children's autonomy in a warm and supportive environment. In contrast, an *authoritarian* parent is less flexible, controlling, emotionally distant, and often arbitrary in enforcing discipline. The third pattern is *permissive* parenting, in which parents are tolerant and accepting towards the child's impulses, use as little punishment as possible, make few demands for mature behaviour, and allow considerable self-regulation by the child. Authoritative parenting has emerged as the most effective parenting style in relation to adolescent school performance (Dornbusch et al. 1987; Steinberg et al. 1989; 1992; 1995; Steinberg 2000), but the relation to adolescent emotional health during developmental transition is unknown, in part, because most studies are cross-sectional in nature and use the parent as the key informant on parenting practices. There is continuing debate whether parenting practices cause – or are a partial consequence of – emotional problems experienced by some adolescents.

To properly assess the influence of family structure and parenting style on the emotional problems experienced by young people in the transition to high school requires controlling for the effects of several characteristics of the adolescents themselves. The intensity of such difficulties has been found to be related to both gender and pubertal timing (Magnusson et al. 1985; Flanagan and Eccles 1993; Simmons et al. 1987; Petersen et al. 1991). Although the findings from middle school transition studies are mixed, research on the differential impact of early versus late maturation generally indicates that early maturing girls have an increased risk for depressive symptoms (Brooks-Gunn 1992; Simmons and Blyth 1987). In addition, pubertal timing has been linked to heightened parent-adolescent conflict, particularly for adolescents who mature 'off-time' compared with their peers (Hill and Holmbeck 1987; Steinberg 1981; 1987a; 1987b; 2000; Sussman et al. 1987; Maccoby and Martin 1983).

By taking into account both contextual and individual influences, this study will be able to give a more comprehensive explanation for the variance found in emotional adjustment outcomes. Research must also move away from a focus on mean level changes in emotional measures and, instead, focus on using innovative approaches (such as growth curve modelling) that are able to take into account intra- as well as inter-individual changes. This study hopes to bridge the gap in the literature on school transitions by examining change in emotional adjustment in light of adolescent (social and biological) and parent-family variables.

Data and Methodology

Data

The longitudinal data for this research come from three cycles (Cycle 1, 1994–95; Cycle 2, 1996–97; and Cycle 3, 1998–99) of the National Longitudinal Survey of Children and Youth (NLSCY), collected jointly by Human Resources Development Canada (HRDC) and Statistics Canada. Data collected from the persons most knowledgeable (PMK) about the children as well as from the children themselves were used in the analyses. A face-to-face interview was used to collect the majority of the data from the PMK, while an age-appropriate self-complete questionnaire was used for the child(ren). A detailed description of the NLSCY methods is available elsewhere (Special Surveys Division 1996). Briefly, the target population was identified using a stratified, multistage probability sample design based on area frames in which dwellings (residences) are the sampling units. Since this study deals with the transition to adolescence we used data collected from children ages 10 and 11 in Cycle 1 from the longitudinal sample (N = 2,065). Imputation of missing values was made using the Lisrel 8.54 software. The present study followed the recommended weighting policy outlined by Statistics Canada.

The variables used in the analyses will be briefly described, while a more detailed description of each variable's measurement can be found in the Technical Appendix. The outcome variable, emotional disorder, is measured using a series of questions from the NLSCY self-complete questionnaire. For the latent growth model, we transformed the original emotional disorder scores into latent scores for each cycle.[1] One of the advantages of using latent scores in the measurement model is the ability to 'purify' the measures by distinguishing between variance related to the items and variance due to measurement error (Bollen 1989). Given that respondents in Cycle 1 were too young to enter high school, we used two variables (from Cycles 2 and 3) to identify when the transition to high school occurred. To account for pubertal timing we used the responses to three gendered maturation questions in the Cycle 2 self-report questionnaire. Gender was also used in the analyses with females coded as the reference category.

To measure family context, the following variables were used: family functioning (previously discussed), family structure, family SES, and parenting style(s). The family structure variables were assumed to be time invariant.[2] Thus, intact families were treated as the reference category, and two dummy variables were used for one-parent and blended families. The family economic condition was also assumed to be time invariant in this study as economic conditions did not change significantly between Cycles 1 and 3. Thus, the PMK's response in Cycle 1 pertaining to income adequacy was used in the analyses. Lastly, following Baumrind's (1990) classification scheme, items were chosen that best reflected the authoritative, authoritarian, and permissive parenting style from the NLSCY's Cycle 1 child self-report questionnaire.

Analyses

The analyses for this study consist of two separate but related parts. The first part used basic descriptives to assess the emotional health of adolescents over time (table 7.1) and related family contexts to adolescent emotional health by using cross tabulations (table 7.2, 7.3, and 7.4).

Given the limitations of other statistical models for analysing repeated measures over time (see Rogasa 1995), the second part of the

TABLE 7.1 Distribution of Emotional Disorder (%), by Age, Sex, and NLSCY Cycle

Level of emotional disorder	Cycle 1 (10–11 years)		Cycle 2 (12–13 years)		Cycle 3 (14–15 years)	
	Male	Female	Male	Female	Male	Female
Low	27.6	23.8	36.7	25.8	40.1	19.7
Moderate	64.2	61.4	57.4	60.2	52.9	60.3
High	8.1	14.8	5.9	14.0	7.0	20.0

Source: NLSCY 1994–95, NLSCY 1996–97, NLSCY 1998–99.

analysis used the SEM (structural equation modeling) – based latent growth modelling technique[3] (figure 7.1). This technique allows analysis of the ways individual attributes change over time, and how these changes (context) affect the emotional health trajectories of adolescents. Briefly, by using this technique we can estimate growth factors (intercepts and slopes) that represent emotional disorder and family functioning scores simultaneously. The intercept latent factor represents the initial levels (or average scores) for both factors. The slope latent factors represent the growth of emotional disorder and family functioning curves (trajectories). By using this type of procedure, we will be able to detect how the *change* (i.e., slope) in family functioning influences the *change* in the outcome variable, and also how initial family functioning scores impact on the initial level of emotional disorder (i.e., Cycle 1) and on the rate of change (i.e., Cycle 3). As well, we can assess how the covariates influence the outcome variable either directly or indirectly via the family functioning scores.

Results

Table 7.1 shows that the majority of students between Cycle 1 and 3 experience moderate levels of emotional disorder scores. But there is a clear difference between male and female scores over time. The percentage of males reporting moderate and high levels of emotional disorder decreases over time, while the pattern for females is the opposite. While fewer males report high levels of emotional disorder in Cycle 3 compared with Cycle 1, there is a substantial increase in the percentage of females who report higher levels.

Since the transition to high school occurs for the majority of students

TABLE 7.2 Distribution of Adolescent Emotional Disorder (%), by Family Structure, Cycle 1 vs Cycle 3

Level of emotional disorder	Cycle 1			Cycle 3		
	One-parent	Two-parent	Blended	One-parent	Two-parent	Blended
Low	23.2	26.6	24.2	24.9	32.1	24.1
Moderate	60.0	63.4	62.9	60.3	55.3	59.4
High	16.8	10.0	12.9	14.8	12.6	16.5

Source: NLSCY 1994–95, NLSCY 1998–99.

in Cycle 3, these findings suggest that the transition is particularly troublesome for adolescent females.

Family Contexts and Emotional Health

Table 7.2 shows the distribution of adolescent emotional disorder scores by family structure and NLSCY cycle. Most adolescents remain in the moderate and low categories across the cycles, but one shift of particular importance is among adolescents living in one-parent and blended families. In Cycle 1, adolescents living in one-parent families report having high disorder levels more often than adolescents living in other family structures. But, in Cycle 3, it is adolescents from blended families who report higher levels of emotional disorder. Perhaps environment changes such as moving to a new high school, in addition to the biological changes associated with puberty, are more difficult for adolescents living in a reconfigured family than for those living with either one or two biological parents.

Table 7.3 shows the distribution of adolescent emotional disorder scores by family functioning scores.[4] As expected, the results reveal that higher levels of family functioning are most often associated with lower levels of adolescent emotional disorder. Thus, for both cycles, adolescents living in cohesive families are more likely to be emotionally healthy during the time of transition to high school. Surprisingly, however, the Cycle 3 results show similar percentages experiencing a high level of emotional disorder for all three categories of family functioning.

Table 7.4 shows the relationship between emotional disorder scores and family SES. While only a minority of young people experienced a high level of emotional disorder at either point in time, those from the

TABLE 7.3 Distribution of Adolescent Emotional Disorder (%), by Level of Family Functioning, Cycle 1 vs Cycle 3

Level of emotional disorder	Cycle 1 Family functioning			Cycle 3 Family functioning		
	Low	Moderate	High	Low	Moderate	High
Low	11.2	26.8	28.2	22.4	28.5	35.5
Moderate	69.1	63.1	60.9	64.3	58.7	50.5
High	19.7	10.1	10.9	13.3	12.8	14.0

Source: NLSCY 1994–95, NLSCY 1998–99.

TABLE 7.4 Distribution of Adolescent Emotional Disorder (%), by Family SES, Cycle 1 vs Cycle 3

Level of emotional disorder	Cycle 1 Family SES			Cycle 3 Family SES		
	Low	Moderate	High	Low	Moderate	High
Low	25.4	26.8	28.2	27.5	31.1	29.7
Moderate	57.7	62.8	63.7	56.1	56.3	61.4
High	16.9	11.1	8.1	16.4	12.7	8.9

Source: NLSCY 1994–95, NLSCY 1998–99.

most disadvantaged homes were approximately twice as likely to do so as were those from the high SES families.

Finally, table 7.5 presents the correlations between the three parenting style variables and the emotional disorder scores reported in Cycles 1 and 3. Permissive and authoritarian parenting styles were positively correlated with the outcome variable. This finding concurs with the literature, as these two parenting styles have been found to be detrimental to healthy child and adolescent emotional development. On the other hand, the negative correlation between emotional disorder scores and authoritative parenting also corresponds with findings in the literature, as authoritative parenting has been linked to the development of emotionally healthy children.

The second part of the analysis introduces the latent growth curve model. As previously stated, an objective of this chapter is to examine associations between changes in adolescent emotional health during a

TABLE 7.5 Parenting Styles and Emotional Disorder Score Correlations, Cycle 1 and Cycle 3

	(1)	(2)	(3)	(4)	(5)
(1) Authoritarian	1				
(2) Authoritative	−.231*	1			
(3) Permissive	.691*	−.219*	1		
(4) Emotional score, Cycle 1	.109*	−.158*	.096*	1	
(5) Emotional score, Cycle 3	.067*	−.094*	.077*	.19*	1

Source: NLSCY 1994–95, NLSCY 1998–99.
Note: Variable names are discussed in the text. Numbers on the horizontal axis of the table refer to variables on the vertical axis of the table.
*$p < .01$.

school transition and changes in family context (most notably changes in family functioning). Figure 7.1 illustrates the significant paths in our model.

Although the family functioning variable was measured using the responses given by the PMK, and not by the adolescent, we believe it still gives us a good indication of the type of family environment in which the adolescents live. As shown in figure 7.1, the initial family functioning scores have no effect on the initial emotional disorder scores, nor do they affect the rate of change in emotional scores (arrow connecting exogenous latent intercept to endogenous latent slope). Surprisingly, figure 7.1 shows that parent(s) described as being author-itative (as indicated by the positive coefficient .46), report higher start-ing values for family functioning (indicating dysfunction). Perhaps these types of parents, compared with those whose parenting is more characteristic of the authoritarian or permissive styles, are harsher in their reporting, as they have relatively higher expectations of how fam-ilies should function. As for the rate of change in emotional disorder over time, males exhibit a significant decrease in emotional disorder scores (−.24) compared with females, while adolescents living with permissive parent(s) exhibit a significant increase in their disorder scores (.05).

Furthermore, the path indicated by the arrow connecting the exoge-nous and endogenous latent slopes illustrates that the rate of change in family functioning has a significant effect on the rate of change in emo-tional disorder scores. This finding indicates that adolescents who experience a decrease in family functioning scores (recall that lower

Figure 7.1 Conditional multi-latent growth curve model of emotional disorder and family context.

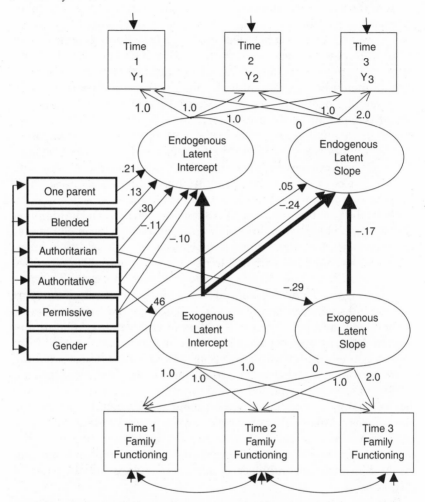

Source: *NLSCY* 1994–95, *NLSCY* 1996–97, *NLSCY* 1998–99.
Note: All paths between exogenous variables and growth factors were estimated but only significant ($p < .05$) paths are displayed. Values associated with each path are standardized regression coefficients.

family functioning scores denote higher family functioning) experience a significant decrease in emotional disorder scores over time.

From the model we found adolescents living in two-parent families to have lower initial emotional disorder scores compared with those living in one-parent and blended families. These findings concur with those from past studies (i.e., Dawson 1991; Steinberg 1987b; Erel and Burman 1995) in that children raised in 'nuclear' families seem to be developmentally better off, at least initially, than their peers living in other familial configurations. We expected parents of adolescents living in two-parent families to report better family functioning rates, both initially and over time, compared with those living in one-parent and blended family structures. In addition, we also expected the family structure variables to have an indirect influence on the outcome growth trajectories through the family functioning trajectories. These expectations were not substantiated by our model.

Given the past research findings (Korenman et al. 1995; Hoddinott et al. 2002) showing that children living in families of lower SES are at significant risk for experiencing poorer levels in various developmental measures compared with children living in higher SES families, we hypothesized that this relationship would affect adolescent children. Our findings did not support this hypothesis. Some studies report indirect links between family economic hardship and increased levels of emotional and behavioural disorders in children (e.g., Offord and Lipman 1996; Lempers et al. 1989). These and other studies cite inconsistent parenting and lower levels of parental nurturance resulting from economic hardship as important indirect factors (e.g., Flanagan 1990). Thus, we too, expected to find family SES to indirectly affect the rate of change in emotional development via the family functioning scores. We postulated that economic hardship would increase the level of stress within the family microsystem, thereby resulting in higher levels of family dysfunction. Surprisingly, our results indicate that family SES does not influence family functioning's initial or rate of change scores.

Lastly, the model shows adolescents with authoritarian parent(s) have significantly higher initial emotional disorder scores (.30), while those with authoritative and permissive parents have significantly lower initial scores (–.11 and –.10, respectively). Because there are no studies to date that have assessed the indirect association between parenting styles and adolescent functioning through the family context, the theoretical foundation of our hypothesis relies on the parenting style literature, which consistently reports on the advantages of the authoritative parenting style on childhood emotional scores. Thus, we hypothesized that this parenting style would also have an indirect, beneficial influence on adolescent outcome scores through the family functioning scores since the functioning of this microsystem is very much dependent on parenting style. However, we found no evidence to support this hypothesis. Instead, we found the authoritarian parenting style had a significant impact on the rate of change in family functioning scores, which indirectly influenced the rate of change in the outcome scores through the family context. Perhaps emotionally disordered adolescents are more receptive to the authoritarian parenting style – resulting in their parents reporting better levels of family functioning and their reporting of better levels of emotional health.

In sum, in contrast to what we originally postulated, namely, that change in pubertal development as well as the transition to high school would significantly impact adolescent emotional growth trajectories, we found that they, in fact, play an insignificant role in explaining intra- or intervariation among adolescents. Data on adolescents' own perceptions of their family functioning were *not* measured by the NLSCY. If such data were available, we suspect that we would have found stronger associations between the family functioning latent factors and the emotional disorder outcome latent factors. Nevertheless, our findings pertaining to the impact of parenting style on the latent emotional and family functioning factors as well as the impact of the rate of change in family functioning on the rate of change of the outcome measure provide a baseline from which to conduct future analyses on adolescent emotional well-being.

Conclusion

This study examined the emotional health of adolescents over time, as well as how emotional health is influenced by family contexts during a school transition. By using descriptive procedures as well as a latent growth model, this study examined the intra- and intervariability of emotional disorder and family functioning, two very important concepts in developmental research. Further, by taking into account the influence of biological (puberty) and social (entering high school) transitions in addition to the family context, this study adhered to the developmental systems view of examining person-context relations. Our findings from the descriptive analyses reveal that adolescents from one-parent and blended families as well as those from lower SES families are at risk of experiencing higher levels of emotional disorder. Also, we found that students who come from cohesive and stable families are less likely to experience high levels of emotional disorder compared with their peers living in less cohesive families. Lastly, our latent growth model indicated that adolescents who experience a more cohesive family between Cycle 1 and Cycle 3 also experience a decrease in emotional disorder scores. Thus, cohesive families are more likely to 'launch' their children into high school with lower levels of emotional disorder. These findings point to the importance of family context as a determinant of adolescent mental health.

Technical Appendix

Measurement of Variables

Variable	Description
Emotional Disorder	Adolescents were asked to rate whether they were unhappy, sad, or depressed; as happy as other children; had trouble enjoying themselves; cried a lot and felt miserable; as well as if they were unhappy and tearful. Three of the items specifically addressed feelings of anxiety. Respondents were asked to rate whether they were too fearful or anxious; were worried and felt nervous, high strung, or tense. The possible scores ranges from 0 to 36, high scores indicating higher levels of emotional disorder.
Family Functioning	PMKs (person most knowledgeable, in most cases, mothers) were asked if their family members misunderstood each other; could turn to each other for support; confided in each other; did not get along well together; could not talk to each other about sadness; whether family members were accepted as they were; felt accepted for what they were; if they avoided discussing fears or concerns; if they expressed feeling to each other; whether there were lots of bad feelings in the family; if making decisions was a problem for the family; and if they were able to make decisions to solve problems. The total score ranges from 0 to 36, a high score indicating family dysfunction.
Family Structure	In the NLSCY, *one-parent family* (16.8% of sample) is defined as the child living with one parent only (includes biological, adoptive, step, and foster parents). A *two-parent family*

(73.0%) refers to a census couple family (married or common law), where all children are the natural and/or adopted offspring of both members of the couple (foster children are not included in the census family). Lastly, the *blended family* category (10.3% of sample) in this study includes couple census families (married or common law) with two or more children, one of whom does not share the same natural and/or adoptive parents as the other child(ren), as well as couple census families in which at least one of the children is in a step relationship with at least one of the parents.

Family Socioeconomic Status (SES)

This ordinal measure was coded 1 (lowest income category) through 5 (highest income category).

Parenting Style Authoritative

Five items, each having four response categories ranging from *never* to *very often* (1 to 4), make up the measure for the construct. Adolescents were asked if their parents wanted to know what they were doing; if their parents told them what time to be home; if their parents made sure that they knew they were appreciated; if their parents made sure their homework was done; and whether their parents spoke of good things that they do. Items were summed and had a total score ranging from 7 to 20, a higher score indicating a greater presence of the authoritative parenting characteristic.

Authoritarian

Adolescents were asked to rate how often their parents hit them or threatened to do so, threatened to punish them more than they did, enforced rules depending on their mood, and nagged them about little things. Items were also summed and had a total score that ranged from 4 to 15, a higher score indicating a higher presence of authoritarian parenting.

Permissive

Adolescents were asked if their parents allowed them to go out any evening, if their parents kept rules when it suited them, and if their parents forgot rules that they made. The items were summed and had a total score that ranged from 3 to 12, a higher score indicating higher levels of permissive parenting.

High School Transition

From cycle 2 and cycle 3's self-complete questionnaire, adolescents were asked if they changed from junior school to high school or from elementary school to high school. Response categories were coded 1 for *yes* and 0 for *no* and *not applicable*. Since anomalies in the data became apparent subsequent to combining both items from each cycle, we created two dummy variables, one for those who transited during cycle 1 and 2 (13.7% of sample) and the other for those who transited during cycle 2 and 3 (38.0% of sample). The reference category for both the dummy variables comprises those who did not make the transition to high school.

Pubertal Timing

For girls, questions pertaining to body hair growth, breast development, and menarche were used. For boys, questions about body hair growth, deepening of voice, and facial hair were used. Pubertal timing scores were derived by summing the three characteristics appropriate to a given individual's sex. The possible scores ranged from 3 to 12. Respondents whose scores were ≥7 were classified as early developers, while scores of less ≤6 were classified as late developers. These two classifications were coded as a dummy variable, whereby early developers were coded as the reference category and late developers as 1. In addition, to account for expected maturational differences between boys and girls in our models, an interaction effect is incorporated into our analyses.

NOTES

1 Latent scores for each cycle were obtained using the LISREL 8.54 software package.
2 The stability and change of family structure between cycle 1 and cycle 3 were tested and found to be not significant, therefore validating our decision to treat this variable as being time invariant.
3 For further details refer to K. Mac Con (2004).
4 Uneven splitting of the categories was necessary because of low frequency counts for certain scores. Thus, data for emotional disorder scores were grouped in the following categories: low (0–1), moderate (2–7), and high (8–16). For the purpose of consistency, reverse coding was done for the family functioning scores: low (14–28), moderate (7–13), and high (0–6).

REFERENCES

Baumrind, D. 1990. 'Parenting Styles and Adolescent Development.' In R.M. Lerner, J. Brooks-Gunn, and A.C. Petersen (eds.), *The Encyclopedia of Adolescence*, 746–58. New York: Garland.
Bollen, K.A. 1989. *Structural Equations with Latent Variables*. New York: Wiley.
Bronfenbrenner, U. 1979. *The Ecology of Human Development*. Cambridge, MA: Harvard University Press.

Bronfenbrenner, U., and P. Morris. 1998. 'The Ecology of Developmental Process.' In W. Damon (series ed.) and R.M. Lerner (vol. ed.), *Handbook of Child Psychology,* vol. 1, *Theoretical Models of Human Development* (5th), 993–1028. New York: Wiley.

Brooks-Gunn, J. 1992. 'Growing Up Female: Stressful Events and the Transition to Adolescence.' In T. Field, P. McCabe, and N. Schneiderman. (eds). *Stress and Coping in Infancy and Childhood,* 119–45. Hillsdale, NJ: Erlbaum.

Byrne, C.M., D.R. Offord, and M.H. Boyle, 1992. *Family Functioning and Emotional/Behavioural Disorders in Children: Results from the Ontario Child Health Study.* Ottawa: Ministry of Community and Social Services.

Clark. J.J., M.G. Sawyer, a.-M.T. Nguyen, and P.A. Baghurst. 1993. 'Emotional and Behavioural Problems Experienced by Children Living in Single-Parent Families: A Pilot Study.' *Journal of Paediatrics and Child Health* 29(5): 338–43.

Craig, W.M., R.D. Peters, and J.D. Willms. 2002. 'The Role of the Peer Group in Pre-Adolescent Behaviour.' In J.D. Willms (ed.), *Vulnerable Children: Findings from Canada's National Longitudinal Survey of Children and Youth,* 317–27. Edmonton: University of Alberta Press.

Dawson, D.A. 1991. 'Family Structure and Children's Health and Well-Being: Data from the 1988 National Health Interview Survey on Child Health.' *Journal of Marriage and the Family* 53(3): 573–84.

Dooley, M.D., L. Curtis, E. Lipman, and D. Feeny. 1998. 'Child Psychiatric Disorders, Poor School Performance and Social Problems: The Roles of Family Structure and Low Income.' In M. Corak (ed.), *Labour Markets, Social Institutions, and the Future of Canada's Children,* 107–27. Ottawa: Statistics Canada.

Dornbusch, S., P. Ritter, H. Leiderman, D. Roberts, and M. Fraleigh. 1987. 'The Relation of Parenting Style to Adolescent School Performance.' *Child Development* 58(5): 1244–57.

Entwisle, D.R., and K.L. Alexander. 1995. 'A Parent's Economic Shadow: Family Structure versus Family Resources as Influences on Early School Achievement. *Journal of Marriage and Family* 57(2): 399–407.

Erel, O., and B. Burman. 1995. 'Interrelatedness of Marital Relations and Parent–Child Relations: A Meta-analytic Review.' *Psychological Bulletin* 118(1): 108–32.

Flanagan, C.A. 1990. 'Change in Family Work Status: Effects on Parent-Adolescent Decision-Making.' *Child Development* 61: 163–77.

Flanagan, C.A., and J.S. Eccles. 1993. 'Changes in Parent's Work Status and Adolescents' Adjustment at School. *Child Development,* 64(1): 246–57.

Haralambos, M., and M. Holborn. 2000. *Sociology: Themes and Perspectives.* London: Harper Collins.

Hill, J.R., and G.N. Holmbeck. 1987. 'Familial Adaptation to Biological Change during Adolescence. In R.M. Lerner and T.T. Foch (eds.), *Biological-Psychoso-cial Interactions in Early Adolescence*, 207–24. Hillsdale, NJ: Erlbaum.

Hirsh, B., and D. DuBois. 1992. 'The Relation of Peer Social Support and Psychological Symptomatology during the Transition to Junior High School: A Two-Year Longitudinal Analysis.' *American Journal of Community Psychology* 20(3): 333–47.

Hoddinott, J., L. Lethbridge. and S. Phipps. 2002. *Is History Destiny? Resources, Transitions and Child Education Attainments in Canada*. Ottawa: Human Resources Development Canada, SP-551-12-02E.

Kashani, J.H., N.C. Beck, E.W. Hoeper, C. Fallahi, C.M. Corcoran, J.A. McAllister, T.K. Rosenberg, and J.C. Reid. 1987. 'Psychiatric Disorders in a Community Sample of Adolescents.' *American Journal of Psychiatry* 144(5): 584–9.

Korenman, S., J. Miller, and J. Sjaadstad. 1995. 'Long-term Poverty and Child Development in the United States: Results from the NLSY.' *Children and Youth Services Review* 17(1–2): 127–55.

Landy, S., and K. Tam. 1998. *Understanding the Contribution of Multiple Risk Factors on Child Development*. Ottawa: Applied Research Branch, Human Resources Development Canada, W-98-22E.

Lempers, J., D. Clark-Lempers, and R.L. Simons. 1989. 'Economic Hardship, Parenting, and Distress in Adolescence. *Child Development* 60(1): 25–39.

Lerner, R.M. 1984. *On the Nature of Human Plasticity*. New York: Cambridge University Press.

– 1985. 'Adolescent Maturational Changes and Psychosocial Development: A Dynamic Interactional Perspective.' *Journal of Youth and Adolescence* 14(4): 355–72.

– 2002. *Adolescence: Development, Diversity, Context, and Application*. Upper Saddle River, NJ: Pearson Education.

Lipman, E.L., D.R. Offord, and M.D. Dooley. 1996. 'What Do We Know about Children from Single-Mother Families? Questions and Answers from the National Longitudinal Survey of Children and Youth.' In *Growing Up in Canada: National Longitudinal Study of Children and Youth*. Ottawa: Human Resources Development Canada and Statistics Canada, cat. no. 89-550-MPE.

Mac Con, K. 2004. 'The Impact of Context on Adolescent Developmental Trajectories during the Time of Transition to High School.' Doctoral dissertation, University of Western Ontario.

Maccoby, E., and J. Martin. 1983. 'Socialization in the Context of the Family: Parent-Child Interaction. In P.H. Mussen (series ed.) and E.M. Hetherington (vol. ed.), *Handbook of Child Psychology*, Vol. 4, *Socialization, Personality, and Social Development* (4th ed.), 103–96. New York: Wiley.

Magnusson, D., H. Stattin, and V. Allen. 1985. 'Biological Maturation and

Social Development: A Longitudinal Study of Some Adjustment Processes from Mid Adolescence to Adulthood.' *Journal of Youth and Adolescence* 14(4): 267–84.

McFarlane, A.H., A. Bellissimo, and G.R. Norman. 1995. Family Structure, Family Functioning and Adolescent Well-being: The Transcendent Influence of Parental Style. *Journal of Child Psychology and Psychiatry* 36(5): 847–64.

Offord, D.R., and E.L. Lipman. 1996. *Emotional and Behavioural Problems*. In *Growing Up in Canada, National Longitudinal Study of Children and Youth*. 119–26. Ottawa, Ontario: Human Resources Development Canada and Statistics Canada, cat. no. 89-550-MPE.

Ohannessian, C., R.M. Lerner, J.V. Lerner, and A. von Eye. 1995. 'Discrepancies in Adolescents' and Parents; Perceptions of Family Functioning and Adolescent Emotional Adjustment. *Journal of Early Adolescence* 15(4): 490–516.

Olson, D.H., C.S. Russell, and D.H. Sprenkle. 1983. 'Circumplex Model of Marital and Family Systems, VI: Theoretical update.' *Family Process* 22(1): 69–83.

Petersen, A.C., P.A. Sarigiani, and R.E. Kennedy. 1991. 'Adolescent Depression: Why More Girls? *Journal of Youth and Adolescence* 20(2): 247–71.

Racine, Y., and M.H. Boyle. 2002. 'Family Functioning and Children's Behaviour Problems.' In J.D. Willms (ed.), *Vulnerable Children: Findings from Canada's National Longitudinal Survey of Children and Youth*, 149–65. Edmonton: University of Alberta Press.

Rogasa, D.R. 1995. 'Myths and Methods: "Myths about Longitudinal Research" plus Supplemental Questions.' In J. Gottman (ed.), *The Analysis of Change*, 2–65. Hillsdale, NJ: Erlbaum.

Simmons, R., and D. Blyth. 1987. *Moving into Adolescence The Impact of Pubertal Change and School Context*. New York: Aldine De Gruyter.

Simmons, R., R. Burgeson, and S. Carlton-Ford. 1987. 'The Impact of Cumulative Change in Early Adolescence.' *Child Development* 58(5), 1220–34.

Special Surveys Division. 1996. *National Longitudinal Survey of Children and Youth: User's Handbook and Microdata Guide*. Ottawa: Human Resources Development Canada and Statistics Canada.

Steinberg, L. 1981. 'Transformations in Family Relations at Puberty. *Developmental Psychology* 17(6): 833–40.

Steinberg, L. 1987a. 'The Impact of Puberty on Family Relations: Effects of Pubertal Status and Pubertal Timing. *Developmental Psychology* 23(3): 451–60.

– 1987b. 'Single Parents, Stepparents, and the Susceptibility of Adolescents to Antisocial Peer Pressure.' *Child Development* 58(1): 269–75.

– 2000. 'We Know Some Things: Parent-Adolescent Relations in Retrospect.' Presidential Address, Society for Research on Adolescence, Chicago, 1 April.

– Steinberg, L., N.E. Darling, A.C. Fletcher, B.B. Brown, and S.M. Dornbusch.

1995. 'Authoritative Parenting and Adolescent Adjustment: An Ecological Journey.' In P. Moen, G. Elder Jr, and K. Luscher (eds.), *Examining Lives in Context* 423–66. Washington, DC: American Psychological Association.

Steinberg, L., J. Elem, and N. Mounts. 1989. 'Authoritative Parenting, Psychosocial Maturity, and Academic Success among Adolescents.' *Child Development* 60(6): 1424–36.

Steinberg, L., S. Lamborn, S. Dornbush, and N. Darling. 1992. 'Impact of Parenting Practices on Adolescent Achievement: Authoritative parenting, School Involvement, and Encouragement to Succeed.' *Child Development* 63(5): 1266–81.

Sussman, E., G. Inoff-Germain, E. Nottelmann, G. Cutler, G., Jr, and G. Chrousos. 1987. 'Hormones, Emotional Dispositions, and Aggressive Attributes in Early Adolescence.' *Child Development* 58(4): 1114–34.

Tremblay, R.E., B. Boulerice, P.W. Harden, P. McDuff, D. Perusse, R.O. Pihl, and M. Zoccolillo. 1996. 'Do Children in Canada Become More Aggressive as They Approach Adolescence?' In *Growing Up in Canada: National Longitudinal Survey of Children and Youth* Human Resources Development Canada and Statistics Canada, 27–37. Ottawa: cat. no. 89-550-MPE.

Zyblock, M. 1996. *Child Poverty Trends in Canada: Exploring Depth and Incidence from a Total Money Perspective, 1975–1992.* Ottawa: Human Resources Development Canada.

8 Intergenerational Transfer: The Impact of Parental Separation on Young Adults' Conjugal Behaviour

CLAUDINE PROVENCHER, CÉLINE LE BOURDAIS,
AND NICOLE MARCIL-GRATTON

Family life has undergone profound transformations over the past thirty years. The rise of conjugal instability has resulted in a growing number of children who are likely to experience parental separation through the course of their life. Do children who grew up in an environment marked by disruption in their parents' conjugal lives, in turn, start their own conjugal lives differently from children who did not experience such family instability? This chapter explores this question by presenting the results of an analysis based on data from 1995 General Social Survey on the family (Statistics Canada 1996). These data allow us to measure the impact of dissolution of the parental union on the conjugal lives of the generations of children who became young adults between the 1970s and the mid-1990s. These young adults were born to parents who experienced union dissolutions in growing numbers, especially after the adoption of Canada's divorce law in 1968 and the subsequent modifications to the law in 1986. Their experience of family life was strongly marked by the major transformations in conjugal life that occurred during the twentieth century, and we can hypothesize that this affected the way in which these young adults started their own conjugal lives.

Transformations in Conjugal Life during the Twentieth Century

In Canada important changes in conjugal behaviours began to take place in the 1970s. Marriage had been the predominant form of union until then, although divorce had become possible, and did occur, and cohabitation had also emerged as a choice for some couples who wanted to test their compatibility before marrying. But it was during the

1980s and 1990s that the attraction of marriage really began to decline, as growing numbers of couples opted for de facto unions. Since 1981 the prevalence of cohabitation has continued to increase, affecting all generations (Statistics Canada 2002). Whereas some cohabiting couples decided to maintain this status, others chose to legalize their de facto union by marrying. By the end of the 1980s, in Canada, more than 40% of cohabiting partners had legalized their unions after five years of living together (Le Bourdais and Marcil-Gratton 1996; see also Dumas and Bélanger 1997; Wu and Balakrishnan 1995). There was also a considerable increase in divorce after the 1968 adoption of the Divorce Act and the 1986 modifications to it. The total divorce rate, which is the proportion of marriages that would end in divorce if the behaviours observed in a given year were to persist, rose from 14% in 1969 to 37% in 1982; aside from the fluctuations associated with the 1986 reform, this rate has since remained at about 40%, a level that continued to be observed in 2000 (Marcil-Gratton et al. 2003; Statistics Canada 2003).

The way people enter into a first conjugal union, experience this union, or choose to end it has changed over time, for both consensual and legal unions. A number of studies have attempted to pinpoint the demographic, cultural, or socioeconomic characteristics that are likely to affect the conjugal lives of individuals.

Determinants of Conjugality

One of the most frequently discussed factors in the literature on the formation and dissolution of unions is clearly the fact of having experienced parental separation. Almost all of the studies concur in the finding that individuals whose parents have separated are more likely to enter into a first union early on in their lives (Kiernan 1992; Keith and Finlay 1988; Le Bourdais and Marcil-Gratton 1998). These individuals are also more likely to have their first sexual experience at a young age, which tends to lead to the early formation of a first union (Kiernan and Hobcraft 1997; Miller and Heaton 1991). In addition, young people who have experienced parental separation are more inclined to choose cohabitation rather than marriage as a way of starting their conjugal life (Furstenberg and Teitler 1994; Clarkberg 1999; Le Bourdais and Marcil-Gratton 1998; Pollard and Wu 1998).

Individuals whose parents have separated are also more likely to face the dissolution of their first union. This finding is at the basis of the theory of 'intergenerational transmission of marital instability,' which was advanced in the late 1970s (Pope and Mueller 1976; Mueller and Pope

1977). Since then studies have chiefly shown that the effect of parental separation is exerted primarily through intermediate factors that are associated with a greater risk of dissolution, such as entering into a first union at a young age (Kiernan and Cherlin 1999; Bumpass et al. 1991), opting for cohabitation rather than marriage as a first conjugal experience (Amato 1996), the birth of a child outside of marriage or at a young age (Berrington and Diamond 1999; McLanahan and Bumpass 1988), or an early interruption of studies (Sandefur and Wells 1999; Powell and Parcel 1997). Some authors have found that children of parents who have separated also have problems with interpersonal relations (Amato 1996; Heaton and Blake 1999), which is said to increase their risk of experiencing dissolution of the union.

Other authors have attempted not only to measure the overall impact of parental separation on children's lives, but also to estimate its effect according to the children's age at the time of the separation (Kiernan 1997; Kiernan and Cherlin 1999). But the studies differ in their findings. Some have shown that experiencing parental separation in childhood increases young people's likelihood of entering into a first union at a younger age (Kiernan 1997) or of experiencing the dissolution of this union (Amato 1996), whereas other studies have not found a significant relation between the children's age at the time of parental separation and their conjugal behaviours in early adulthood (Kiernan and Cherlin 1999; McLanahan and Bumpass 1988).

In the wake of the studies on the impact of parental separation on the conjugal lives of children in early adulthood, another theory more specifically dealing with family instability was advanced. This theory suggests that a certain level of stress is associated with each family change that the child experiences, which increases with the number of family changes experienced (Furstenberg and Cherlin 1991; Wu and Martinson 1993; Wu 1996). These effects are said to persist for a longer period in individuals' lives. The changes referred to are the transition to a situation of single parenthood at the time of parental separation or the death of a parent, the formation of a stepfamily subsequent to a new union, or the remarriage of one of the parents. These kinds of events lead to one or several changes in the parental figures that are involved in children's lives; and such changes are said to increase the chances of early pregnancy (Wu 1996) and the level of conjugal dissatisfaction (Amato and Booth 1991), two factors associated with an increased likelihood of separation.

Other demographic, cultural, or socioeconomic factors may also influence the way in which individuals start their conjugal lives, as well as their risk of experiencing separation or divorce. The demographic factors include behavioural changes observed across generations. More recent generations seem more likely to choose cohabitation as a way of starting their conjugal lives, whereas older generations were more inclined to marry directly (Goldscheider et al. 1999; Bracher and Santow 1998); likewise, younger generations seem to have a greater risk of union dissolution compared with older birth cohorts (Hall and Zhao 1995; Neill and Le Bourdais 1998). Other studies have shown that the more recent is the period of union formation, whether through marriage or cohabitation, the greater is the risk of dissolution (Wu and Balakrishnan 1995; Glenn 1998; Kposowa 1998). Also, for both consensual and legal unions, the studies unanimously conclude that the younger the individual is at the moment of entering into the union, the greater are the chances of a breakdown of the union (Ono 1999; Manning and Smock 1995; Le Bourdais et al. 2000).

The arrival of a child is an event that is likely to change a couple's conjugal relationship. Some studies have shown that the conception of a child hastens the entry into a union (Pollard and Wu 1998; Blossfeld and Huinink 1991; Dumas and Bélanger 1997); it has also been found that the birth of a child conceived during a union often has a stabilizing effect on the partners' conjugal life (Tzeng and Mare 1995; Waite and Lillard 1991). Finally, a marriage to a partner who had been married previously is said to increase the risk of separation (Amato 1996; Heaton and Blake 1999), but this effect was not found to be significant for cohabiting couples (Wu and Balakrishnan 1995).

With regard to cultural determinants, it has been found that Quebekers are more likely to choose cohabitation as a first conjugal experience than are residents of other provinces of Canada (Le Bourdais and Marcil-Gratton 1998; Wu 1999; Goldscheider et al. 1999); they are also less inclined to marry directly or to transform their de facto union into a marriage. Individuals whose mother tongue is French show similar behaviours to those of Quebekers, the majority of whom are French-speaking (Bélanger and Turcotte 1999; Turcotte and Goldscheider 1998). However, it seems that the effects of the place of residence or mother tongue are not as clear with regard to dissolution of the union. It has also been found that immigrants are less likely to cohabit, when compared with people born in Canada. Finally, people who frequently attend religious services or meetings tend to choose marriage rather than cohabitation (Dumas and Bélanger 1997), and they appear to have a more stable relationship as a couple (Berrington and Diamond 1999).

Certain socioeconomic factors are closely linked to the processes of formation and dissolution of the first union. Being a student postpones the entry into conjugal life, whereas being employed is associated with an earlier start to conjugal life (Bracher and Santow 1998; Clarkberg 1999). Moreover, there is a greater risk of union dissolution for individuals who were still pursuing their studies when the relationship began (Le Bourdais et al. 2000). The findings are not as clear regarding the effect of the level of education completed, or of socioeconomic status, on the first union. Some studies have found that education does not significantly affect the likelihood of forming a first union (Blossfeld and Huinink 1991; Goldscheider et al. 1999; McLaughlin and Lichter 1997), while others have shown that the chances of entering into a union (Bracher and Santow 1998; Raley 1996), through cohabitation (Bélanger and Turcotte 1999) or marriage (Clarkberg 1999; Pollard and Wu 1998; Thornton et al. 1995), or of experiencing dissolution of the union (Berrington and Diamond 1999; Bumpass et al. 1991) rise as the level of education increases. Likewise, some of these studies show a positive association between socioeconomic status and formation of a first union, whereas others find a negative association. But they all agree that the socioeconomic status of the family of origin does not really influence the likelihood of dissolution of the first union (see, e.g., Thornton 1985).

In the analysis that follows we are interested in the formation and dissolution of the first union, and more specifically, in identifying the impact of parental separation on the behaviours of the children in early adulthood, after controlling for all the other factors that are likely to affect these behaviours. We will also briefly describe how these other factors influence the dynamics of formation and dissolution of the first union.

Data and Methodology[1]

Our analysis is based on data from the 1995 General Social Survey (GSS) on the family, a survey conducted on a sample of 10,749 individuals age 15 years and older and residing in Canada[2] (Statistics Canada 1996). This retrospective survey collected information on the respondents' family histories up to the time of their leaving the parental home and on their subsequent conjugal and family lives. The survey, thus, provides us with information on many of the family changes experienced by these individuals during their childhood and, particularly, on changes in the parents' conjugal relationship that affected the children's family life. We also have information on the circumstances surrounding the first union entered into by the respondents, that is, the type of union chosen at the outset (cohabitation or marriage), some of the subsequent changes (e.g., dissolution of the union), and the timing of conjugal events; we also know the respondents' age at the time of the birth of their first biological child.

Since we are interested in the impact of parental separation on the lives of young adults, we only considered respondents born between 1951 and 1980, that is, the generations who had been affected in relatively large numbers by the separation of their parents. After excluding individuals for whom some basic information on parental separation or on the first union was missing, our sample, for the study of union formation, comprised 2,807 men and 3,157 women who were between 15 and 44 years of age in 1995. For our study of union dissolution, we only selected respondents who had entered into a first union and who were between 25 and 44 years of age at the time of the survey. We excluded from our analysis individuals aged between 15 and 24 at the time of the survey, who had barely had the time to be exposed to the risk of a breakup, with the exception of those who had formed a union at a very young age. The sample used to study union dissolution, thus, consisted of 1,766 men who had formed a first union, through either marriage (939 men) or cohabitation (827 men), and 2,192 women (1,228 marriages and 964 cohabitations).

We used the method of life tables coupled with 'event history analysis' to study the processes of formation and dissolution of the first union, according to whether or not the individuals had grown up with both of their parents. First, life tables enable us to determine the intensity and timing of union formation and dissolution (see below). Event history analysis is then used to measure the effect of each independent factor considered (demographic, cultural, or socioeconomic) on the chances that individuals will enter into a first union (or experience dissolution of the union), after controlling for the impact of all other variables. This method allows us to consider characteristics whose value may change over the course of an individual's life (see below).

Timing of Union Formation and Union Dissolution According to Experience of Parental Separation

Let us start by looking at the intensity and timing of young adults' formation of a first union. To do so, we constructed multiple decrement life tables, in which the probability of entering into a union, through either marriage or cohabitation, is calculated at each age by relating the number of individuals who enter into a union at this age to those who have not yet done so and are still at risk of forming a union; in this case, cohabitation and marriage are treated as competing risks, that is, as alternative ways of entering into a union. Individuals are removed from the group at risk of entering into a union as they exit the observation period, for example, a 19-year-old respondent who had not yet entered into a union at the time of the survey when calculating the probability of forming a union at age 20; this individual is treated as a censored case.

To contrast the behaviours of young adults according to whether they had experienced parental separation, we constructed separate multiple decrement life tables for young people who had grown up with both parents and for those whose parents had separated before the individual had reached age 19.[3] In this case, the analysis focuses only on individuals who were born (or adopted) into a two-parent family, that is, on individuals in a family with both of their biological (or adoptive) parents.[4] Moreover, since we are interested in the beginning of the conjugal lives of young adults, we chose to limit the analysis to first unions formed before the age of 25. Figure 8.1 shows the results of the life tables for men and women.

Let us look at the situation for women first, and then for men. The cumulative probabilities of entering into a union, as depicted in Figure 8.1, indicate that women who have seen their parents separate tend to form their first union earlier, and a greater proportion opt for cohabitation, than is the case for women whose parents remained together. The latter tend to start their conjugal lives at a later age and are more likely to choose marriage. At age 20, for example, nearly 30% of women who had experienced parental separation or divorce had already started to cohabit with a partner, and only 9% had chosen to marry directly; by age 25, these proportions are about 52% and 25% respectively. Women who did not experience parental separation show no preference as to the type of union chosen (note the overlapping curves) until age 20: at that age, 11% were cohabiting with a partner and 13% had chosen to enter directly into marriage. By contrast, at age 25, some 44% of these women had chosen marriage for their first conjugal union, and 27% had opted for cohabitation.

In contrast to women, men start their conjugal lives a little later on. This finding concurs with vital statistics, which show that the average age for men to start a first marriage is 26, that is, about two years later

Figure 8.1 Cumulative probabilities (%) of entering into a conjugal union through cohabitation or marriage before age 25, according to whether or not parents had separated, women and men.

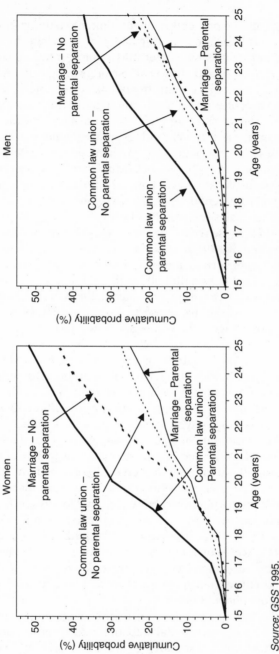

Source: GSS 1995.
Notes: Samples comprised 3,057 women and 2,742 men born into two-parent families and who were 15 to 44 years of age at time of survey.

than the average age for women (Bélanger and Dumas 1998). This may explain the fact that men whose parents did not separate show no preference as to the type of first union chosen: in their case, the age threshold of 25 may limit the analysis too prematurely, since at that age, barely 20% of men have already entered into a first marriage. However, Figure 8.1 clearly shows that a larger proportion of men whose parents had separated tend to choose cohabitation, and do so at a younger age: at age 20 about 16% have already cohabited with a partner, which is on average four times higher than for the other groups. At age 25 some 37% of men who had experienced parental separation had started a first union through cohabitation, which is 14 percentage points higher on average than for the other groups of men.

Figure 8.2 shows the cumulative probabilities of separation before the twelfth year of the union for women and men between age 25 and 44 at the time of the survey, by the type of union chosen at the outset of conjugal life.[5] Here, the cumulative probabilities of a breakdown are calculated separately for young people opting for marriage and for those opting for cohabitation, and according to whether the respondents had experienced parental separation before they reached adulthood. The results are fairly similar for men and women. First, unions that begin with cohabitation clearly more often end in a breakdown than do unions formed by marriage at the outset, regardless of the family histories of the respondents; and second, regardless of whether individuals choose marriage or cohabitation to start their conjugal life, those who have experienced parental separation during their childhood or adolescence are more likely to experience a conjugal breakdown.

For women whose parents had separated, one-third of de facto spouses and only 10% of married women had had their relationships end after three years of conjugal life. At the end of the eleventh year of the union, these proportions were 63% and 29%, respectively. So we find that legal unions tend to last longer than consensual unions. This observation is also true for women whose childhood was not affected by parental separation. But a smaller proportion of the latter experienced a conjugal separation than did the women whose parents had separated: after three years of the union, for example, 18% of de facto spouses and 4% of married women who had grown up with both parents were separated (compared with 34% and 10% of those whose parents had broken up); by the twelfth year of the union, these proportions were 47% and 20%, respectively (compared with 63% and 29%).

Figure 8.2 Cumulative probabilities (%) of union dissolution before the 12th year of the union by type of union at the outset and according to whether parents had separated, women and men.

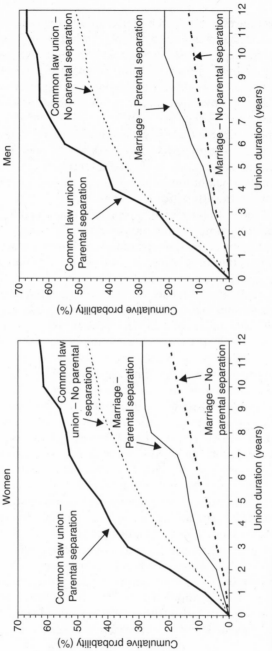

Source: GSS 1995.
Notes: Samples comprised 1,183 marriages and 889 cohabitations for women, and 921 marriages and 782 cohabitations for men. Individuals selected were born into two-parent families and were 25 to 44 years of age at time of survey.

The tendencies observed are very similar for men, although at the beginning of the union, the probability of union dissolution remains virtually the same for the two types of union, whether or not the men had experienced parental separation. Compared with women, the family histories of the young men seemed to have slightly less influence, and indeed had almost no influence before the third year of the union.

Impact of the Parents' Conjugal Life on the Conjugal Life of Their Children

This section now attempts to measure the net effect of family changes experienced by young people during their childhood or adolescence on the dynamics of formation and dissolution of their first conjugal union, after controlling for the potential effect of other factors recognized as also having an influence on the first union. For this purpose, we used the method of event history analysis, which combines the use of life tables with multiple regression analysis.

For this part of the study, two variables were constructed to take into account changes in the respondents' family life: a first variable characterizes respondents according to their experience of parental separation and their age at the time of this event (variable called 'parental situation'); and a second variable takes into account the family environment at the time of the respondents' birth (single-parent or two-parent family) and subsequent changes that they had experienced during their childhood or adolescence (variable known as 'family trajectories'). In the first case, we only look at respondents born into two-parent families, and we only consider the first family change experienced (parental separation); in the second case, the analysis includes all of the respondents, regardless of the family environment at the time of their birth, and we consider all of the family changes experienced.

The various cultural and socioeconomic variables considered in the analysis are the same in the study of both union formation and union dissolution (see the detailed list of variables in the Appendix). Cultural variables include the respondents' mother tongue, region of residence, place of birth, and religious practice; and socioeconomic variables include the level of education completed,[6] whether the respondent is employed,[7] and the highest level of education completed by the parents. In the study of first union formation, demographic characteristics include the respondents' birth cohort, and the conception and birth of the first child; in the study of union dissolution, they include the respondents' age at the beginning of the union, the period of union formation, the type of union (taking into account cohabitations that evolved into marriage), the conception and birth of the first child, and whether the spouse had been married previously or had previously cohabited with a partner. Some of these characteristics may take on a value that changes over the course of an individual's life. This is the case, for example, with the parents' conjugal situation or young people's employment status; event history analysis allows us to take into account parental separation or entry into the job market only from the moment these events occur in the individual's life.

The independent variables were successively integrated into the event history analysis to allow us to see how these variables influence the conjugal life of individuals and to identify the potential direct and indirect (or intermediate) effects of the variables. For example, we would say that parental separation has a direct effect on the formation or dissolution of the first union if the effect of this factor is still statistically significant after we have controlled for the effects of all the other variables; and we would say that it has an indirect influence if the effect of this factor disappears as we include other variables which also affect the risks of forming a union or experiencing a separation.

The risk ratios (or relative risks) generated by the event history analysis should be interpreted as follows: when the value of the coefficients shown in the tables is greater than 1, this means that the effect of this variable increases the risk of experiencing the event being studied compared with the reference category (shown in parentheses in the table); conversely, a coefficient of less than 1 indicates that there is a reduced risk of experiencing the event compared with the reference category. For example, in table 8.1, the relative risk of entering into a first marriage before the age of 25 is 0.59 for a woman who, between the ages of 11 and 14, witnessed the separation of her parents. This means that a woman who experienced parental separation between the ages of 11 and 14 has 59% of the chance of marrying before the age of 25 that women who grew up with both parents do; in other words, experiencing parental separation during adolescence reduces a woman's chances of marrying by 41%.

In the following sections, we compare the gross effect and net effect of parental separation and family changes experienced prior to adulthood on the conjugal life of the respondents. The results are drawn from a partial model, which measures only the influence of the family situation experienced, and from a complete model, which takes into account all of the independent variables described above. However, to make it easier to read the tables, we only give the coefficients associated with the family changes that are of primary interest to us.

Formation of the First Union

Table 8.1 measures the impact of parental separation, according to the age of the children at the time of the conjugal breakdown, on the formation of the first union before the age of 25, for both men and women. The analysis is conducted separately according to whether the type of union chosen at the outset is a cohabitation or marriage. When we look at first unions formed through marriage, individuals opting for cohabitation, who are no longer at risk of starting their conjugal life with a marriage, are removed from the group being studied from the moment their cohabitation begins. Similarly, individuals who married directly are excluded from the study of cohabitations from the moment their marriage occurs.

We see that, in general, the way individuals start their lives as couples is influenced by their previous family experience. The partial model, in fact, shows that individuals who experienced family disruption during childhood have a significantly greater likelihood of beginning a cohabitation before the age of 25, compared with individuals whose parents stayed together, regardless of how old they were when their parents separated. Women who experienced parental separation are thus 2.0 to 2.9 times more likely to cohabit with a partner than women who grew up with both parents, and men are 1.6 to 2.4 times more likely to do so.

However, while generally remaining significant, the risk of cohabitation decreases slightly when we include all of the variables considered (complete model). In other words, parental separation appears to have a direct and indirect effect on the risk of cohabitation, except for men and women aged 0 to 5 years at the time of the conjugal breakdown, and for men aged 11 to 14, where it appears to have an indirect effect only. In this case, the effect of parental separation is apparently mediated by intervening factors that are, in turn, linked to formation of a first de facto union. A detailed examination of the data showed that a larger proportion of women who had experienced parental separation are from more recent generations, and they are more likely to conceive a first child before the start of the union, which appears to result in their beginning a cohabitation at a younger age (data not shown). Men whose parents had separated seem to be more likely to have a first child before the first

TABLE 8.1 Effect of Parental Situation on the Risk of Entering into a First Cohabitation or First Marriage before Age 25 for Young Adults Born into Two-Parent Families

Variable	Category	Women Common law union Models Partial[a]	Women Common law union Models Complete[b]	Women Marriage Models Partial[a]	Women Marriage Models Complete[b]	Men Common law union Models Partial[c]	Men Common law union Models Complete[d]	Men Marriage Models Partial[c]	Men Marriage Models Complete[d]
Parental situation: (Parents together)	Age at PS (years)								
	0–5	2.01***	1.37	0.92	0.92	2.27***	1.39	1.76*	1.58
	6–10	2.93***	1.74***	0.82	0.85	1.62*	1.65*	0.59	0.78
	11–14	2.04***	1.47*	0.43**	0.59*	1.84**	1.22	0.86	0.82
	15–18	2.80***	2.18***	0.42**	0.46*	2.39***	2.09**	0.90	1.40
	Parent deceased	0.96	1.11	1.03	1.05	1.12	1.06	1.01	0.99
	Other	1.53	1.09	1.29	1.11	1.75	1.18	1.39	1.78

Source: GSS 1995.

Note: The variables in italics vary over time, i.e., they may take on a different value over time. The reference category is shown in parentheses. See Appendix for a detailed list of the variables included in the complete models. Risk ratios obtained using Cox semi-parametric model and weighted data.

*$p < .05$; **$p < .01$; ***$p < .001$.

[a] Sample comprised 3,032 women.

[b] Sample comprised 2,714 women (information missing for some variables for 318 respondents).

[c] Sample comprised 2,722 men.

[d] Sample comprised 2,428 men (information missing for some variables for 294 respondents).

PS = Parental Separation

union, to not practice a religion, and to enter the job market earlier, all factors that appear to favour a subsequent cohabitation.

Moreover, for women, experiencing parental separation during adolescence (age 11–18) significantly lowers their risk of marrying before the age of 25, and this effect is direct in that it is not mediated by intervening factors. We may surmise that these women are still affected by their parents' experience and are especially cautious about entering into a more committed type of union, such as a marriage. For men, parental separation has little influence on their risk of marrying, except if the separation occurred very early on in their lives; men who were under 6 years of age at the time of the separation have a 76% greater likelihood of marrying before the age of 25 than do men who grew up with both parents. This effect is reduced and becomes non-significant when we take into account the other variables included in the analysis; this is apparently due to the greater propensity of these men to procreate at a young age and to enter the job market early on, two factors that favour marriage (data not shown). Finally, we see that experiencing the death of a parent as a first family event or experiencing any other type of family situation does not result in a different start to conjugal life when compared with individuals who grew up with both parents.

The same type of analysis was repeated, as we considered this time not only the breakdown of the parents' union but also all the other family changes that might have occurred before the respondents' nineteenth birthday (table 8.2). This model compares the likelihood of men and women entering into a cohabitation or marriage, according to whether their original family trajectory remained intact or was affected by various types of changes. For individuals born into two-parent families, we separated out young adults who had lived with both parents up to the age of 19, those who had experienced only one family change (separation or death of a parent), those who had experienced at least one other change in their family environment after this event (e.g., a parent entering into a new union), and those who reported, as a first family change, living in some 'other' kind of family (living with a foster family or with relatives other than their biological father or mother). For individuals born into single-parent families, we separated out those who grew up in that type of family, those who experienced at least one change, and those who lived in some 'other' kind of family.

Compared with individuals who grew up with both parents, in both the complete and partial models, we see a significantly greater likelihood of experiencing a first cohabitation before age 25 for individuals

TABLE 8.2 Effect of Family Trajectories on the Risk of Entering into a First Cohabitation or First Marriage before the Age 25

Variable	Category	Women Common law union Models Partial[a]	Women Common law union Models Complete[b]	Women Marriage Models Partial[a]	Women Marriage Models Complete[b]	Men Common law union Models Partial[c]	Men Common law union Models Complete[d]	Men Marriage Models Partial[c]	Men Marriage Models Complete[d]
Family trajectories: (Has always lived with both parents)	Born into two-parent family								
	Separated only	2.12***	1.52***	0.60***	0.69*	2.12***	1.65***	0.93	1.09
	Separated with changes	2.65***	1.86***	0.89	0.93	1.99***	1.48*	1.18	1.19
	Death only	0.90	1.07	1.02	1.07	1.21	1.10	1.04	0.94
	Death with changes	1.48	1.47	1.31	1.09	0.71	0.80	0.87	1.37
	Other	1.55	1.14	1.28	1.13	1.77	1.20	1.38	1.80
	Born into one-parent family								
	Stable	1.76*	1.82	0.67	0.66	1.31	1.50	1.82	2.85*
	With changes	2.58***	2.28**	0.65	0.65	1.52	0.88	0.69	0.84
	Other	2.08*	1.36	1.04	1.22	2.01	1.69	1.76	2.41

Source: GSS 1995.

Note: The reference category is shown in parentheses. See Appendix for a detailed list of the variables included in the complete models. Risk ratios obtained using Cox semi-parametric model and weighted data.

*p < .05; **p < .01; ***p < .001.

[a] Sample comprised 3,150 women.
[b] Sample comprised 2,807 women (information missing for some variables for 343 respondents).
[c] Sample comprised 2,795 men.
[d] Sample comprised 2,489 men (information missing for some variables for 306 respondents).

who experienced parental separation, whether or not this was followed by other changes. This same relationship is also found for women born into single-parent families whose family environment changed after the single parent entered into a union: these women show a significantly greater risk of beginning a first cohabitation before age 25 than do women who always lived with both of their parents, and this association persists in the complete model. For men, on the other hand, being born into a single-parent family does not seem to lead to any significant differences in the likelihood of entering into cohabitation at a young age.

Finally, we see that a family trajectory other than growing up with both parents has relatively little impact on young adults' risk of marrying before age 25, with two exceptions. The first involves women who lived in a single-parent family after their parents separated: even after controlling for all the variables included in the complete model, these women have a risk of marrying before age 25 that is 31% lower than the risk for women whose parents remained together. The second exception involves young men who were born into and grew up in a single-parent family, and who are nearly three times more likely to marry than young men who grew up in a two-parent family. In this case, the net effect of the family situation, which is estimated when we take all the sociodemographic variables into account, is greater than the gross effect observed in the partial model. This suggests that having only a mother figure as a parent reinforces these young men's tendency to marry, after controlling for the effects of their other characteristics.

Dissolution of the First Union

The analysis of the risk of dissolution of the first union only involves the generations born between 1951 and 1970. As we noted earlier, respondents aged 15 to 24 at the time of the survey were removed from the sample; these generations did not really have the time to be exposed to the risk of a breakup, except for individuals who entered into a union at a very early age and are more likely to separate. Including them in the analysis would increase the risk of overestimating the likelihood of union dissolution for these generations. Moreover, the analysis is conducted separately according to the type of union chosen at the outset of conjugal life. For the study of cohabitations, a variable was introduced into the complete model in order to take cohabitations that evolved into marriages into account from the moment the marriage occurred.

Table 8.3 shows the effect of parental separation on young adults' chances of experiencing the dissolution of their own conjugal union, according to their age at the time their parents separated. As we saw earlier when looking at the life tables, parental separation is generally associated with an increased risk of dissolution, regardless of how individuals started their conjugal life. However, the effect of this event on the conjugal life of the children varies according to the children's age at the time the separation occurred.

Except for women who were very young (under 6 years of age) when their parents separated, women entering into a union through cohabitation who saw their parents separate are themselves more likely to separate from their de facto spouses (Table 8.3); and they are 65% to 96% more likely to experience a breakup than are women from stable two-parent families (partial model). However, this effect is largely indirect, in the sense that the risk ratios become statistically non-significant after controlling for the effect of all the sociodemographic variables (complete model). As we saw in the previous section, women who experienced the separation of their parents are more inclined to begin cohabitation early on; they tend to start their conjugal life at a young age and while they are still at school, two factors that, in turn, increase the risks of experiencing a separation (data not shown).

For men living in a de facto union, the influence of parental separation operates in a different fashion. Men who were under 11 years of age when their parents separated are more likely to experience a breakdown of their de facto union: their risk of separating is about twice as high as the risk for men whose parents stayed together (partial model). For men who experienced parental separation when they were very young, the effect appears to be direct, in the sense that it persists even when we take all the sociodemographic variables into account. For men who were aged 6 to 10 at the time of parental separation, the effect of this event seems, in part, to be linked to their greater likelihood of starting their first union at a young age, which increases the risk of dissolution (data not shown).

Women who entered into a marriage directly without previously cohabiting with their spouse and who saw their parents separate do not seem more likely to separate from their spouse than women who grew up in a stable two-parent family, after we take all the variables considered into account. On the other hand, married men who experi-

TABLE 8.3 Effect of Parental Situation on the Risk of Union Dissolution before the 12th Year of the Union, by Type of Union at the Outset for Young Adults Born into Two-Parent Families

		Women				Men			
		Common law union		Marriage		Common law union		Marriage	
Variable	Category	Models Partial[a]	Models Complete[b]	Models Partial[a]	Models Complete[b]	Models Partial[c]	Models Complete[d]	Models Partial[c]	Models Complete[d]
Parental situation: (Parents together)	Age at PS (years)								
	0–5	1.16	0.66	1.83	1.68	2.14***	1.88*	1.00	0.62
	6–10	1.65*	1.18	2.05*	1.66	1.87*	1.60	5.80***	5.26***
	11–14	1.94***	1.14	0.20	0.19	0.87	1.05	2.32	1.31
	15–18	1.96**	1.49	1.93	1.61	1.43	1.45	0.74	0.54
	Parent deceased	1.05	0.88	0.74	1.00	0.70	0.82	1.33	1.20
	Other	1.71	1.10	3.39***	2.43*	1.63	1.48	3.98**	2.89

Source: GSS 1995.

Note: The reference category is shown in parentheses. See Appendix for a detailed list of the variables included in the complete models. Risk ratios obtained using Cox semi-parametric model and weighted data.

*p < .05; **p < .01; ***p < .001.

[a] Sample comprised 1,178 married women and 896 de facto spouses.

[b] Sample comprised 1,103 married women and 867 de facto spouses (data missing for some variables for 75 married women and 29 de facto spouses).

[c] Sample comprised 912 married men and 785 de facto spouses.

[d] Sample comprised 839 married men and 746 de facto spouses (data missing for some variables for 73 married men and 39 de factor spouses).

PS = Parental Separation

enced parental separation when they were between 6 and 10 years of age seem to be much more likely to have their union break down, and the influence of the separation persists after controlling for the effect of other factors (complete model). It is also interesting to note that both men and women who married directly and who had experienced a family situation other than that of living with one or both of their birth parents clearly have more chances of facing marital dissolution than those who grew up with both of their parents. However, this category combines a series of very different situations (e.g., living with grandparents or with a foster family), and it is difficult to identify the mechanisms that are operating here, except to say that these family situations may be associated with behavioural problems on the part of the children or the parents' inability to assume their roles as couples and parents and thus act as role models for their children.

Table 8.4 presents the effect of various family trajectories experienced during childhood on men's and women's risk of experiencing a breakdown of their conjugal union. Given the small number of men who were born into single-parent families, it was not possible to separate out those who had experienced subsequent family changes and those who had not.

The only one of the various family trajectories examined that seems to be associated with an increased risk of dissolution of a consensual union is the situation of young adults who saw their parents separate but did not experience a subsequent change in their family situation. Women in this situation show a gross risk of separation that is twice as high as the risk for women cohabitors whose parents remained together (partial model). However, the effect appears to be largely mediated by intervening factors. The greater propensity to separate among women who had experienced parental separation, thus, seems to be due to the fact that a larger proportion of these women do not practice a religion and tend to enter into a union earlier and often while they are still at school – and it is all these factors that are apparently influencing their risk of having their union break down. Young men who grew up in a single-parent family after their parents separated are 45% more likely to see their de facto union end, and the effect of parental separation is direct and persists after controlling for the socioeconomic variables (complete model).

For individuals who married directly, the only family trajectories that are associated with an increased risk of union dissolution involve being born into a single-parent family or having lived in a family other than

TABLE 8.4 Effect of Family Trajectories on the Risk of Union Dissolution before the 12th Year of the Union by Type of Union at the Outset

		Women				Men			
		Common law union		Marriage		Common law union		Marriage	
Variable	Category	Models Partial[a]	Models Complete[b]	Models Partial[a]	Models Complete[b]	Models Partial[c]	Models Complete[d]	Models Partial[c]	Models Complete[d]
Family trajectories: (Has always lived with both parents)	Born into two-parent family								
	Separated only	2.00***	1.33	1.24	1.16	1.48*	1.45*	2.06*	1.41
	Separated with changes	1.18	0.76	1.43	0.98	1.45	1.29	1.76	1.29
	Death only	1.19	0.93	0.84	1.23	0.63	0.78	1.37	1.27
	Death with changes	0.48	0.43	0.62	0.52	1.60	1.23	0.93	0.89
	Other	1.67	1.05	3.41***	2.51*	1.63	1.50	4.00**	2.74
	Born into one-parent family								
	Stable	1.33	1.00	2.94*	1.73	0.75	0.81	1.12	1.01
	With changes	1.34	1.00	5.77***	4.68**				
	Other	0.97	0.72	2.41	2.51				

Source: GSS 1995.

Note: The reference category is shown in parentheses. See Appendix for a detailed list of the variables included in the complete models. Coefficients obtained using Cox semi-parametric model and weighted data.

*p < .05; **p < .01; ***p < .001.

[a] Sample comprised 1,214 married women and 929 de facto spouses.

[b] Sample comprised 1,131 married women and 899 de facto spouses (data missing for some variables for 83 married women and 30 de facto spouses)

[c] Sample comprised 928 married men and 808 de facto spouses.

[d] Sample comprised 854 married men and 765 de facto spouses (data missing for some variables for 74 married men and 43 de facto spouses).

that of one's birth parents. Women born into a single-parent family are 1.7 to 4.7 times more likely to experience separation (complete model). The small number of women in our sample born into this family context in part explains the fact that two of the three coefficients associated with this type of family trajectory are large but non-significant.

Other Results

Let us now briefly present the effect of the other variables included in the analysis of the processes of formation and dissolution of the first union.[8] The results confirm that these behaviours have changed over time. More recent generations are clearly more inclined than are older generations to choose cohabitation as a way of starting their conjugal life, and they are less likely to opt for marriage. Also, the more recent the period of union formation, the greater are the risks for both men and women of facing dissolution of the union, regardless of the type of union chosen. The individual's age at the beginning of the conjugal relationship is also linked to the probability of young adults separating, with relationships formed earlier on in life being more likely to end quickly. But this is not the case for men who married directly; the postponement of marriage to a later age among more recent cohorts may in part explain the lack of a statistical link. Moreover, the risks of separation decline substantially from the moment the cohabitation changes into a marriage: men and women who married their partner have only a third of the chances of those still living in a de facto union of facing dissolution of the union, after controlling for all of the respondents' other characteristics.

The conception of a child is associated with an earlier start to conjugal life. This event increases the propensity of both men and women to enter into a cohabitation or marriage, but it tends to influence men's behaviour more strongly and is more closely linked to entry into marriage. Having a child outside of the union does not at first glance seem to be linked to a greater risk of separation (except for men in a de facto union). On the other hand, the stabilizing effect of a child on the conjugal relationship is only seen when the child was conceived during the union. Finally, the fact that the spouse had been married previously does not seem to affect the chances of a breakup, but this risk increases when the spouse had previously cohabited with another partner.

The influence of cultural and economic variables on formation and dissolution of the first union is much less clear than the effect of the demographic variables, except in the case of religious practice, where the impact is very clear. Individuals who attend religious services or meetings on a regular basis are much more inclined to marry directly; they are also less likely to experience separation, regardless of whether the partners are married or cohabiting. Moreover, individuals whose mother tongue is French are more likely to cohabit than individuals whose mother tongue is English or a language other than French or English, as are respondents born in North America compared with immigrants from other continents. Finally, when we take all their characteristics into account, residents of Quebec do not seem to be more inclined to cohabit than people living elsewhere in Canada, but they are less likely to marry directly.

Like several other studies, our analysis does not show strong statistical links between the level of education completed and conjugal life. Not having completed one's education postpones the entry into conjugal life and, conversely, entry into the job market favours the formation of a conjugal union, and these variables more strongly influence the choice of marriage rather than cohabitation. Finally, starting one's conjugal life while still attending school is linked to an increased risk of separation, but this is only true for women.

Conclusion

Our results confirm the existence of a link between disruption during childhood and adolescence in an individual's family life and the individual's behaviours associated with the first conjugal experience in early adulthood. Young adults who were affected as children by the separation of their parents tend to begin their own conjugal lives earlier on than individuals who grew up with both of their parents, and to do so through cohabitation. The effect of parental separation is exerted both directly and indirectly, through the adoption of particular attitudes and behaviours that, in turn, influence the formation of the union. As Kiernan and Hobcraft (1997) suggest, the separation of their parents may lead individuals to seek affection outside of the home by forming intimate relationships, which increase their chances of an early start to conjugal life and parenthood.

We also examined the effects of parental separation on the risk of dissolution of the conjugal union during the first twelve years of the union. In this case, the impact is less clear than is the effect of parental separation on the beginning of conjugal life. Also, the effect of the young adults' age at the time of their parents' separation is not as clear as we had surmised. While parental separation increases the risk of a conjugal breakdown for men and women who choose to cohabit, this phenomenon seems to be more marked when the parents had separated when the women were 6 years of age or older, and when the men were under 6 years of age. The impact of parental separation for men is direct and persists after controlling for all of the variables considered, whereas separation has a more immediate effect for women in leading to particular behaviours, which in turn increase the risks of experiencing a conjugal breakdown.

Women whose parents separated during their adolescence are less likely to marry before the age of 25. However, only men whose parents separated when they were under 6 years of age are more likely to marry than men who grew up with both parents. Furthermore, only married men who experienced this event between the ages of 6 and 10 seem more inclined to separate from their spouse, compared with married men who grew up with both parents. A possible explanation for this is that men who experienced parental separation during childhood may have difficulties in dealing with their interpersonal relations with their partner (Amato 1996). Our results also show that men who were born to and grew up with a single parent, often the mother, seem more likely to marry before the age of 25. Finally, the fact of having lived in some 'other' type of family, for both men and women, or of being born into a single-parent family for women, appears to be linked to an increased risk of divorce when these individuals are married.

Generally speaking, the family environment in which children are born and raised has undergone major transformations. It has gradually changed from a stable family environment characterized by ascribed gender parental roles towards a context marked by a greater emphasis on the parents' personal growth through their relationship as a couple. It seems that this tendency found within the family reflects the gradual emergence of changes in societal values, including a growing trend towards individualism (Lesthaeghe 1988). This period of change was also marked by a transition from a context where women were financially dependent on their spouses, and took on the role of raising their children in a situation where there was a relationship of interdependence between the father and mother, to a context where women had entered the job market and had become economically independent.

The simple fact of not growing up in a stable two-parent family exposes the child to the risk of experiencing various economic and social problems; for example, single-parent families formed after parental separation are often forced to move – which, for the children, means breaking up with their peers – and often face a substantial reduction in income. Moreover, as our results show, the fact of having lived in a family environment outside the 'normal' context of the stable two-parent family leads to individuals adopting different behaviours, such as forming a union at a young age, having a child outside of a union, entering into a union before the age of 25 while still in the process of completing one's education, and in turn, facing the breakup of one's own conjugal union. These behaviours are likely to have long-term effects on the living conditions experienced by individuals and their children.

In sum, individuals who experience family disruption show a greater risk of adopting behaviours that are different from those of individuals who grow up with both of their parents, especially behaviours associated with the beginning of conjugal life. In that respect, the breakdown of the family is likely to have wide-reaching effects on the life course of individuals and on the fabric of society as a whole.

Appendix: List of Variables Included in the Event History Analysis

- *Parental situation*: parents together; age at parental separation 0–5 years, 6–10 years, 11–14 years, 15–18 years; parent deceased; other situation
- *Family trajectory*: always lived with both parents; born into two-parent family and experienced separation only, separation followed by other changes, death of a parent only, death followed by changes, or other situation; born into and grew up in single-parent family; born into single-parent family and experienced changes, or other situation
- *Generation*: born 1951–60; 1961–70; 1971–80 (only in the analysis of union formation)
- *Period of union formation*: before 1980; 1980–89; 1990–95 (only in the analysis of union dissolution)
- *Age at beginning of union*: for women: <18; 18–19; 20–1; 22–4; ≥25; for men: <20; 20–1; 22–3; 24–6; ≥27 (only in the analysis of union dissolution)
- *Cohabitation evolved into marriage*:[9] yes; no (only in the analysis of union dissolution)

- *First child:*[10] no children; conception of a child; birth of a child (in the analysis of union formation); no children; child born prior to the union; child conceived prior to the union; child conceived during the union (in the analysis of union dissolution)
- *Spouse previously married*: yes; no (only in the analysis of union dissolution)
- *Spouse had previously cohabited with a partner*: yes; no (only in the analysis of union dissolution)
- *Mother tongue*: French only; English only; French and English; other language
- *Region of residence*: Quebec; elsewhere in Canada
- *Place of birth*: Canada; elsewhere in North America; Europe; developing country
- *Religious practice*: regular (at least once a week or once a month); sporadic (a few times or once a year); no religion or no religious practice
- *Level of education completed*: less than high school diploma; high school diploma; post-secondary diploma; university degree
- *Education completed:*[11] yes; no
- *Employed in first regular job* (lasting at least six months):[12] yes; no
- *Highest level of education completed by father or mother*: less than high school; high school; post-secondary; university; unknown

NOTES

1 For a more in-depth explanation of the methodology used for the analysis and the operationalization of variables, see chapter 2 in Provencher (2002).
2 Except in the Northwest Territories (including Nunavut) and the Yukon.
3 The group of respondents who did not experience parental separation is mostly comprised of individuals who grew up with both of their parents, but also includes a small proportion of individuals who experienced the death of a parent or some other type of family situation (e.g., lived with another family member or with a foster family). Even though we might expect these individuals to have different conjugal behaviours from individuals who grew up with both parents, we can assume that the impact of this group of individuals will be relatively minor due to their small number.
4 From this point on in the text, when we refer to 'biological' children or parents, we will also be including children and parents brought together by adoption.

5 The analysis was limited to the first twelve years of the union so that unions of longer duration would not be overrepresented among older generations.
6 We only have the level of education completed at the time of the survey. However, using a pre-established grid, we attempted to estimate the level of education completed according to the respondents' age. For example, for an individual with a university degree who completed his or her studies at age 22.4 years, we proceeded as follows: at age 15, the respondent is classified as having less than a high school diploma; at age 16.7, a high school diploma, a level retained until the individual is 18.7 years of age, at which point he or she is attributed a college diploma, and at age 22.4, a university degree (for more details, see Provencher 2002).
7 We conducted separate analyses to take into account the situation of being employed or a student, given the strong correlation that exists between these two variables. We only present here the results of analyses that included the variable of being employed.
8 For a detailed description of the effect of these variables, see Provencher (2002).
9 Variable whose value changes from the moment the cohabitation changes into a marriage.
10 In the analysis of union formation, variable whose value changes from the moment the child is conceived or born; in the analysis of union dissolution, variable whose value changes from the moment the child is conceived during the union.
11 In the analysis of union formation, variable whose value changes from the moment the studies end; in the analysis of union dissolution, fixed variable whose value is measured from the moment the union begins.
12 In the analysis of union formation, variable whose value changes from the moment the regular job begins; in the analysis of union dissolution, fixed variable whose value is measured from the moment the union begins.

REFERENCES

Amato, P.R. 1996. 'Explaining the Intergenerational Transmission of Divorce.' *Journal of Marriage and the Family* 58(3): 628–40.
Amato, P.R., and A. Booth. 1991. 'The Consequences of Parental Divorce and Marital Unhappiness for Adult Well-Being.' *Social Forces* 69(3): 895–914.
Bélanger, A., and J. Dumas (with the collaboration of C. Oikawa and L. Martel). 1998. *Report on the Demographic Situation in Canada 1997*, Ottawa: Statistics Canada, cat. no. 91-209-XPF.

Bélanger, A., and P. Turcotte. 1999. 'L'influence des caractéristiques sociodémo-graphiques sur le début de la vie conjugale des Québécoises.' *Cahiers québécois de démographie* 28(1–2): 173–97.

Berrington, A., and I. Diamond. 1999. 'Marital Dissolution among the 1958 British Birth Cohort: The Role of Cohabitation.' *Population Studies* 53(1): 19–38.

Blossfeld, H.P., and J. Huinink. 1991. 'Human Capital Investments or Norms of Role Transition? How Women's Schooling and Career Affects the Process of Family Formation.' *American Journal of Sociology* 97(1): 143–68.

Bracher, M., and G. Santow. 1998. 'Economic Independence and Union Formation in Sweden.' *Population Studies* 52(3): 275–94.

Bumpass, L.L., T. Castro Martin, and J.A. Sweet. 1991. 'The Impact of Family Background and Early Marital Factors on Marital Disruption.' *Journal of Family Issues* 12(1): 22–42.

Clarkberg, M. 1999. 'The Price of Partnering: The Role of Economic Well-Being in Young Adults' First Union Experiences.' *Social Forces* 77(3): 945–68.

Dumas, J., and A. Bélanger (with the collaboration of G. Smith). 1997. *Report on the Demographic Situation in Canada 1996*. Ottawa: Statistics Canada, cat. no. 91-209-XPF.

Furstenberg, F.F. Jr., and A.J. Cherlin. 1991. *Divided Families: What Happens to Children When Parents Part*. Cambridge, MA: Harvard University Press.

Furstenberg, F.F. Jr., and J. O. Teitler. 1994. 'Reconsidering the Effects of Marital Disruption. What Happens to Children of Divorce in Early Adulthood?' *Journal of Family Issues* 15(2): 173–90.

Glenn, N. 1998. 'The Course of Marital Success and Failure in Five American 10-Year Marriage Cohorts.' *Journal of Marriage and the Family* 60(3): 569–76.

Goldscheider, F.K., P. Turcotte, and A. Kopp. 1999. 'The Changing Determinants of Women's First Union Formation in Industrialized Countries: The United States, Canada, Italy and Sweden.' Paper presented at the European Population Conference, The Hague, 30 Aug. to 3 Sept.

Hall, D.R., and J.Z. Zhao. 1995. 'Cohabitation and Divorce in Canada: Testing the Selectivity Hypothesis.' *Journal of Marriage and the Family* 57(2): 421–7.

Heaton, T.B., and A.M. Blake. 1999. 'Gender Differences in Determinants of Marital Disruption.' *Journal of Family Issues* 20(1): 25–45.

Keith, V.M., and B. Finlay. 1988. 'The Impact of Parental Divorce on Children's Educational Attainment, Marital Timing, and Likelihood of Divorce.' *Journal of Marriage and the Family* 50(2): 797–809.

Kiernan, K.E. 1992. 'The Impact of Family Disruption in Childhood on Transitions Made in Young Adult Life.' *Population Studies* 46(2): 213–34.

– 1997. *The Legacy of Parental Divorce: Social, Economic and Demographic Experi-*

ences in Adulthood. London: London School of Economics, Centre for Analysis of Social Exclusion, CASE Paper, no. 1.

Kiernan, K.E., and A.J. Cherlin. 1999. 'Parental Divorce and Partnership Dissolution in Adulthood: Evidence from a British Cohort Study.' *Population Studies* 53(1): 39–48.

Kiernan, K.E., and J. Hobcraft. 1997. 'Parental Divorce during Childhood: Age at First Intercourse, Partnership and Parenthood.' *Population Studies* 51(1): 41–55.

Kposowa, A.J. 1998. 'The Impact of Race on Divorce in the United States.' *Journal of Comparative Family Studies* 29(3): 529–47.

Le Bourdais, C., and N. Marcil-Gratton. 1996. 'Family Transformations across the Canadian/American Border: When the Laggard Becomes the Leader.' *Journal of Comparative Family Studies* 27(2): 415–36.

– 1998. 'The Impact of Family Disruption in Childhood on Demographic Outcomes in Young Adulthood.' In M. Corak (ed.), *Labour Markets, Social Institutions, and the Future of Canada's Children*, 91–105. Ottawa: Statistics Canada and Human Resources Development Canada.

Le Bourdais, C., G. Neill, and N. Vachon. 2000. 'Family Disruption in Canada: Impact of the Changing Patterns of Family Formation and of Female Employment.' *Canadian Studies in Population* 27(1): 85–105.

Lesthaeghe, R. 1988. 'Cultural Dynamics and Economic Theories of Fertility Change. *Population Development Review* 14(1): 1–44.

Manning, W.D., and P.J. Smock. 1995. 'Why Marry? Race and the Transition to Marriage among Cohabitors.' *Demography* 32(4): 509–20.

Marcil-Gratton, N., C. Le Bourdais, and H. Juby. 2003. 'Etre père au XXIᵉ siècle: vers une redéfinition du rôle des hommes auprès des enfants.' In V. Piché and C. Le Bourdais (eds.), *La démographie québécoise: Enjeux du XXIᵉ siècle*, 144–75. Montreal: Presses de l'Université de Montréal.

McLanahan, S., and L. Bumpass. 1988. 'Intergenerational Consequences of Family Disruption.' *American Journal of Sociology* 94(1): 130–52.

McLaughlin, D.K., and D.T. Lichter. 1997. 'Poverty and the Marital Behavior of Young Women.' *Journal of Marriage and the Family* 59(3): 582–94.

Miller, B.C., and T.B. Heaton. 1991. 'Age at First Sexual Intercourse and the Timing of Marriage and Childbirth.' *Journal of Marriage and the Family* 53(3): 719–32.

Mueller, C.W., and H. Pope. 1977. 'Marital Instability: A Study of Its Transmission Between Generations.' *Journal of Marriage and the Family* 39(1): 83–93.

Neill, G., and C. Le Bourdais (with the collaboration of N. Vachon). 1998. *Dissolution des premières unions fécondes au Canada: une analyse de risques dans un contexte de changements.* Paper presented at Chaire Quetelet 1998 – Ménages, comportements démographiques et sociétés en mutation, Louvain-la-Neuve, Nov.

Ono, H. 1999. 'Historical Time and U.S. Marital Dissolution.' *Social Forces* 77(3): 969–97.

Pollard, M.S., and Z. Wu. 1998. 'Divergence of Marriage Patterns in Quebec and Elsewhere in Canada.' *Population and Development Review* 24(2): 329–56.

Pope, H., and C.W. Mueller. 1976. 'The Intergenerational Transmission of Marital Instability: Comparisons by Race and Sex.' *Journal of Social Issues* 32(1): 49–66.

Powell, M.A., and T.L. Parcel. 1997. 'Effects of Family Structure on the Earnings Attainment Process: Differences by Gender.' *Journal of Marriage and the Family* 59(2): 419–33.

Provencher, C. 2002. *La conjugalité des jeunes adultes ayant vécu la séparation de leurs parents.* Master's thesis. Montreal: Université de Montréal.

Raley, R.K. 1996. 'A Shortage of Marriageable Men? A Note on the Role of Cohabitation in Black-White Differences in Marriage Rates.' *American Sociological Review* 61(6): 973–83.

Sandefur, G.D., and T. Wells. 1999. 'Does Family Structure Really Influence Educational Attainment?' *Social Science Research* 28(4): 331–57.

Statistics Canada. 1996 *General Social Survey.* Canada: author.

– 2002. *Changing Conjugal Life in Canada.* Ottawa: Statistics Canada, cat. no. 89-576-XIE.

– 2003. *Annual Demographic Statistics 2002.* Ottawa: Statistics Canada, cat. no. 91-213-XIB.

Thornton, A. 1985. 'Changing Attitudes toward Separation and Divorce: Causes and Consequences.' *American Journal of Sociology* 90(4): 856–72.

Thornton, A., W.G. Axinn, and J.D. Teachman. 1995. 'The Influence of School Enrollment and Accumulation on Cohabitation and Marriage in Early Adulthood.' *American Sociological Review* 60(5): 762–74.

Turcotte, P., and F.K. Goldscheider. 1998. 'Evolution of Factors Influencing First Union Formation in Canada.' *Canadian Studies in Population* 25(2): 145–73.

Tzeng, J.M., and R.D. Mare. 1995. 'Labor Market and Socioeconomic Effects on Marital Stability.' *Social Science Research* 24(4): 329–51.

Waite, L.J., and L.A. Lillard. 1991. 'Children and Marital Disruption.' *American Journal of Sociology* 96(4): 930–53.

Wu, L.L., and B.C. Martinson. 1993. 'Family Structure and the Risk of Premarital Birth.' *American Sociological Review* 58(2): 210–32.

Wu, L.L. 1996. 'Effects of Family Instability, Income, and Income Instability on the Risk of a Premarital Birth.' *American Sociological Review* 61(3): 386–406.

Wu, Z. 1999. 'Premarital Cohabitation and the Timing of First Marriage.' *Canadian Review of Sociology and Anthropology* 36(1): 109–27.

Wu, Z., and T.R. Balakrishman. 1995. 'Dissolution of Premarital Cohabitation in Canada.' *Demography* 32(4): 521–32.

9 Single Parenthood and Labour Force Participation: The Effect of Social Policies

NANCY MEILLEUR AND ÉVELYNE LAPIERRE-ADAMCYK

This chapter aims to shed light on variations in the labour force participation rates of single mothers and to explore how social policies may influence their involvement in paid work. A focus on single mothers and their families is especially pertinent in the context of concerns about social cohesion, because the manner in which society arranges support for particularly vulnerable groups reveals its capacity to avoid social exclusion and the resulting problems.

Changes in family structure over the past three decades have brought about an increase in the number and the relative importance of single-parent families and have profoundly modified the sociodemographic profile of mothers living alone with their children. The increase in divorce, the diminishing numbers of legalized marriages, and the rise of cohabitation have contributed to the emergence of numerous family units in which one of the two parents, most often the mother, takes on the responsibility of raising the children, with or without the support of the other partner, who does not share the same residence. Numerous studies demonstrate that single-parent families are often poor. For many single-parent families these circumstances prove to be temporary, but there is always a danger that such families may become mired in a situation from which it is difficult to escape. We know that for some, single motherhood may last quite a long time and that, during this period, these mothers' situation is difficult because they need to assure the economic well-being of their children, and, at the same time, their physical and emotional security. How is it possible to achieve this double objective, already quite a challenge, even for a two-parent family with their combined resources and energies?

Participation in economic activity constitutes one of the principal means by which Canadians ensure their well-being and integrate fully into society. The case of single mothers deserves particular attention: the statistical data show that their labour force participation varies substantially as a function of their personal characteristics, that it is lower than is true for other mothers, and that it is not uniform across Canadian regions. In the latter case, it seems likely that social policies exert a significant influence.

This chapter addresses these diverse questions, commencing with a description of the variations in economic activity of single mothers in Quebec, Ontario, and Alberta. Next, the emphasis will be placed on an exploratory analysis, again comparative, of certain pertinent elements of social policy in these three provinces. Many difficulties, among others the impossibility of satisfactorily documenting all of the measures taken at different points in time by the various governments, as well as their frequent modifications, prevent a thorough analysis of the links between labour force participation and social policies. Nonetheless, in establishing a particular point in time, in this case 1996, it becomes possible to explore the relations between variations in provincial social policies and the work patterns of single mothers. The text is divided into three sections: a brief outline of what we know of the factors associated with the economic activity of single mothers; a statistical description of their varying rates of activity in the three Canadian provinces examined; and, finally, an analysis of the elements of single-mothers' income from which the impact of certain aspects of social policies may be discerned.

The Issue of Single Mothers' Economic Activity

From 1961 to 1996 single-parent families increased from 11% of families with children to 22%; during this period 80% of these families were headed by single mothers (Péron et al. 1999). Matricentric single-parent families increased a bit more rapidly during this time than families led by a single father, and Gunderson (1998) warns that this growth will have a negative effect on family income.

The paths to becoming a single parent vary. While single parenthood used to be most frequently because of the death of a spouse, today it is more likely to result from the dissolution of a union. Some separations have a legal basis while others do not; furthermore, the age of the children at the time of the rupture can affect the ease of adaptation to the

new situation. Men and women experience single parenthood differently; in particular, their income is not the same. For example, in 1996
mothers had a lower average salary ($24,044) than single fathers
($39,428) and were almost twice as likely to live below the poverty line
(60.8% vs 31.3%; Statistics Canada 2000). Furthermore, it would seem
that the economic consequences of union breakup are not quite the same
for men and women. Women, much more than men, see their income
decline sharply immediately after separation, but after a period of five
years, the difference is substantially reduced, with men gaining slightly,
and women still behind but by 5% only (Beaujot 1999). Those who enter
a new union are favoured; however, women are less likely than men to
be in a new union after five years.

To understand the situation of single mothers, an approach that situ-
ates them in their social context seems appropriate, since social policies
constitute a mirror of society's concerns. Thus, in investigating the
relationship between mothers' economic activity and social policies,
we will determine whether, indeed, policies facilitate the employment
of people in a most precarious situation. But first, let us examine
women and the workplace.

Séguin (1996; 1997) studied single mothers' employment strategies
and concluded that 'the characteristics of women's work, the emergence of an economy based on two-income households, the asymmet-
ric sharing of parental responsibilities and the exclusion of a large
proportion of single mothers from the labour force seem to be the principal factors explaining this greater economic vulnerability of female-
headed single-parent families' (1996: 28). Usually, there is only one
income-earner in single-parent families. Since governmental assistance
is often insufficient, the sine qua non to escape from poverty is usually
to hold down a well-paying job. At the same time, for some, a new
union may appear to provide a way out of a perilous situation.

In Canada the median duration of single parenthood is five years
(Desrosiers et al. 1993). It is generally a transitory situation between the
rupture of one union and the establishment of another, or between the
breakup of a union and the departure of the children from the parental
home (Péron et al. 1999). However, while single parenthood often constitutes a bridge between two unions, it is nonetheless not a marginal
phenomenon. Though the return to a conjugal relationship (or the
development of a new union) may strongly contribute to an escape
from economic difficulties (OECD 1990; Galarneau and Sturrock 1997),
this is not always the case (Séguin 1996). On the one hand, entry into a

new union favours single mothers who are more economically advantaged; on the other hand, it does not reflect the desires of all mothers, some of whom are not anxious to enter another relationship (Bellware and Charest 1986; Séguin et al. 1996). Finally, the reconstituted family is also fragile and the risk of rupture is always present. Mothers who enter a new union are not assured relief from economic difficulties. Also, the professional involvement of single mothers remains, in the long term, the best guarantee of their ability to escape from poverty (Séguin 1996).

Research on the problems encountered by single mothers at work is scant (Séguin 1996), though considerable attention has been paid to the larger question of women and work, particularly from the perspective of the sexual division of labour. It has been observed that, even if mothers' participation has increased, they do not yet play an equal role in the labour force. They are more likely than men to have part-time positions and are more apt to be segregated in the less skilled, and thus poorly remunerated, employment sectors (Dandurand 1994). Saint-Jean (1987) reminds us nonetheless that part-time work is an important element of women's integration into the workforce, even if it is not always their preference. Indeed, for certain women, part-time employment constitutes a means of gradually joining the workforce, or of better balancing work and family, but for one-income families, part-time work does not provide an escape from poverty.

The problems facing single mothers in the labour market are exacerbated by their low education level, lack of familiarity with the labor market, and insufficient work experience. Analyses reveal that education is the most significant determining factor in the employment of single parents (Beaupré 1982). This is linked, in turn, to the mother's age, the responsibility for young children (Lero and Brockman 1993), and the salary offered in the workplace. Less educated single mothers are more likely to confine themselves to their role of mother, and they are more inclined to consider their presence as vital to their children (Séguin 1996; Bellware and Charest 1986; Dandurand 1994). Thus, many turn to social assistance to meet their needs.

Other considerations of a family nature may be linked to single mothers' difficulties in joining the professional world. Nowadays, the father is more likely to be present in the child's environment, contrary to what prevailed when single parenthood resulted from widowhood. Still, data from the middle of the 1990s show that only 7% of children of divorced or separated parents were in joint custody arrangements while more than 85% lived only with their mothers. Of these, 30% saw their fathers once a week, 16% every two weeks, and 40% saw their fathers sporadically or not at all (Marcil-Gratton and Le Bourdais 1999). When children live with their mother, it is customary for the father to look after them only intermittently. It is difficult to envisage the father contributing other forms of assistance that could facilitate the mother's working (such as childcare, visits to the doctor, and transportation). This is why, short of substituting for the non-custodial parent's role, it falls to the state to put in place measures to alleviate family responsibilities and permit single mothers to balance their dual roles and acquire financial autonomy.

It is not just the presence of a child (or children) but the number and ages of the children that influence mothers' labour force participation (Lapierre-Adamcyk and Marcil-Gratton 1995; Hardey and Glover 1991; Lero and Brockman 1993; Ray, 1990; Beaupré 1982; Nakamura and Nakamura 1986; Martin 1998). Lero and Brockman (1993) contend that when it is difficult to find affordable and accessible daycare, having a young child of preschool age reduces the chances of a parent being employed. As children age, they may require less time but may become more costly in terms of goods required (Beaupré 1982). Thus, when female behaviour in the labour force is studied, it is essential to provide information on family configuration (Nakamura and Nakamura 1986).

Sociodemographic Profile of Single Mothers

Before undertaking a study of labour force participation, a sociodemographic profile of single mothers in the three provinces will be presented. An analysis of the 1996 census data reveals that single mothers in all three provinces differ from those in unions on all sociodemographic characteristics shown to affect economic activity. These characteristics include the following: age, education level, marital status, and the number and ages of children present in the home. Single mothers are much younger than mothers in unions (more than 10% vs less than 5% are 15 to 24 years of age); they have fewer children at home than mothers in unions (more than 40% vs less than 30% have only one child), and they are less likely to have preschool-aged children at home (less than 45% vs over 50%). They are also less likely to have a university education (around 17% vs more than 25%; Meilleur 2001, chapter 3, tables 3.1 and 3.2).

A comparison of the profiles of single mothers in the three provinces is more complex. Quebec is distinguished from the rest of Canada by its low fertility rate and its high incidence of cohabitation. This is reflected in the characteristics of the single mothers. In comparison with Ontario and Alberta, we find more families with only one child, and fewer with three or more. We also observe fewer families with children from both age groups, (0–5 years and 6–14), and more families with preschool-aged children. Moreover, we find a larger proportion of unmarried mothers in Quebec: 47% of single mothers have never been married, while this proportion is 34% in Ontario and 32% in Alberta. It has been demonstrated that cohabitation is more fragile than marriage and that children of unmarried parents are exposed to a greater risk of seeing their parents separate than are those children whose parents are married (Le Bourdais and Neill 1998; Marcil-Gratton 1998). It is, above all, the high incidence of cohabitation, which is particularly the case in Quebec, that contributes to the great proportion of unmarried people among single parents, rather than the incidence of births outside marriage or common law relationships, which have increased very little over the past few decades. Furthermore, we can observe that an enormous gap separates the three provinces from the point of view of education. In Alberta 62% of single mothers have some post-secondary education, while this proportion is 53% in Ontario and 44% in Quebec. Finally, while a similar proportion of single mothers everywhere have children aged 15 and older, these youngsters are more likely to contribute to the family income in Alberta.

In short, this comparison highlights the fact that single mothers have many common characteristics in the three provinces: they are relatively young, they have a lower level of education, fewer preschool children, and more children who are between 6 and 14 years old. They also have a few differences: Quebec's single mothers are more likely to have never married, whereas single mothers in Alberta stand out for their high level of education.

Variations in Mothers' Labour Force Participation

The economic situation of lone parent families depends, in an important respect, on the social policies of the society. (Gustafsson 1990). We can attempt to determine whether this claim is well founded, because in Canada each province has a certain degree of autonomy regarding social policies related to employment, and the extensive data available allow us to measure labour force participation. Figure 9.1 demonstrates that labour force participation has long differed from one region to another.

While the labour force participation rates of mothers in unions show an upward tendency across the provinces, the situation for single mothers is more varied. Until 1981 in Quebec and 1987 in Ontario, single-mothers' activity exceeded that of mothers in unions. Beyond those years, participation rates for mothers in union were consistently higher. The situation in Alberta was quite different. Except for the period from 1987 to 1995, single mothers have demonstrated much greater activity than mothers in unions. However, the evolution of the activity of Albertan two-parent families follows that of other regions. Albertan single parents have always shown a level of activity superior to that of their counterparts in Quebec and Ontario, and this gap has increased since the start of the 1990s. In Ontario, on the other hand, single-mothers' activity, which was nearing that of Albertans, fell at the end of the 1980s to join that of Quebeckers.

Theoretically, one might expect that the activity of mothers in unions should surpass that of single mothers. To a certain extent, mothers in unions are less constrained to work since their partners can provide for the household needs, but on the other hand, they have more means at their disposal to balance work and family: financial assistance to pay for childcare and shared childrearing and household tasks.

In fact, this situation is observed in Quebec and Ontario where the ratio between single-mothers' activity and that of mothers in unions is slightly less than one (0.9). In contrast, in Alberta, the ratio exceeds one (1.1). Among young Alberta mothers (age 15–24) and among those with children in both of the age categories, the ratio exceeds 1.2 In Ontario, by contrast, the ratios are fairly homogeneous and systematically less than one; they are lower by more than 20% in the case of less educated mothers (ratio, < 0.8). It is in Quebec where the variations are the greatest and the ratio is less than 0.8 for mothers age 15–24, mothers who are less educated, and mothers who have a child under 6. These are the circumstances which we must bear in mind when scrutinizing social policies. Henceforth, our attention will be directed to the actual level of activity of single mothers in an interprovincial comparison. These rates may be found in table 9.1.

The effects of age are almost identical across the provinces. The general tendency is for the activity rate of single mothers to increase until the age of 45, and then stabilize. A multiplicity of factors account for the

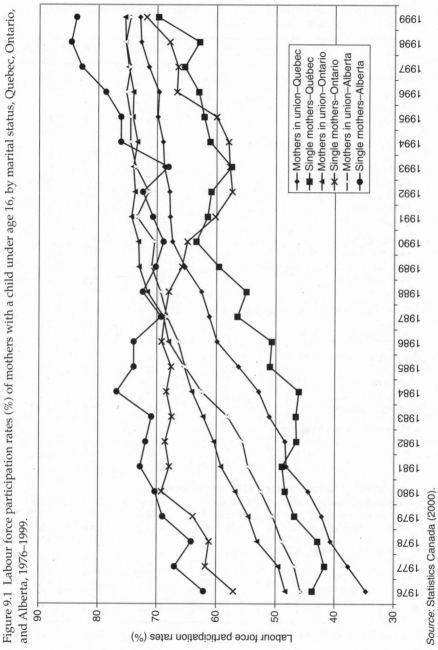

Figure 9.1 Labour force participation rates (%) of mothers with a child under age 16, by marital status, Quebec, Ontario, and Alberta, 1976–1999.

Labour force participation rates (%)

Mothers in union–Quebec
Single mothers–Québec
Mothers in union–Ontario
Single mothers–Ontario
Mothers in union–Alberta
Single mothers–Alberta

Source: Statistics Canada (2000).

TABLE 9.1 Labour Force Participation Rates of Single Mothers in Quebec, Ontario and Alberta, Selected Variables, 1996

Categories	Quebec	Ontario	Alberta
Overall Activity Rate	62.9	67.7	82.2
Age (years)			
15–24	29.8	46.2	75.7
25–34	55.5	65.6	80.4
35–44	73.6	75.1	85.1
45–54	76.0	73.7	85.1
Marital status			
Divorced	74.5	73.2	87.0
Separated	70.4	73.7	82.8
Unmarried	52.1	57.5	76.9
Widowed	67.7	66.7	77.5
Level of education			
Less than high school	37.8	46.4	67.4
High school graduate or equivalent	66.9	70.2	81.3
Post-secondary	76.1	76.8	87.7
University	84.1	81.4	88.8
Region of residence, census metropolitan areas			
Within	62.6	67.4	81.5
Outside	63.7	68.7	83.6
Child suppport income (annual)			
None	61.0	65.1	80.3
<$1,999	51.8	61.8	82.6
$2,000–4,999	73.8	80.4	89.6
≥$5,000 and up	75.5	81.3	84.1
Never-married Children at Home			
1	66.6	70.0	83.6
2	62.1	69.2	83.0
≥3	52.7	59.4	77.4
Combinations of children under age 15 (years) at home			
Presence of child 0–5, absence of child 6–14	49.2	59.3	79.3
Presence of child 0–5, presence of child 6–14	42.0	57.3	83.3
Presence of child 6–14, absence of child 0–5	74.6	75.9	85.1
Children 15 and older at home			
None	60.9	66.8	81.4
One, with support	77.6	77.2	87.3
One, without support	66.1	67.4	82.5
N	3,672	5,233	1,201

Source: Census of Canada 1996, Public Use Microdata File.

growth of activity with age. As one ages, one has more experience, credentials, training, less chance of having young children, and a greater chance of having older children who can help with the household tasks and the care of younger offspring, allowing the mother to leave home to work. From the age of 45 on, we see a levelling of activity because of early retirement or it may simply be a generational effect. Two distinctive provincial features capture our attention. First, in Alberta, 85% of women between 35 and 55 years of age are in the labour force; in Quebec and Ontario, this rate is nearer 75%.

Of particular interest is the remarkable situation of young single mothers: on the one hand, the limited involvement of young single mothers in Quebec and, on the other hand, the very high participation rates for Albertans of the same age. In Quebec only 30% of single mothers age 15–24 are in the labour force, while this proportion rises to 46% in Ontario and almost 76% in Alberta. A variety of social factors lie behind these provincial differences. Young Quebec mothers are more likely to be unmarried, doubtless because they became mothers during a short-lived period of cohabitation. They are more likely to have young children and, as a result, are less able to leave the home to work, but they are also more prone to be receiving benefits. We believe that these considerations are insufficient to explain the underactivity of this group. These mothers have income markedly inferior to that of other women and are more likely to fall below the low income cut-off (LICO) than are older women. Paradoxically, in Alberta, single parents age 15–24 are 40% more likely to be employed than are those of the same age in two-parent families. These various observations highlight the need to pursue an analysis of family policies.

Everywhere, unmarried women are less likely to be employed than women who are separated or divorced. In addition, labour force participation rises with education level. Single mothers with only primary or secondary education are more disadvantaged than are other mothers. As with all these considerations, activity rates are higher in Alberta. The gulf between the provinces narrows, however, with an advance in education level: 30 points separate Quebec and Alberta for primary level, whereas for university level, the gap is a mere 5 points.

Most single mothers, 71% of those in Ontario and Quebec and 64% of those in Alberta, claimed that they received no child support payments. In the two former provinces, the activity of mothers who did not receive child support payments was higher than those who received small sums of between $1 and $1,999. One might have expected that this activity would diminish with the amount of child support payments received. However, it seems that for those who received $2,000 and up, activity increased considerably; in Ontario and Quebec the rate of activity jumps approximately 20%. It is difficult to interpret this relationship; the results of a multivariate analysis show that the higher rate of activity related to higher child support payments persists, although the differences are less pronounced, even when education is controlled for (Meilleur 2001). One might suggest that the level of education of partners should be considered, as it might be related to their ability to pay child support; however, data on this question are not available in the 1996 census.

Furthermore, regardless of the province and the parental situation, more children resulted in diminished activity. Also, mothers of younger children were less likely to be in the labour force, and the combined presence of children from 0 to 5 years and those from 6 to 14 years of age likewise resulted in less activity. Indeed, single mothers with no child under age 6 had high participation rates: 75% in Quebec and Ontario and 85% in Alberta. Children older than 5 require different care then younger ones do; furthermore, school assumes responsibility for their care for part of the day. Alberta is distinguished by a greater activity level of mothers with children in either age group. In this category, the average activity level, at 83% in Alberta, was far beyond that of Ontario at 57%, and double that of Quebec. Clearly, Alberta has a higher overall activity rate, but the participation rates for mothers with children from 0 to 5 and 6 to 14 indicate a striking gulf between the provinces.

In general, the findings regarding participation rates fit with the expectations arising from a review of the literature. A higher education level promotes greater labour force participation, while the presence of young children, as well as the number of children, hinder integration into the labour force. Never-married mothers are also less likely to be in the labour force than mothers who are divorced or separated Although these patterns are evident in all three provinces, it is also true that Alberta is distinctive in its heightened activity level. Even in the categories where participation rates are low, Albertan mothers are much more likely to be in the labour force than their counterparts in other parts of Canada. Multivariate statistical analysis (Meilleur 2001) does not significantly reduce the disparities observed between the provinces and, thus, an analysis of relevant social policies, which vary among these three provinces, is needed to better understand provincial differences.

TABLE 9.2 Comparative Average and Median Income ($) of
Single Mothers, Three Provinces, 1995

	Average income	Median income
Quebec	20,048	15,512
Ontario	21,438	17,126
Alberta	21,932	18,107

Source: Census of Canada 1996, Public Use Microdata File.

Social Policies and Labour Force Participation of Single Mothers

To better define the impact of policies related to the labour force participation of single mothers in 1996, one must first list all the policy measures in place at the start of the 1990s: policies linked to the family, work, and income. The consultation of relevant works to chart the precise indicators particularly affecting single mothers is arduous and yields disappointing results. The different governmental bodies are constantly changing and do not keep meticulous records of their policies before 1996, or the measures presented in their documentation do not solely concern single mothers. Despite these difficulties, there are three avenues that may be explored: an examination of income, the description of social assistance, and the examination of daycare services.

Based on census data from 1996, table 9.2 shows single-mothers' average and median incomes. Income is defined as the sum of the following elements: salary and income from self-employment, the total amount of government transfers, investment income, and other cash income. We find little difference among the three provinces. Annual income varied from $20,000 to $22,000. The median income, which corresponds to an income level above which 50% of the population is situated and below which the other 50% falls, allows us to see that in Quebec, income was lower than in Alberta and Ontario.

A breakdown of single-parents' income demonstrates that government transfers represented a higher proportion of income in Quebec and Ontario (33% and 35%) than in Alberta (24%; figure 9.2.)

The total income of single-parent families in which the mother is employed was approximately twice that of those in which the mother was not (table 9.3). It is in Quebec where single mothers at home had the lowest average income, 15% less than in Ontario and Alberta. This

Figure 9.2 Relative importance (%) of various sources of income among single mothers with a child less than 15 years old, Quebec, Ontario, and Alberta, 1996.

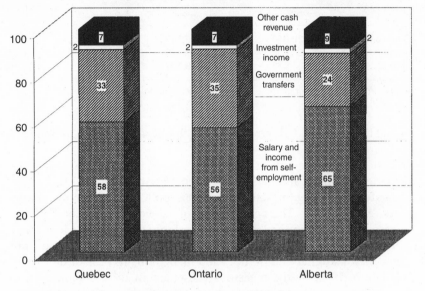

Source: Census of Canada 1996, Public Use Microdata File.

TABLE 9.3 Comparative Average Income ($) of Single Mothers, at Home and Employed, Three Provinces, 1995

	At home	Employed
Quebec	11,383	25,157
Ontario	13,061	25,429
Alberta	13,114	23,844

Source: Census of Canada 1996, Public Use Microdata File.

may lead to speculation that Quebeckers received less public money than those in other provinces.

Table 9.4, based on 1996 census data, offers a three-way glimpse of government transfers, by province, by family situation, and by activity status. The province which is most generous towards single mothers is Ontario, while for two-parent families, it is Quebec. In Ontario, single parents at home received 15% more in government transfers than in

TABLE 9.4 Comparative Average of All Government Transfers ($) to Mothers, Single and in Two-Parent Families, at Home and Employed, Three Provinces, 1995

	Single mothers		Mothers in two-parent families	
	At home	Employed	At home	Employed
Quebec	8,683	5,166	1,724	1,966
Ontario	10,018	6,360	1,614	1,520
Alberta	7,699	4,617	1,247	1,357

Source: Census of Canada 1996, Public Use Microdata File.

TABLE 9.5 Ratio of Average of All Government Transfers to Mothers, Single and in Two-Parent Families, at Home and Employed, 1995

	Single mothers: at home/ employed	At home mothers: single in two-parent familes	Employed mothers: single in two-parent families
Quebec	1.68	4.0	1.6
Ontario	1.58	5.2	3.2
Alberta	1.67	5.2	2.4

Source: Census of Canada 1996, Public Use Microdata File.

Quebec, and 30% more than in Alberta. Among employed single parents, the gap was slightly larger, with Ontarians receiving 23% more than Quebeckers and 38% more than Albertans. Not only were the government transfers less in Alberta, but the difference between what employed single parents and those at home received was less in Alberta ($3,082 in Alberta, $3,517 in Quebec, and $3,658 in Ontario).

The differences in the level of government transfers are not only linked to the province, but also to family situation and activity level (table 9.5). Single mothers who were not employed received between 58% and 68% more in transfer payments than employed single mothers. This is explained by the fact that the earnings of certain working women exceed the admissible ceiling for social programs.

The amount received from government transfers is, above all, related to the family situation, to a degree that varies across the provinces. Single mothers, whether employed or at home, received significantly more than mothers in unions. Among employed mothers, for

TABLE 9.6 Proportion (%) of Income According to Sources, Single Mothers Not Employed outside the Home, Three Provinces, 1995

	Quebec	Ontario	Alberta
Salary and income from self-employment	10.5	12.0	20.9
Total governmental transfer payments	77.4	77.7	60.8
Other cash income	9.9	7.9	15.4
Investment income	2.2	2.3	2.9
Total	100.0	100.0	100.0

Source: Census of Canada 1996, Public Use Microdata File.

example, the ratio ranges from 2.6 in Quebec to 4.2 in Ontario. Some of the transfers single mothers received are related to their status as lone parents, while others reflect their low family income.

In sum, government transfers are an important component of the family income of single parents. However, the level of transfers varies among the provinces with Alberta being less generous than the other provinces, while Ontarians are more likely to enjoy the fruits of public transfers. Ontario is distinguished, above all, in emphasizing the family situation more than the other provinces. For instance, the ratio of employed single parents' transfer income and that of other parents was 1.6 times that of Quebec, while, when one examines single parents according to activity level, the ratio was smaller in Ontario than elsewhere. This situation is a result of provincial policies developed in the 1990s (see Statistics Canada 1997b).

Turning to other sources of income, analysis demonstrates that the situation is not homogeneous across provinces. Two observations emerge concerning the situation of single parents at home: in Alberta they received considerably less government transfers than in Ontario and Quebec; on the other hand, their total income was equivalent to that in Ontario.

Table 9.6 amply demonstrates that in Alberta the share of income coming from government transfers was considerably lower. Albertans relied more on their salaries (or income derived from self-employment) and other sources of cash income, probably child support payments. But above all, Albertans not in the labour force at the time of the census had higher salaries, which seems paradoxical since these women were classified as not working. This incongruity is simply the result of certain anomalies in the census; the income indicators referred to the year 1995, whereas the data regarding activity level were based on the week preceding the census. A mother could have worked in 1995 and thus have received some salary, but been classified as not employed at the time of the census in 1996. This again underlines the greater labour force involvement of single mothers in Alberta.

Social Assistance

To better appreciate the impact of government transfers, social assistance, a policy closely linked to employment, must be studied. In all the provinces, social assistance is a measure of last resort, which takes into account, when evaluating need, the value of one's assets, as well as income from all possible sources.

The expression 'social assistance' may refer to benefits linked to insufficient income, to housing assistance, or to other forms of support. In this case, we are concerned with benefits linked to income. During the early 1990s, across the provinces, we find important differences in criteria of admissibility that shed some light on the results for labour force participation rates. In Alberta single mothers are deemed able to work when the youngest child reaches two years of age. In Ontario the exemption from work is extended until a child reaches the age of 16, and in Quebec age 5. This interprovincial gap brings about a flood of consequences. We can better understand why Albertan mothers of young children are very likely to be in the labour force. This policy constitutes a good example of a coercive measure linked to employment. Fortunately, other more positive measures are put forward to encourage work (Canada 1994).

COMPLEMENTARY PROGRAMS

A worker's admissibility for social assistance is subject to an income ceiling. When net employment income is higher than the admissible levels, the amount of benefits is reduced. For many single mothers, the starting salary offered is often less than the social benefits for which they would be eligible. The result is a dilemma: whether to stay at home or to accept less remunerative employment to gain the experience or skills required to procure better paid work. In response, some provinces have put in place programs that allow individuals to earn income, up to a certain level, while continuing to receive social assistance. These programs are intended to encourage people to become self-supporting.

In Quebec, for example, the program APPORT (*Aide aux parents pour leurs revenus de travail* – Support for parents for their employment income) encourages low-income workers with children under 18 to remain in the workforce, and social assistance recipients with children to return to work. To be eligible, single-parent families must earn between $1,200 and $15,000 a year. According to the size of the family and certain conditions, benefits can go as high as $3,784 a year. In Ontario the families must have an annual income of between $5,000 and $20,000, or failing that, must undergo training. The annual benefits are $1,020 for each child under 7. Alberta, for its part, is flexible but less generous. Income may fall between $6,500 and $50,000, with the maximum amount available for those earning less than $25,000. These families benefit from tax exemptions and an annual credit of $500 per child or $1,000 for two children (Canada 1994: 28).[1] At first glance, the Quebec program appears more financially advantageous, although the comparison is problematic. It would be foolhardy to draw conclusions from these few indicators. First, one must acquire more details on the conditions of application of these measures and their joint application with programs for returning to work, training, professional development, etc. Even with the available statistical data, these measures are not necessarily equivalent, as an income of $15,000 does not have the same value in Toronto, Calgary, and Trois-Rivières.

In sum, the provinces have recently turned towards the promotion of greater labour force participation. Finding ways for single mothers to balance family and work remains in the forefront of public debates. The summary data presented here remain more descriptive than explanatory. Nonetheless, they reveal a notable difference among the provinces with regard to a child's age when a mother is required to work. This measure alone may contribute greatly to the higher activity level of Albertan single mothers.

Childcare Services

The 1984 commission of inquiry on employment equity reaffirmed that childcare services are key to providing mothers equal access to the workforce (Doherty et al. 1998). Moreover, such services are an essential element in the social and professional integration of single parents. Many studies have demonstrated that the possibility and ease of finding daycare services near work or home constitute a determining factor in the decision to work (Zouali and Rousseau 1992).

Finding well-paid employment provides greater income than does social assistance, allows a mother to expand her social network, and to cope with additional costs such as transport, clothing, and medical expenses. But to find such work, these mothers must have the possibility of educating themselves or upgrading their professional qualifications. Thus, childcare services assume tremendous importance. Aside from offering mothers without work the possibility of a respite or providing additional pedagogical opportunities for child development, such services provide an option in case of emergency or if the mother should fall sick. For all the above reasons, effective childcare policies are especially important for single mothers.

Unfortunately, uniform national data on childcare services do not exist, since the provinces are not required to provide the federal government with comparable data on the expenses related to such services. This is why we will rely on a document by Doherty et al. (1998) which addresses this issue. This study refers to data collected by the provinces with estimates, and information provided by respondents. After defining what constitutes childcare services in Canada, we will assess accessibility to these services, their availability, and their quality.

In Canada the expressions 'childcare services,' 'early childhood services,' and 'preschool and primary education' designate services based on the development of children under the age of 12 years. They comprise the services of daycares centres, daycare in a family setting, nursery schools, and community action programs for children. When we speak of childcare services, we are not referring to care provided by a member of the family or a third person (a nanny or young babysitter) in the home setting. Instead, we will study provincially regulated childcare services, whether daycare centres, programs for the care of school-aged children, or family-run daycare centres. This will allow us to pinpoint the interprovincial differences ascribed to the division of costs between the federal and provincial governments (Doherty et al. 1998: 1).

The viability and growth of childcare services have always been related to the availability of federal subsidies, and to the political will and financial capacity of the provinces (ibid.: 10). Since 1977 the government of Canada has gradually withdrawn from sharing the costs of social services with the provinces. In the 1980s the provinces, realizing their increased responsibility for supporting childcare, established regulations and provided subsidies to regulated services. 'These provincial funds have assured childcare services a certain financial stability and encouraged their growth' (Ibid.: 19).

TABLE 9.7 Comparative Average Fees, Full-Time Regulated
Daycare Services ($ per month), Three Provinces, 1983–1995

	1983	1993	1995
Quebec			
Infants	352	407	404[a]
Preschool	350	328	
Ontario			
Infants	509	502–1,109	N/A
Preschool	447	460–753	N/A
Alberta			
Infants	300	382	430
Preschool	N/A	348	375

Source: Doherty et al. (1998: 23).
[a] Average for both infants and preschool-aged children.
N/A = data not available.

Nevertheless, the withdrawal of the federal government seems to have had an impact on the accessibility and availability of services. Between 1990 and 1996 Quebec and Ontario reduced their periodic subsidies to childcare services while Alberta froze its contribution. As a result, new services could not obtain any subsidies. Fees for childcare rose in all the provinces at a time when real family income was decreasing. The result was a shortage of childcare spaces, though the extent of the shortage varied by province.

ACCESSIBILITY

To determine whether childcare services are affordable, two factors are taken into account: fees paid by the parents and government financing offered for these services. In Canada childcare is, above all, financed by the parents. Between 1989 and 1993 average income (after taxes) of single-parent families decreased in most provinces. While it went from $22,066 to $22,427 in Quebec it fell from $27,170 to $24,404 in Ontario and from $22,665 to $21,063 in Alberta. At the same time, childcare costs increased. In Quebec, the increase was approximately $50 a month between 1983 and 1995. In Ontario there was similarly an upward trend which varied by municipality, and in Alberta there was a significant rise for infants as well as other preschool-aged children.

In 1993, a year for which we have complete data, average childcare fees differed tremendously from one region to another. Moreover, the

TABLE 9.8 Comparative Subsidies for Childcare, for Children Aged 0 to 6 Years, for Regulated Daycare Programs, Three Provinces, 1989–1995 ($ per month)

Province	1989	1993	1995
Quebec			
Maximum	254	485.80	285
User fees	20	20	20
Ontario[a]			
Alberta			
Maximum	280	300–370[b]	Same as in 1993
User fees	40	40	40

Source: Doherty et al. (1998: 25–6).
[a] The subsidy amount for childcare, the existence of user fees and their amount are left to the discretion of the municipality that administers the subsidy programs; for all years shown on this table.
[b] According to the age of the child.

fees were not uniform across the provinces. Nevertheless, fees in Ontario were considerably higher, on average, than in Alberta, though the difference between Alberta and Quebec is less clear. All the provinces provide additional subsidies for low-income parents who meet certain criteria. Nonetheless, in Ontario the availability of this contribution is limited by a ceiling on total subsidies or a defined number of families eligible for it. Some families that have sufficiently low income to be eligible are thus refused this assistance.

Subsidies for childcare do not always rise at the same pace as the fees demanded of parents. In Alberta these contributions stagnated between 1993 and 1996. In Quebec they increased, but parents must still make up for the difference between the childcare fees, which have risen, and the provincial grants, while in many Ontarian municipalities the subsidies have diminished (Doherty et al. 1998: 24). All this underscores the fact that it is difficult, especially in Ontario, to afford daycare that will allow mothers to enter the labour force.

Affordable childcare fees may encourage workforce participation, but again, there must be a space at the daycare facility for one's child! Figure 9.1 shows that in Ontario and in Quebec the official number of daycare places has increased each year. It is in Ontario that the progress has been most significant. In contrast, in Alberta, since 1991 the situation has fluctuated greatly. While there were 54,872 places in 1990, there were only 43,262 in 1995.

Figure 9.3 Number of full-time regulated daycare places (000s), three provinces, 1989–1995.

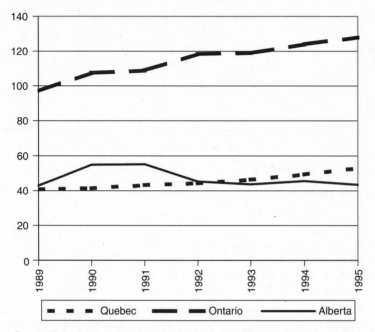

Source: Doherty et al. (1998); estimates based on Statistics Canada (1986–1996).

In all provinces childcare services seem to be insufficient relative to the demand. We have compared the data for children aged 0 to 6 over the same period, to calculate a ratio corresponding to the number of children relative to the number of places in care. To do so, the population age 0–6 for each year was extrapolated from the census data of 1991 and 1996 and compared with the number of places. While this ratio is not a perfect measure of needs, we find the results very interesting. First, Quebec stands out for its very high ratio, more than double that of Alberta. While in Alberta, in 1989 there were seven children for each daycare place, in Quebec that same year there were fifteen. Ontario was mid-way between the two, with ten children for each spot. Fortunately, conditions subsequently improved in Quebec, so that in 1995 this ratio had declined to 12.2 while in Alberta and Ontario it was, respectively, 8.0 and 6.5 (Figure 9.4).

Figure 9.4 Number of children per available full-time regulated daycare place, by provinces, 1989–1995.

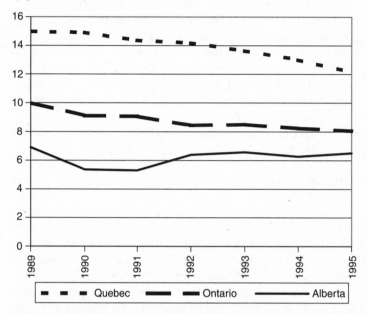

Source: Doherty et al. (1998); estimates based on Statistics Canada (1986–1996).

In short, the availability of childcare differs in the three provinces. While the number of daycare places is clearly higher in Ontario than elsewhere, and while in Alberta we only perceive a slight increase in places between 1989 and 1995, considering the number of children permits us to conclude that childcare is most accessible in Alberta. The Quebec situation in 1989 was alarming because many children were awaiting a place. Fortunately, since 1996 the new Quebec family policy arrangements have led to a significant improvement.

QUALITY OF SERVICES

The reduction in financing for daycare services has important repercussions for the quality of services offered. American research has demonstrated that a low level of financing is the most important factor affecting quality. To control costs, salaries are kept low and a high ratio of children per educator is maintained. The employees are thus less qualified or simply overwhelmed, contributing to a high turnover in personnel. Studies have revealed that the quality is higher in regulated daycare centres than in other settings (Doherty et al. 1998: 32). Similarly, the quality is greater in the provinces where the training of personnel, the number of children per educator, or the equipment of daycare centres is regulated. Thus, most provinces have established their own regulatory norms. Since 1991 Alberta has, nonetheless, raised its ratio of the number of children aged 13 to 18 months per educator from three to one to four to one, and has increased the permissible size of this age group from six to eight children. For its part, Ontario has announced its intention to increase by two children its ratio of school-aged children in home-based before- and after-school care. No figures are mentioned for the situation in Quebec.

General Conclusion

While it is still true that most families with children are headed by two parents, single-parent families represent two out of every ten Canadian families with children. In Canada between 1991 and 1996, this type of family grew at a rate four times that of married couples. These families attract our interest because of their particular vulnerability and the poverty in which their children often live. Nonetheless, a good number of such families manage to break free of this situation and attain a comfortable standard of living. Paid employment seems to provide the surest escape route. It is through integration into the labour force that the single mother can manage to become financially self-sufficient and able to provide for her family's needs. But research has demonstrated that single mothers are often disadvantaged when they try to enter the labour force. Thus, society, through the actions undertaken by the state, can facilitate their economic activity and reinforce their sense of belonging to the community.

This examination of single mothers' characteristics and their economic activity in three Canadian provinces highlights some profound differences that are only partially explained by the variations in the mothers' characteristics. An analysis of several aspects of social polices in place at the beginning of the 1990s casts some light on the way in which these three environments approach the issue of single parenthood.

Whatever the province, many single mothers face the following dilemma: whether to stay at home and survive on meagre social assistance benefits or integrate into the workforce, knowing that it may take a few years to earn a salary greater than their social assistance benefits. Integration into the labour force is, however, greatly influenced by measures that can facilitate the reconciliation of work and family life for single mothers.

The results presented in this chapter illustrate the clearly greater employment activity of Albertan single mothers, in comparison with Quebeckers and Ontarians. For the period preceding the point at which economic activity was measured, we can also observe some striking contrasts in the relevant social programs of the three provinces considered. More particularly, we can conclude that Alberta's lower level of social assistance benefits, as well as the much younger age required for Albertan children to be considered admissible for social assistance programs, constitute a major incentive for mothers to enter the workforce. On the other hand, Alberta's abundance of reasonably priced public daycare centres serves to facilitate labour force participation.

This analysis, while exploratory, suggests the existence of links between social programs and economic participation. To further investigate this topic, a longitudinal, rather than a cross-sectional, analysis is required. We must also examine the direct association between the individual situation and access to social programs. Furthermore, we should take into account the duration of single parenthood, and the periods of work, and conjugal unions, in order to reach more conclusive results. In addition, the particular economic situation of each province must be considered, including such factors as the availability of work and the unemployment rate.

As a function of social cohesion, it would be useful to verify whether policies designed to encourage single mothers' labour force participation attain their long-term objective, which is to permanently lift them out of insecurity, and the poverty that often accompanies this. This would be especially pertinent for young single mothers: does strongly encouraging them to work outside the home allow them to remain employed in the long run and to not fall behind in their careers through prolonged periods of inactivity? From this perspective, do Albertans fare better than other Canadians?

It would also be relevant and significant to examine the development of children of these mothers. Do children of single mothers at home who are raised by mothers supported by more generous social programs develop in a more balanced and harmonious fashion than do children of mothers who entered the workforce under strong pressures, driven by less generous social programs?

The results of this study, though incomplete, are thought-provoking and demonstrate the relevance of an analysis of social behaviour in the light of policies in place at the time. Canada constitutes, in this regard, a veritable social laboratory; social policies vary across the provinces and lend themselves to a significant comparative analysis.

NOTES

1 This chapter is a condensed version of Meilleur (2001).
2 This study fails to mention the year for these statistics.

REFERENCES

Beaujot, Rod. 1999. *Earning and Caring in Canadian Families*. Peterborough, ON: Broadview Press.

Beaupré, Lucille. 1982. 'Les déterminants des heures de travail des femmes québécoises.' Master's thesis, Montreal: Université de Montréal, Département des sciences économiques.

Bellware, Jo-Ann, and Diane Charest. 1986. *Monoparentalité féminine et aide sociale*. Quebec: Service des politiques et de la recherche en sécurité du revenu.

Canada. 1994. Développement des ressources humaines Canada, *L'aide sociale au Canada, 1994*. Ottawa: Human Resources and Development Canada, Political and Social Directorate. Consulted 17 Jan. 2001 at http://www.hrdc-drhc.gc.ca/socpo/reports/social94/partie1_f.shtml#a

Canada, Statistique Canada. Division des enquêtes-ménages. 1986–1995. *Revue chronologique de la population active*. Ottawa: Statistics Canada. Available at http://ivt.crepuq.qc.ca/rcpa/index.html.

– 1997a. 'Recensement de 1996: état matrimonial, unions libres et familles.' In *Le Quotidien*, Ottawa: Statistes Canada. Consulted 10 Dec. 1999 at: http://www.statcan.ca/Daily/Francais/971014/q971014.htm.

– 1997b. *Revue chronologique du revenu*. Series: *Anciennement Tendances du revenu au Canada (1980–1997)*. Ottawa: Statistes Canada. Available at: http://www.bibl.ulaval.ca/bd/sdn/b2020/rcr/.

– 1986–1999. *Recensement de 1996, Fichier de microdonnées à grande diffusion de 1996 sur les familles. Documentation de l'utilisateur*. Ottawa: Minister of Industry. Available at http://sherlock.bib.umontreal.ca/ENQ-10063/doc/fmgdf.pdf

– 2000. *Revue chronologique de la population active*. Canada: Statisties Canada.

Dandurand, Renée B. 1994. 'Divorce et nouvelle monoparentalité.' In Fernand Dumont, Simon Langlois, and Yves Martin (eds.), *Traité des problèmes sociaux*, 519–44. Quebec: Institut québécois de recherche sur la culture.

Desrosiers, Hélène, Céline Le Bourdais, and Yves Peron. 1993. 'La dynamique de la monoparentalité au Canada.' *European Journal of Population / Revue européenne de démographie* 9(2): 197–224.

Doherty, Gillian, Martha Friendly, and Mab Oloman. 1998. *Le soutien aux femmes, le travail des femmes et la garde des enfants à l'ère de la réduction du déficit, du transfert des responsabilités, de la réduction de la taille de l'État et de la déréglementation*. Ottawa: Status of Women, Research Division.

Galarneau, Diane, and Jim Sturrock. 1997. 'Family Income after Separation.' *Perspetives on Labour and Income*, 9(2): 18–28.

Gunderson, Morley. 1998. *Les femmes et le marché du travail canadien: Transition vers l'avenir*. Ottawa: Statisties Canada.

Gustafsson, Siv. 1990. 'Participation à la vie active et gains des parents seuls en Suède: comparaison avec la situation en Allemagne.' In *Les familles monoparentales. Les enjeux économiques*, 175–97. Paris: OECD.

Hardey, Michael, and Judith Glover. 1991. 'Income, Employment, Daycare and Lone Parenthood.' In *Lone Parenthood – Coping with Constraints and Making Opportunities in Single-Parent Families*, 88–109. Toronto and Buffalo: University of Toronto Press.

Lapierre-Adamcyk, E., and N. Marcil-Gratton. 1995. 'Prise en charge des enfants: stratégies individuelles et organisation sociale.' *Sociologie et sociétés*, 27(2): 121–42.

Le Bourdais, Céline, and Ghyslaine Neill . 1998. 'L'effet du type d'union sur la stabilité des familles "intactes."' Paper presented at Séminaires du partenariat Familles en mouvance et dynamiques intergénérationnelles, Montreal, 21 Oct.

Lero, Donna S., and Lois M. Brockman. 1993. 'Single Parent Families in Canada: A Closer Look.' In Joe Hudson and Burt Galaway (eds.). *Single Parent Families. Perspectives on Resarch and Policy*, 91–114. Toronto: Thompson Educational.

Marcil-Gratton, Nicole. 1998. *Grandir avec maman et papa? Les trajectoires familiales complexes des enfants canadiens*. Ottawa: Statisties Canada, cat. no. 89-566-XIF.

Marcil-Gratton, Nicole, and Céline Le Bourdais. 1999. *Garde des enfants, droits de visite et pension alimentaire: résultats tirés de l'Enquête longitudinale nationale sur les enfants et les jeunes*. Ottawa: Ministry of Justice.

Martin, Jacqueline. 1998. 'Politique familiale et travail des mères de famille: perspective historique 1942–1982.' *Population* 53(6): 1119–54.

Meilleur, N. 2001. 'Analyse des déterminants socio-démographiques et politiques provinciales associées à l'activité des mères monoparentales en Alberta, au Québec et en Ontario.' Master's thesis, Département de démographie, Université de Montréal.

Nakamura, Alice, and Masao Nakamura. 1986. 'Une vue d'ensemble des études sur le comportement des Canadiennes sur le marché du travail.' In W. Craig Riddell (ed.), *Le travail et le salaire: le marché du travail au Canada*, 193–246. Ottawa: Ministry of Supply and Services.

Organisation of Economic Cooperation and Development. 1990. *Les familles monoparentales. Les enjeux économiques*. Paris: OECD.

Péron, Yves, Hélène Desrosiers, Heather Juby, Évelyne Lapierre-Adamcyk, Céline Le Bourdais, Nicole Marcil-Gratton, and Jaël Mongeau. 1999. *Les familles canadiennes à l'approche de l'an 2000*. Ottawa: Statistics Canada.

Ray, Jean-Claude. 1990. 'Mères isolées, aide sociale et incitations au travail: le cas de la France.' In *Les familles monoparentales. Les enjeux économiques*, 257–77. Paris: OECD.

Saint-Jean, Lise. 1987. 'La pauvreté des femmes: la monoparentalité féminine.' In *Les nouveaux visages de la pauvreté*, 19–44. Quebec: Institut québécois de recherche sur la culture.

Séguin, Céline. 1996. *La conciliation emploi-famille dans le contexte de la monoparentalité féminine. Analyse des pratiques, des stratégies et des attitudes de mères seules en emploi*. Mémoire de maîtrise, Montreal: Université du Québec à Montréal, Département de sociologie.

– 1997. 'Conjuguer emploi et famille en situation de monoparentalité: les stratégies déployées par les mères seules.' In Angelo Soares (ed.), *Stratégies de résistance et travail des femmes*, 151–83. Montreal: Harmattan.

Séguin, Céline, Francine Descarries, and Christine Corbeil. 1996. *Famille et emploi dans le contexte de la monoparentalité féminine. Une analyse comparative menée dans le cadre d'une enquête auprès de 493 mères en emploi de la région montréalaise*. Montreal: Université du Québec à Montréal, Institut de recherches et d'études féministes.

Zouali, Siham, and Claire Rousseau. 1992. 'Les problèmes d'intégration au marché du travail des familles monoparentales au Québec.' In Gilles Pronovost (ed.), *Comprendre la famille*, 275–306. Sainte-Foy, Que: Presses de l'Université du Québec.

PART THREE

Family Solidarity and Social Integration

10 Family Solidarity in Canada: An Exploration with the General Social Survey on Family and Community Support

FERNANDO RAJULTON AND ZENAIDA R. RAVANERA

The transformation of family structures, duration of family roles, and members' relationships to one another could be traced to demographic changes in fertility and mortality. Blum and LeBras (1985) called the change 'verticalization' of the family, as opposed to the 'horizontal' relationships that existed in traditional societies. The horizontal family structure had two or at most three generations, each with four or five siblings. It typically involved relationships between members of the same generation, near and distant cousins. In contrast, the vertical family structure of today is typically multigenerational, having three to five generations, each with fewer siblings. Moreover, the relationships between members run across generations.

Not only the changes in fertility and mortality but also, more importantly, the changes in marital behaviour and living arrangements have brought about more conspicuous transformations in the family. Added to these changes are the sweeping trends of individualism, identified as an impetus behind the 'second demographic transition' (see, e.g., Lesthaeghe 1995; Van de Kaa 1987). These shifts in attitudes and behaviour have raised questions about the age-old assumption that the family provides important resources to sustain the well-being of its members and that providing and receiving support among family members is a lifelong activity. A general argument known as the 'family decline hypothesis' (Popenoe 1988; 1993) contends that the family of today has become ill-equipped to ensure the well-being of its members, let alone the support enduring as a lifetime activity. The 'cancer of individualism' has eaten away at the family fabric and has spread to such an extent that current social norms themselves are increasingly legitimating the pursuit of individual goals to the neglect of family or societal goals (Bengtson et al. 1995).

In addition, recent changes in sociopolitical realities brought about by globalization and cultural shrinkage have also dramatically altered and reshaped family members' capacity to function as sources of support to each other (Hutton and Giddens 2000). The situation has been made worse by globalization and concomitant 'commodification' of all our needs and resources.[1] Commodification in particular has weakened the nurturing role of the family by making available alternative social groups or social services that can satisfy our basic needs for which we were once dependent on family and kinship relationships. Echoing the structural-functional argument that nuclear family isolation was an inevitable outcome of economic development (Parsons 1944), globalization is also thought to have led to the decline of intergenerational co-residence – children living far away from their parents, which in turn inevitably leads to the decline in the strength and intensity of family relationships.[2] A counter-argument, once again echoing an argument prevalent in the 1960s and 1970s (Litwak 1960; Bengtson and Black 1973), claims that in spite of the long distances separating the parents from their adult children, there is still communication and support (hence solidarity) between them, thanks to modern technology.

The gloomy outlook of a 'family decline' hypothesis seems to be the dominant one encountered in public debates, as well as in the research literature, which sees in particular a sharp decline in the potential for mobilizing the family as an interpersonal support system (see, e.g., Blossfeld et al. 1993; Wolf et al. 1997). But, as Silverstein and Bengtson point out, 'contemporary social commentaries that paint the family as an institution in decline have used too broad a brush to characterize intergenerational family relationships.' (1997: 450). A recent study by Scott and Brook (2001), using the data from the British Household Panel Study, suggests that family concerns are still of utmost importance in people's lives and that fears of 'family decline' are unwarranted. In other words, recent studies make it clear that, in spite of all the changes in marital behaviour and in family structure, intergenerational kinship relationships still constitute a viable resource for the majority of family members of whatever age or whatever stage of the life course.

Another view even goes further. Riley (1983) and Riley and Riley (1992; 1993), for example, envisioned more potential relationships awaiting older people because of the present family transformations. They argue that changes in the nature and meaning of the family would definitely replace the traditional forms by new forms of kinship bonds. Although these new forms would involve fewer ascribed and obligatory relationships, they would yield more potential relationships to choose from, especially for older people. Riley and Riley see these new forms of relationships constituting a 'latent matrix' in that these relationships are not readily visible but still exist and can be called upon when needed. Cohabitation, surrogate kin, and new biosocial relationships are all traces of this latent matrix structure that exists today and that may be very common tomorrow. Thus, older generations in the near future, and future generations in general, will enjoy a safety net of significant connections to choose from in case of need.

In the context of the two opposing views, this chapter examines how Canadians express their family solidarity (or intensity of interpersonal relationships) in terms of providing *and* receiving support among their own family members. It aims at finding which view is substantiated by national-level data on family support, and measures the *degree* of family solidarity through the information on types of support that family members provide to each other. As will be shown by the analysis, in spite of the dramatic changes taking place in the family and in spite of the gloomy forecasts by some studies, the family support system is still working in Canada.

Theories on Family Support

That the family is still the viable unit for nurturing the young is obvious. In contrast, it is not always apparent why adults, particularly the elderly, are involved in the family support system. Thus, for greater insight into the working of the family support system, we turn to gerontology, which has developed major paradigms on the topic, a few of which are salient to our study. 'Attachment theory,' for example, argues that there is and always will be a strong sense of responsibility and commitment of (adult) children towards their (aging) parents and vice versa. Studies show that this is the case, even among those who have experienced estrangement or a history of childhood abuse or neglect (see, e.g., Ainsworth and Bowlby 1991; Goldberg et al. 1995). Early patterns of family interaction and strong emotional attachments seem to persist over time. More frequently expressed as a 'warm-glow' hypothesis (Andreoni 1989), this idea implies that parents and children give support to one another because of the satisfaction of giving, nothing more.

From the point of view of economics, one frequently comes across two main paradigms, altruism and exchange, as the motives of support among family members. Becker's (1974) concept of 'altruistic motives' assumes a moral duty or obligation, that is, that children would provide support to parents in most need and vice versa (*need* being defined in terms of health or financial status). The idea of exchange (see, e.g., Homans 1974; Blau 1975; Henretta et al. 1997; Kotlikoff and Morris 1989) is that one gives to others because one expects to receive in return. Parents provide services to (adult) children, such as childcare, in return for financial support and co-residence, while children provide help to (elderly) parents to increase their chances of receiving an inheritance in the future. According to some studies, the anticipation of an inheritance serving as a motive for support provided by children does seem to play a role (Bernheim et al. 1985; Schoeni 1997). Kotlikoff and Morris (1989) offer an even more provocative extension of this idea by saying that transfers from parents to their children are not debts or obligations but simply bribes.

Paradigms from economics have also focused on the impact of a mature welfare system on family solidarity and on the level and pattern of giving and receiving services between parents and their children. Quite divergent views and explanations are given by these paradigms for the continuation of family support, among which are the 'crowding out' and 'crowding in' hypotheses (Abrams and Schmitz 1984; World Bank 1994; Kunemund and Rein 1999). 'Crowding out' argues that a strong welfare state reduces the willingness of children to provide support and services to their parents (implying less family solidarity); 'crowding in' argues that the more resources the aged have beyond bare necessities for economic survival, the more scope they have for participating in reciprocal giving and receiving.

These and similar paradigms imply that the family support system will somehow endure, although under a multiplicity of motives that can range from pure altruism to pure selfishness. It is possible to examine the validity of these paradigms if relevant information on the types of support given and received by family members is available. Thus, for example, if the 'crowding out' phenomenon works, the elderly who normally receive sufficient support from the welfare system will be less likely to cite their children as their main source of support. On the other hand, if 'crowding in' works, the elderly who are well off as a result of sufficient public transfers and other incomes are more likely to report instrumental and emotional support provided by family members. If altruism works, socioeconomic characteristics of parents and/or children will have little influence on the types of support given and received (Chan and Cheung 1997). Many studies on family support reveal that an exchange motive is dominant. To examine these hypotheses in depth, we would need specific information on financial support between parents and children as well as information on wealth and property investments, which unfortunately is not available in the data set used in this study. However, we do have information on income, and we use it together with information on the types of support to explore, albeit in limited way, which hypothesis is the most likely explanation for the degrees of family solidarity that this paper measures and examines.

Measuring Family Solidarity

One can think of family solidarity, or its degrees, as a latent construct and measure it through many indicators (see, e.g., Schmitt 2000; Silverstein and Bengtson 1997; Olson et al. 1979). In our attempt at measuring this unobservable, we take advantage of the knowledge gained from gerontological research on intergenerational support. Intergenerational support (or intrafamily support) can be considered to be essentially of four basic types:

1 Instrumental support that includes all tangible forms of help given and received by family members such as housework, transportation, shopping, and personal care
2 Emotional support given and received by family members of different generations such as confiding, comforting, and reassuring one another; and listening to one another's problems – in essence 'being there' for one another
3 Informational support that includes giving and receiving advice when necessary, for example, in seeking medical treatment, referrals to agencies, and sharing family news
4 Financial and housing support

These four types of support give rise to a three-dimensional measure of intergenerational (or intrafamily) relationships (Silverstein and Bengtson 1997) that involve:

1 *Affinity*, which essentially implies emotional closeness, comprising activities that fall under emotional support
2 *Opportunity structure*, which refers to frequency of contact and residential proximity, thus, comprising activities that fall under the informational and financial types of support

TABLE 10.1 Degrees of Family Solidarity Based on Three Dimensions of Support

Affinity	Opportunity structure	Functional exchange	Solidarity type	Score
0	0	0	Detached	0
0	0	1	Purely functional	1
0	1	0	Pure proximity	1
1	0	0	Pure affinity	1
0	1	1	Obligatory	2
1	0	1	Empathic	2
1	1	0	Sociable	2
1	1	1	Tight-knit	3

Source: GSS 1996.

3 *Functional exchange*, which refers to flows of various kinds of help, essentially comprising all tangible forms of help and falling under instrumental support (see also Roberts et al. 1991, and Millward 1998, and citations therein for more details)

Making use of these three dimensions and assigning dichotomous values of 0 and 1 for the absence and presence of a specific type of support, we can categorize intergenerational (or intrafamily) relationships into eight (2^3) different types, which refer to the way family members exhibit their solidarity in one way or another, some to a very high degree and others to a low degree. Table 10.1 illustrates how these eight types are formed and the labels attached to them (some borrowed from the gerontological literature; see Silverstein and Bengtson 1997).

These eight categories form a 'scale' reflecting the degree of family solidarity. Those individuals who have no score on all the three dimensions represent those who are *detached* from their families (i.e., they are not involved in any type of support activities), while those who have scores on all represent those who are *tight-knit* with their families. In between these two scores are six other types representing various degrees of support, and hence of family solidarity. A score of 1 can represent three types: *purely functional*, representing those involved in tangible forms of help only; *pure proximity*, representing those who live close to their family members and/or involved in frequent contact with them; or *pure affinity*, representing those involved in providing only emotional support. Similarly, a score of 2 represents three groups with a higher degree of solidarity, higher in the sense that they are involved in more than one dimension of service. For convenience, let us call them *obligatory* (those involved in both opportunity structure and functional exchange), *empathic* (those involved in both affinity and functional exchange), and *sociable* (those involved in both affinity and opportunity structure).

A few observations are in order regarding this scale of solidarity. First, the measures are solely based on support services in a family. In other words, it is assumed that support services given and received by family members are good indicators of the latent construct, *family solidarity*. One can think of including other indicators as well if relevant data are available (e.g., regarding financial support).

Second, the 'degree' of solidarity is measured by a combination of involvement in the three major dimensions of intergenerational support. Thus, those individuals who are involved in more than one dimension of support (and hence have a score of 2 or more) supposedly have a higher degree of solidarity than those who are involved in only one dimension (and have a score of 1 only). Such an imperfect measure can be improved upon if additional information is available, for example, about the amount of time spent in rendering each service. Any one of these types (except the *detached*) can in reality encompass a higher or lower degree of solidarity than the classification here allows.

Third, surveys most often collect information on support services from individuals. However, from such individual-level information we make inferences on family solidarity, thus passing from one level of analysis to another – the well-known individualistic or atomistic fallacy in research methods. Careful reflection shows that there is no such fallacy here, or that even if such a fallacy exists it is not serious, because the information on support services obtained from individuals is actually information on family *relationships*, not just on individual characteristics or behaviour. Support services occur in the context of the family members' needs and thus essentially imply family solidarity.

An underlying rationale in devising such a measure for family solidarity is that support among family members covers a wide range of behaviour – physical, psychological, emotional, economic, and instrumental – and that different types of help received and given by family members need to be taken into account. Thus, family solidarity cannot be examined with only one kind of information, such as data regarding 'emotional support,' as is often encountered in the literature.

With these theoretical backgrounds underpinning the data analysis, this chapter presents the results in two parts. The first covers the levels of different types of support given and received by the Canadian population with particular focus on elderly persons. The second part centers on the measures of family solidarity and factors that influence it. But first, we discuss the data and methodology.

Data, Methods, and Models

This study uses the General Social Survey (GSS) Cycle 11 on Social and Community Support, conducted in 1996, with the sample representing all Canadians aged 15 years and older except residents of Yukon and Northwest Territories and full-time residents of institutions (Statistics Canada 1998). Basic information on services given and received was gathered from *all* the respondents of the survey (12,756 total weighted sample[3]). It collected data on instrumental and emotional support, frequency of contact, and proximity of residence but not on financial support. The survey did collect information on 'care relationships'; that is, to whom services were given or from whom services were obtained, but these data were gathered only from those who had temporary difficulties and from those who had long-term health or physical limitations. Had this specific information on care relationships been obtained from *all* the respondents, it would have given us deeper insights into the prevalence and degree of family solidarity in Canada.

Making the best use of information that is available for all respondents, the following procedure was adopted for the indicators of affinity, opportunity structure and functional exchange described in Table 10.1. Individuals who gave emotional support to or received it from family members only (i.e., excluding friends, government agencies, and nongovernmental organizations) were given a score of 1 for affinity. Individuals who reported that they had contact with the roster members daily or at least once a week (i.e., excluding at least once a month or less than once a month) and, individuals who reported that they lived with the roster member in the same household or in surrounding area (that is, excluding less than half day's journey or more than half day's journey) were given a score of 1 for opportunity structure. Individuals who reported giving *or* receiving services of *any* kind (i.e., childcare, meal preparation and clean-up, house cleaning, laundry and sewing, house maintenance, shopping for groceries and other necessities, transportation, banking and bill paying, and personal care such as assistance in bathing, toiletry, cutting finger nails, brushing teeth, shampooing, or hair dressing) were given a score of 1.

Adding the scores for each respondent provides a measure of the degree of family solidarity, which is an ordinal variable that takes values from 0 to 3. To examine the factors that influence family solidarity, the resulting ordinal score is used as a dependent variable in a multivariate technique of analysis. As will be seen below, the proportion belonging to the *detached* category is small and is excluded in building an explanatory model. Moreover, since the dependent variable is ordinal, we paid special attention to the statistical technique to be used.[4] In this study, we employ nested logistic regression for the advantages it offers (Fox 1984).

The logic of nested logistic regression is as follows. If there are three ordered categories, say low, medium, and high (standing for the three scores 1, 2, and 3 on the scale of solidarity seen above), then we can build two logistic regression models by nesting the categories low versus medium and high together in one model, and then medium versus high in the other. The first model would estimate the probabilities of falling into the medium/high versus low degree of solidarity, and the second would separate the probabilities of falling into the high versus medium degree. The impact of socioeconomic characteristics, which for this study are described below, can be estimated in the same manner as with any ordinary logistic regression model.

Results of Analysis and Interpretations

Types and Extent of Family Support

As can be seen in Panel A of Table 10.2, Canadians are involved in all types of support, the most common being the functional type; that is, more than 80% are involved in giving or receiving tangible help. About half live in close proximity to or are in frequent contact with family members; and about a quarter are involved in giving or receiving emotional support. Panel B, which presents the most common types of help given and received, shows that the percentages of respondents who receive help in meal preparation and shopping are generally much higher than those who receive help for personal care. This is normal, because personal care involves more intimacy and trust than other types of services. Also, receiving childcare services from family members is obviously limited to women, to women of childbearing ages at that (therefore not shown). In contrast, the proportions of respondents providing childcare are quite appreciable for both women and men.

TABLE 10.2 Proportions of Men and Women Involved in Forms of Support (%)

Panel A Involvement in Three Forms of Support

	Men	Women
Affinity	24	26
Opportunity structure	44	52
Functional	84	83
N	5,527	7,229

Panel B Involvement in Functional Type of Support

	Men	Women
Received service		
Meal preparation	28	25
Shopping	64	62
Personal care	8	13
N	4,081	4,935
Provided service		
Meal preparation	22	19
Shopping	54	43
Personal care	8	16
Child care	16	22
N	2,823	3,872

Source: GSS 1996.

Since the data used in this study essentially capture the relationships among family members, one major source of diversity is gender. Women are socialized early in life to adopt nurturing roles. Their caretaking responsibility continues even late in life, and thus, there is a perception that women provide the majority of support. It is also widely acknowledged that many women are 'sandwiched' between giving childcare and elder care. However, men are involved in the support system as well, and in particular are more involved in things that do not involve 'personal' care, such as financial management, home and auto repair, and arranging for and coordinating formal services, all of which are grouped under the category of functional exchange here. When the focus is not primarily on personal and 'hands-on' type of care, there is greater gender equity in the division of support services than reported. In general, a slightly higher percentage of men than women receive help in meal preparation. Women generally give *and* receive more help for personal care and provide more help for childcare. Men generally tend to provide more help in shopping and management services.

Of specific interest is the information on the proportions of men and women who are aged 60 and over (the elderly, 1,120 men and 1,386 women in the sample) and who are involved in the three main forms of support. Table 10.3, Panel A presents these, further classified by personal income, which for the elderly, comes from self-employment, unemployment insurance, pensions, old age security, welfare payments, and so on. The results presented in this table are useful for checking the validity of the three important paradigms discussed above. As seen from table 10.3, the elderly are definitely involved in different forms of support, the largest involvement falling into the *functional* type; that is, they give or receive various types of help. As seen in the table, there is a nearly uniform distribution of involvement across different income groups, except for minor fluctuations.[5] The elderly whose annual personal income is as low as $20,000 or less are as involved as those whose personal income is as high as $60,000 or more. This implies that, irrespective of their income, the elderly are involved in all the three forms of support, and thus there is no substantial evidence for 'crowding out' or 'crowding in' phenomena here. It would seem from the information on various forms of family support, except for financial support not gathered through the survey, that the more valid paradigm is that of altruism or attachment proposed by Becker. That is, family members support each other mainly out of a strong sense of responsibility or commitment.

Since the *functional* type of support comprises so many different types of services given *and* received, we examined more closely the proportions of the elderly who are involved in specific types of services, again classified by their personal income. Panel B of Table 10.3 presents these results. Apart from the obvious differences between men and women,[6] these again point to a number of remarkable observations. While the proportions of those receiving help are higher than of those giving help, the elderly are not merely at the receiving end of the support system. More than half of elderly men, for example, provide services for shopping and close to a third of elderly women provide childcare. Moreover, similar to the results shown in Panel A, the distribution across income categories is almost uniform – thus, again invalidating the 'crowding in'

TABLE 10.3 Proportions (%) of Men and Women Aged 60+ Involved in Forms of Support, Classified by Personal Income

Panel A   Involvement in Three Forms of Support

	<$20,000	$20–39,000	$40–59,000	>$60,000	Total
Men					
Affinity	17	15	17	15	16
Opportunity structure	39	36	30	37	37
Functional	85	83	76	85	84
Women					
Affinity	20	17	18	18	19
Opportunity structure	46	45	42	49	46
Functional	80	85	81	83	82

Panel B   Involvement in Functional Type of Support

	<$20,000	$20–39,000	$40–59,000	>$60,000	Total
Received service					
Men					
Meal preparation	30	28	25	30	29
Shopping	59	62	67	57	60
Personal care	11	10	9	13	11
Women					
Meal preparation	22	19	18	21	21
Shopping	62	66	63	61	62
Personal care	16	15	19	18	17
Provided service					
Men					
Meal preparation	18	9	14	19	17
Shopping	51	68	59	54	55
Personal care	10	5	3	10	9
Child care	21	17	24	17	20
Women					
Meal preparation	18	15	9	20	17
Shopping	42	37	54	39	41
Personal care	14	17	6	11	13
Child care	26	30	30	30	28

Source: GSS 1996.

TABLE 10.4 Types and Degrees of Family Solidarity (%) Classified by Gender

Types	Total	Men	Women
Detached	10.0	10.0	9.0
Purely functional	39.0	44.0	34.0
Pure proximity	2.0	2.0	2.0
Pure affinity	0.5	0.4	0.5
Obligatory	21.0	18.0	24.0
Empathic	3.0	3.0	4.0
Sociable	1.5	1.3	1.7
Tight-knit	23.0	21.0	25.0
N	12,756	6,279	6,477

Source: 1996 GSS.

and 'crowding out' hypotheses. Finally, both elderly men and women are involved even in the types of services that are often considered to be exclusively or predominantly 'gendered,' for example, childcare or personal care.

Degrees of Family Solidarity

FAMILY SOLIDARITY AND GENDER DIFFERENTIAL

Table 10.4 presents the distribution of the eight categories of family solidarity for the entire sample and for male and female respondents separately. Nine in ten Canadians are involved in the family support system in varying degrees (excepting the *detached*). About one-quarter belong to the *tight-knit* category; that is, family members give or receive emotional support, have contacts on daily or weekly basis, and are involved in helping relationships. The highest proportion (about 40%) of Canadians fall into the *purely functional* category; that is, they receive or give help, but report neither emotional support given or received nor daily or weekly contacts with family members. Another 20% fall into the *obligatory* type of being involved in functional exchange or opportunity structure but not involved in giving or providing emotional support. These three types, together with those belonging to the *detached* category (10%), cover 95% of Canadians. The remaining 5% belong to the other four types of family solidarity.

As far as gender difference is concerned, a significantly greater proportion of men are involved in simply receiving and giving help, the *purely functional* type of support (a difference of 10%), while a significantly greater proportion of women fall into the *obligatory* and *tight-knit* categories (a difference of 6% and 4%, respectively), indicating more frequent contact and more involvement in giving or receiving emotional support. In all other categories, however, the distribution by gender is about the same.

FACTORS INFLUENCING FAMILY SOLIDARITY: RESULTS OF NESTED
LOGISTIC MODELS

We have used the nested logistic regression models to examine the factors that influence the degree of family solidarity exhibited by Canadians, first modelling high/medium score versus low score (which is the reference), and then modelling high score versus medium score (which is the reference). The logit coefficients (or the log-odds) obtained from the analysis are to be interpreted as follows: A positive coefficient implies a higher probability of being classified under the given dependent category, and a negative coefficient implies a lower probability, all in comparison to the reference group. It is easier to interpret the results in terms of odds by taking the exponents of the coefficients. The odds tell us how much more (when odds are greater than 1) or how much less (when odds are less than 1) is the probability of being classified under the given dependent category in comparison to the reference group. These odds, presented in table 10.5, are obtained from the nested logistic models that were built using the forward selection procedure. Thus, those variables that do not significantly add to a model's fit or explanatory power are dropped from model building; hence the absence of some variables in certain columns of table 10.5. As seen at the bottom of Table 10.5, the model *p* values are all highly significant.[7] Thus, the specific explanatory variables included in each model explain very well the odds of falling into specific dependent categories.

As degrees of family solidarity differ by gender of the respondents, analyses are done separately for men and women, which would allow capture of possible differences in the impact of the various factors

Living Arrangements. Functionality, opportunity structure, and affinity are all more easily realizable in the context of marital relationships and living arrangements. It is sufficient to consider one of these two contexts since they are closely related and, between marital and parental statuses, the latter is more important because the presence of children (of whatever age) at home invariably leads to expressions of all the three forms of intergenerational exchange and support. As the GSS did not explicitly collect information on the parental status of respondents,

TABLE 10.5 Odds, or exp(ß), from the Nested Logistic Models of Degree of Family Solidarity

Covariates	Model 1 High/Medium vs Low		Model 2 High vs Medium	
	Male	Female	Male	Female
Living arrangement				
Alone	0.86	0.70***	0.57*	0.88
Couples, no children at home	1.27*	0.81	3.51***	2.69***
Couples, children at home	1.13	0.95	4.28***	2.96***
Single parent, children at home	1.27	1.09	2.34***	1.87***
Other[a]	1.00	1.00	1.00	1.00
Birth cohort				
1926 or earlier	0.53***	0.60***	0.45***	0.59***
1927–36	0.45***	0.70*	0.48***	0.58***
1937–46	0.61***	0.83	0.46***	0.78
1947–56	0.67***	0.83	0.69	0.82
1957–66	0.73*	0.89	0.92	0.87
1967–76	0.69*	0.99	0.90	0.93
1977–81[a]	1.00	1.00	1.00	1.00
Birthplace				
Canada		1.35***		
Outside Canada[a]		1.00		
Language				
English only				0.87
French only				1.75***
Others and mixed[a]				1.00
Education				
Above high school			1.43*	1.06
High school			0.96	0.75*
Elementary			1.00	1.00
Region of residence				
Atlantic	2.02***	1.85***	1.12	1.20
Quebec	1.72***	1.77***	0.68***	0.49***
Ontario	0.77***	0.85*	0.59***	0.55***
Prairies and BC[a]	1.00	1.00	1.00	1.00
N	4,702	6,236	2,334	3,599
Model p value	0.000	0.000	0.000	0.000
Goodness-of-fit p value	0.41	0.09	0.13	0.17
Pseudo-R^2	0.06	0.06	0.19	0.14
Correct classification	(Low)		(Medium)	
	61%	31%	69%	80%

Source: GSS 1996.
[a] Reference variable, group, at item.
*p < .10; **p <.05; ***p < .01.

we use the information on living arrangements as a proxy variable. The categories include: Alone, couples without children, couples with children, single parent with children, and others (comprising all other types including no spouse but living with non-single child, living with two parents, and others, covering about 24% of respondents). The last category serves as the reference.

From Model 1 that compares the odds of falling into high/medium category versus the odds of falling into the low category, we see that male respondents who are living alone have the odds 0.86 of falling into high/medium category, compared with the respondents who are classified into the 'other' living arrangement. Expressed in percentages, this means that men who are living alone are 14% (1 − 0.86 × 100) less likely to fall into the high/medium category than those in the 'other' living arrangement group, although this inference is not statistically significant. Similarly, women living alone are 30% less likely to fall into the high/medium category, which is significant at the 1% level.

Although the odds associated with living arrangement or parental status are not generally significant for both women and men in Model 1, living arrangement does have definite and significant impact on the odds of falling into the *tight-knit* category (i.e., getting a score of 3 vs getting a score of 2) as seen in the results for Model 2. Couples, with or without children, have three to four times higher probabilities of falling into the *tight-knit* category than those who are in the Other living arrangement group. Single parents with children also have about two-fold higher odds of falling into the *tight-knit* category. Women and men living alone have the lowest probabilities of falling into the *tight-knit* category.

Life Course Effects Indicated by Birth Cohorts. The ways in which family members provide and receive support from one another depend much on the life course stages of the members themselves. Thus, family solidarity exhibited through various forms of support can be expected to change over the life course. For example, many elderly persons would have completed their parental roles and are therefore less likely to be involved in all three forms of support. On the contrary, a higher degree of solidarity can be exhibited by young adult men and women who are in the midst of performing the supportive roles in their life course stage. Longitudinal data will be needed to show these changes over the life course in intergenerational and family support. For lack of such data, we have used the birth cohort information that could capture the impact of life course stages on family solidarity. The birth cohorts have been classified as follows: born before 1926, by decades to 1967–76, and also 1977–81, with the youngest cohort as the reference category.

The variable birth cohort brings out clearly the odds of falling into a higher degree of family solidarity. Controlling for the other variables in the model, the youngest cohorts of men and women (the reference group) have the highest probability of getting higher scores (that is, falling into the medium or high solidarity categories). The differentials are striking when we compare men and women. While the oldest two cohorts of women have significantly lower probability (40% lower) of getting scores of 2 or higher (high/medium category in Model 1 and high category in Model 2) in comparison with the youngest cohort of women, the mid-cohorts of women (i.e., women born from the mid-1930s to the mid-1970s) do not differ significantly from the youngest cohort. This is because women are fully engaged in support services well into their old age until they can no longer provide such services. But the picture is quite different for men, particularly in Model 1. The oldest two cohorts of men are less likely to get scores of 2 or higher, just like the oldest cohorts of women. But the mid-cohorts of men also have lower probability of getting higher scores of solidarity, although one sees a definite trend over cohorts. As men age, they are progressively less likely to fall into higher forms of solidarity in terms of providing and receiving services of all types. These differentials by cohorts and by gender capture the life-course stages in which individuals are and the ability to manifest family solidarity through the various forms of support services.

Cultural Differences and Migration Status Effects. As family solidarity may vary by cultural traditions and norms, we incorporate two variables that capture this characteristic. Immigrant status is given by the information on country of birth, Canada and outside Canada, the latter as the reference. The effect of this variable on family solidarity could go in either direction. We could expect those born outside Canada to be more involved in all three types of support because of the high degree of family solidarity in non-western cultures. However, they may also have less opportunity for family support as they are less likely to live in close proximity to as large a number of family members as those born in Canada. We have used 'first language spoken at home' as another variable to capture a multidimensional notion of 'culture.' The categories have been collapsed into three categories: English only, French only, and Others and Mixed to encompass all other non-official languages, the last serving as the reference. We might expect the Other and Mixed language group to be more involved in all three forms of support, other things being equal.

These two variables show significant differentials only for women (the former in Model 1 and the latter in Model 2). Women born in Canada have a 35% higher probability of getting a score of 2 or higher than women born outside Canada, which possibly captures their greater opportunity for interaction with a greater number of family members. Women whose home language is French have a 75% higher probability of getting a score of 3 or falling into the *tight-knit* category than do women of other language groups. Why these cultural variables come out with significant differences only for women can perhaps be explained by the role women play either in looking after the family or in passing on the cultural traditions and norms to their children. But why French-speaking women have higher probability of falling into the *tight-knit* category needs to be further explored. To have a better understanding of the influence of cultural differences on family solidarity, we would need more detailed information on ethnic background.

Education. The Education variable is often used to capture differences in socioeconomic status and thus, like income that was shown to have no significant effect on the levels and types of family support (at least among those aged 60 or more), we expected that education level would not have a significant effect on degree of solidarity. And indeed education does not distinguish between those who have a low level of solidarity from those who have medium or high level (Model 1). However, education seems to distinguish between the medium and high degrees of solidarity as shown in Model 2. Men who are highly educated are more likely to fall into the *tight-knit* category. This is somewhat similar to the effect on women: compared to those with high or low education, women with medium level of education are less likely to fall into the *tight-knit* category. Given that most Canadians are involved in functional exchange and opportunity structures, the difference by education in level of family solidarity could most likely be due to greater emotional involvement (or affinity) among those with high education, particularly among men. It is possible that higher education engenders openness to service relationships and makes easier activities related to emotional support, such as confiding, reassuring, or listening to problems and anxieties of other family members.

Regional Differences. Besides these individual characteristics, there could also be structural influences at various levels on family solidarity.

Although neighbourhood, and neighbourhood characteristics, would be ideal for our purpose, it is difficult to pin down what a neighbourhood is and to obtain the relevant data. For lack of such information, and since it is well known that provinces in Canada are conspicuously distinct in their demographic, economic, and social structures, we use provinces, and for practical purposes, group them into the following regions: Atlantic, Quebec, Ontario, and Prairies and British Columbia, the last serving as the reference.

As it turns out, in the forward selection procedure used in model building, the region variable has the largest explanatory power among the variables included in all the models. In Model 1, we find that respondents in the Atlantic region, both men and women, have a two-fold higher probability of falling into high/medium category than respondents from the western provinces of Canada; and they are also somewhat likely to be in the *tight-knit* category (although the coefficients are not significant in Model 2). Men and women in Quebec are about 70% more likely to fall into high/medium category (Model 1) but are 30% to 50% respectively less likely to fall into the *tight-knit* category (Model 2). As these are two nested models, these two results together indicate that men and women in Quebec are most likely to fall into the medium level of family solidarity. In contrast, Ontarians are more likely to have a low level of family solidarity, as indicated by the (less than one) odds in both Model 1 and Model 2.

That the geographic variable 'region of residence' has a definite impact on the degree of family solidarity reinforces the impression that family and social solidarity is stronger in the East than in other parts of the country – an indication of stronger cultural support for family solidarity in the Atlantic Provinces. However, this could also point to the diversity in economic conditions and opportunities. Where economic conditions are difficult, families compensate by helping each other out. Furthermore, the commodification principle may be in force; that is, alternatives to services traditionally provided by the family may be more available in places with more vibrant economies, notably, in Ontario and in the West.

Conclusions

By measuring the degree of family solidarity in terms of as many services as possible that family members render to support one another, we are able to establish that the family support system in Canada is still in 'good shape' in spite of the many transformations it has undergone in recent times. That the younger cohorts of men and women are fully involved in the system is surely an indication that the support system continues in spite of changes in the nature and function of families of today. In particular, it is quite clear that the presence or absence of children, and couple or single status are important determinants of family solidarity. This study has also shown that other individual socioeconomic characteristics (such as income and, to certain extent, education and place of birth)[8] offer weaker explanations of family solidarity than the family-related variables (e.g., presence of children and life course stage).

The family has undergone changes, and one can envision more changes in the future. But as long as the support system continues in some form or other, perhaps with new kinds of kinship forms as Riley and Riley speculate, there will surely be a lot of giving and receiving among family members. It needs to be stressed here that the term 'lower' or 'higher' degree of family solidarity carries no pejorative connotation. While we have used, for example, *tight-knit* to describe families that are assigned the highest score of 3, and *purely functional* those that get a score of 1, there is a lot of giving and receiving taking place even under the *purely functional* type. Thus, we can confidently say that an intergenerational or intrafamilial support system still constitutes, and will most likely continue to be, a viable resource for the majority of family members of whatever age, stage of the life course, or form of kinship relations.

It may be possible to include other dimensions than intergenerational or family support in measuring family solidarity, and this is definitely a task for the future. At the moment, however, it is rather difficult to find anything better than the support system. Although the support system is the best indicator of family solidarity, data collection strategies could be further improved. As mentioned in an earlier section, detailed information about from whom or to whom services were given need to be collected, not only from those who were in temporary difficulty or those who have long-term disability but from everyone. Moreover, information on financial help given and received needs to be gathered. It would also enrich our knowledge if cross-national comparisons can be done to see how well Canadian society fares in a global perspective.[9]

NOTES

1 The term *commodification* refers to the process of transforming everything into a commodity, such that personal relations simply become market rela-

tions. As a by-product of economic determinism, commodification fosters the idea that markets can provide society (and family) with whatever it needs, including education, health, and social programs. See Dizard and Gadlin (1990) for details.

2 The phenomenon of declining intergenerational co-residence can be found even in those societies where co-residence and support of the aged was the norm. See, e.g., Qureshi (1990), Kunemund and Rein (1990), Aykan and Wolf (2000), and Kauh (1997) for some interesting studies.

3 The survey data come with individual sampling weights, and according to the directives given by Statistics Canada, these weights have been used for all subsequent analyses for the sake of generalization.

4 The most useful technique is the ordinal logistic regression, which estimates the threshold probabilities of falling into the ordered categories in addition to the impact of the socioeconomic characteristics one can think of in explaining the probabilities of falling into those categories. However, it uses an assumption that may not always be realistic, namely, that the socioeconomic characteristics have the same impact on all the dependent categories (known as the parallel lines assumption).

5 Scheffe's tests on differences between these percentages across income categories clearly show that there are absolutely no significant differences between these percentages. (For details in Scheffe's test, see Scheffe 1959).

6 Again, Scheffe's tests on differences between these percentages across income categories *within each sex* show no significant differences.

7 In addition, the chi-square value for goodness of fit should *not* be significant if the fitted frequencies are to be close to the observed frequencies. Thus, the p values for goodness of fit tests should normally be greater than .05, and as these values indicate, all the models are good fits. The explanatory powers of these models range from 6% to 19% depending on the models (given by the pseudo-R^2).

8 Respondents' personal income was first included in the logistic models but was later dropped since this variable not only had no significant impact whatsoever in both the models but also reduced the goodness of fit of these models. An important point learned in this exercise is that Canadian men and women are really involved in the family support system, no matter what their income level is.

9 At the time of completing this chapter, the authors received an announcement from the International Sociological Association about the Inter-Congress Conference on Ageing Societies and Ageing Sociology: Diversity and Change in a Global World, to be held on 7 Sept. 2004 at the University of Surrey Roehampton, U.K. It is encouraging to see among the list of papers to be presented in the conference that similar works are being done in a few other

countries (although not with national level data) and that the abstracts of these papers offer conclusions similar to what we have arrived at here.

REFERENCES

Abrams, B.A., and M.D. Schmitz. 1984. 'The Crowding-Out Effect of Governmental Transfers on Private Charitable Contributions: Cross-Sectional Evidence.' *National Tax Journal* 37(4): 563–8.

Ainsworth, M., and J. Bowlby. 1991. 'An Ethological Approach to Personality Development.' *American Psychologist* 46(4): 333–41.

Andreoni, J. 1989. 'Giving with Impure Altruism: Applications to Charity and Ricardian Equivalence.' *Journal of Political Economy* 97(6): 1447–58.

Aykan, H., and D.A. Wolf. 2000. 'Traditionality, Modernity, and Househoild Composition: Parent-Child Coresidence in Contemporary Turkey.' *Research on Aging* 22(4): 395–421.

Barbagli, M. 1992. 'Asymmetry in Intergenerational Family Relationships in Italy. In T. Hareven (ed.), *Aging and Generational Relations: Life Course and Cross-Cultural Perspectives.* New York: Aldine de Gruyter.

Becker, G.S. 1974. 'A Theory of Social Interactions.' *Journal of Political Economy* 82(6): 1063–93.

Bengtson, V.L., and K.D. Black. 1973. 'Inter-generational Relations and Continuities in Socialization.' In P.B. Baltes and K.W. Schaie (eds.), *Life-Span Developmental Psychology: Personality and Socialization*, 208–34. New York: Academic Press.

Bengtson, V.L., C. Rosenthal, and L. Burton. 1995. 'Paradoxes of Families and Aging.' In R. Binstock and L. George (eds.), *Handbook of Aging and the Social Sciences*, 234-59. New York: Academic Press.

Bernheim, B.D., A. Schleifer, and L.H. Summers. 1985. 'The Strategic Bequest Motive.' *Journal of Political Economy* 93(6): 1045–76.

Blau, P.M. (Ed.). 1975. *Approaches to the Study of Social Structure.* New York: Free Press.

Blossfeld, H.-P., D. Manting and G. Rohwer. 1993. 'Patterns of Change in Family Formation in the Federal Republic of Germany and the Netherlands: Some Consequences for Solidarity between Generations.' In H.A. Becker and P.L.J. Hermkens (eds), *Solidarity of Generations. Demographic Economic and Social Change, and Its Consequences*, 175–96. Amsterdam: Thesis Publishers.

Blum, A., and H. Le Bras. 1985. 'Solidarité familiale, solidarité sociale.' In D. Kessler and A. Masson (eds.), *Cycle de Vie et Generations*, 157–176. Paris: Economica.

Chan, A., and P. Cheung, 1997. 'The Interrelationship between public and Private Support of the Elderly: What Can We Learn from the Singaporean Case?' Paper presented at the 1997 meetings of the Population Association of America, Washington, DC.

Dizard, J.E., and H. Gadlin. 1990. *The Minimal Family*. Amherst, MA: University of Amherst Press.

Fox, J. 1984. *Linear Statistical Models and Related Methods*. New York: Wiley.

Goldberg, S., R. Muir, and J. Kerr. 1995. *Attachment Theory: Social, Developmental and Clinical Perspectives*. Hillsdale, NJ: Analytic Press.

Hareven, T. (ed.). 1992. *Aging and Generational Relations, Life Course and Cross-cultural Perspectives*. New York: Aldine de Gruyter.

Henretta, J.C., M.S.Hill, W. Li, B.J. Soldo, and D.A. Wolf. 1997. 'Selection of Children to Provide Care: The Effect of Earlier Parental Transfers.' *Journals of Gerontology, Psychological Sciences and Social Sciences, Series B* 52B (Special Issue): 110–4.

Homans, G.C. 1974. *Social Behavior: Its Elementary Forms*. NY: Harcourt Brace Jovanovich.

Hutton, W., and A. Giddens. (Eds.). 2000. *On the Edge:Living with Global Capitalism*. London: Jonathan Cape.

Kauh, Tae-Ock. 1997. 'Intergenerational Relations: Older Korean-Americans' Experiences. *Journal of Cross-cultural Gerontology* 12: 3245–71.

Kotlikoff, L.J., and J.N. Morris. 1989. 'How Much Care Do the Aged Receive from Their Children? A Bimodal Picture of Contact and Assistance. In D.A. Wise, (ed.), *The Economics of Ageing*, 149–72. Chicago: University of Chicago Press.

Kunemund, Harald, and Martin Rein, 1999. 'There Is More to Receiving than Needing: Theoretical Arguments and Empirical Explorations of Crowding In and Crowding Out. *Ageing and Society* 19(1): 93–121.

Lesthaeghe, R. 1995. 'The Second Demographic Transition in Western Countries: An Interpretation. In K.O. Mason and A. Jensen (eds.), *Gender and Family Change in Industrialized Countries*, 17–62. New York: Oxford University Press.

Litwak, E. 1960. 'Geographic Mobility and Extended Family Cohesion. *American Sociological Review* 25: 3385–94.

Millward, C. 1998. *Family Relationships and Intergenerational Exchange in Later Life*. Working Paper No.15. Melbourne: Australian Institute of Family Studies.

Olson, D.H., D.H. Sprenkle, and C.S. Russell. 1979. 'Circumplex Model of Marital and Family Systems: I. Cohesion and Adaptability Dimensions, Family Types, and Clinical Applications.' *Family Process* 18(1): 3–28.

Parsons, T. 1944. 'The Social Structure of the Family.' In *The Family: Its Functions and Destiny,* 173–201. Edited by R.N. Anshen. New York: Harper.

Popenoe, D. 1988. *Disturbing the Nest: Family Change and Decline in Modern Societies.* New York: Aldine de Gruyter.

Popenoe, D., N.D. Glenn, J. Stacey, P.A. Cowan. 1993. 'American Family Decline, 1960–1990: A Review and Appraisal.' Comment/Reply *Journal of Marriage and the Family* 55: 327–55.

Qureshi, H. 1990. 'A Research Note on the Hierarchy of Obligations among Informal Carers – A Response to Finch and Mason. *Ageing and Society* 10: 455–8.

Riley, M.W. 1983. 'The Family in an Aging Society: A Matrix of Latent Relationships.' *Journal of Family Issues* 4: 3439–54.

Riley M.W., and J.W. Riley, Jr,1992. Generational Relations: A Future Perspective.' In T. Hareven (ed.), *Aging and Generational Relations, Life Course and Cross-Cultural Perspectives.* 283–92 New York: Aldine de Gruyter.

– 1993. 'Connections: Kin and Cohort.' In V.L. Bengtson and W.A. Achenbaum (eds.), *The Changing Contract across Generations* 169–90.

Roberts, R.E.L., L.N. Richards, and V.L. Bengtson. 1991. 'Intergenerational Solidarity in Families Untangling the Ties That Bind.' *Marriage and Family Review* 16(1/2): 11–46.

Scheffe, H. 1959. *The Analysis of Variance.* New York: John Wiley & Sons. *Intergenerational and Generational Connections.* New York: Howarth Press.

Schmitt, M. 2000. Mother-Daughter Attachment and Family Cohesion: Single and Multi-construct Latent State-Trait Models of Current and Retrospective Perceptions. Magdeburg: Institut fur Psychologie, Otto-von-Guericke-Universitat.

Schoeni, R.F. 1997. 'Private Interhousehold Transfers of Money and Time: New Empirical Evidence. *Review of Income and Wealth* 43: 423–48.

Scott, J., and L. Brook. 2001. 'Family Change: Demographic and Attitudinal Trends across Nations and Time. Available at: http://www.brookes.ac.uk/schools/social/population-and-household-change/1_scott.html.

Silverstein, M., and V.L. Bengtson. 1997. 'Intergenerational Solidarity and the Structure of Adult Child-Parent Relationships in American Families.' *American Journal of Sociology* 103: 2429–60.

Statistics Canada. 1998. *1996 General Social Survey, Cycle 11: Social and Community Support.* Public Use Microdata File Documentation and User's Guide. Ottawa: Statistics Canada, cat. no. 12M0011GPE.

Van de Kaa, D.J. 1987. 'Europe's Second Demographic Transition.' *Population Bulletin* 42(1): 1–58.

Wolf, D.A., V. Freedman, and B.J. Soldo. 1997. 'The Division of Family Labor:

Care for the Elderly Parents. *Journals of Gerontology, Psychological Sciences and Social Sciences, Series B* 52B (Special Issue): 102–9.

World Bank. 1994. *Averting the Old Age Crisis: Policies to Protect and Promote Growth.* New York: Oxford University Press.

11 Social Integration over the Life Course: Influences of Individual, Family, and Community Characteristics

ZENAIDA R. RAVANERA AND FERNANDO RAJULTON

Social integration, or the process through which individuals are included in the economic, political, and social fabric of society, differs by life course stages, with each stage broadly characterized by different channels of integration. For children, formal integration into society is mainly through school. Youth's integration is still largely through school, but they also go through the process of getting integrated through work. For adults, the most likely means of integration is through work, although this is truer for men than for women. Many women are integrated into society through volunteering, mainly in child-oriented organizations in schools and in communities. At later life, the channel of integration changes yet again from one that is work-oriented to one that is community-oriented through volunteering. For some elderly people, the change may also be from integration to disengagement.

All of the above are formal channels of integration that involve institutions such as schools, workplaces, and organizations. But there are informal ones as well, such as neighborhood playgrounds in childhood, socializing with families, kin, peer groups, and friends in youth and adulthood, and through leisure activities, particularly in later life. Both the formal and informal channels of integration could differ for each individual over the life course, not only by his or her attributes but also by social, geographic, and historical contexts within which his or her life course unfolds.

Jenson (1998) and Bernard (1999) identified six dimensions of social cohesion: the sociocultural dimensions of *recognition* and *belonging*, the political dimensions of *legitimacy* and *participation*, and the economic dimensions of *inclusion* and *equality*. The same six dimensions can also be used for integration, an individual-level indicator of societal cohesion (Ravanera, Rajulton, and Turcotte 2003). However, only three are examined in this study, mainly because of data availability. Economic *inclusion* refers to an individual's attachment to the labour force and is indicated by employment status, or for young persons, preparation for entry into the labour force through schooling. *Participation* signifies involvement in politics through voting, membership in associations, political parties, union, etc., and volunteering in organizations. And, *belonging* refers to the feeling of being part of community and connotes a sense of identity and sharing of values and norms.

Data and Methodology

We make use of the General Social Survey on Time Use conducted by Statistics Canada in 1998 with a cross-sectional sample of 10,749 respondents who are representative of the Canadian population 15 years of age and over but excluding the residents of Yukon and Northwest Territories and full-time residents institutions of (Statistics Canada 1999). The survey asked respondents to record in a diary how they spent their time over a period of 24 hours. However, this study uses only the information on volunteer work, significant life events experienced over the past year, and respondents' social and demographic backgrounds. In addition, community characteristics derived for enumeration areas from the 1996 census were appended to the 1998 General Social Survey, thus allowing an examination of influences of community characteristics on integration. Sample weights are used throughout the analysis.

From the survey, we took the following as indicators of the three selected dimensions of integration:

- *Inclusion* – whether the respondent has a full-time job, is a full-time student, or a student with a part-time job
- *Participation* – whether the respondent volunteered in the past year
- *Belonging* – whether the respondent feels a strong sense of belonging to the community

These indicators assume that integration is achieved through active participation in the economy and in voluntary organizations and through social involvement that engenders a sense of belonging, most likely through interaction with friends, relatives, and neighbours in the community. By no means do these indicators comprehensively cover all the dimensions of integration. Information on levels and sources of income would have covered the *equality* dimension; however, a substantial proportion of respondents did not provide information on income. Political *participation* could be measured using other variables such as voting and donating, but volunteering, the variable used here, is probably a better measure since it demands much more from an individual in terms of time, effort, and commitment. Measures of *recognition*, referring to tolerance of pluralism where people of different beliefs and values peacefully coexist (Berger 1998), require data on values that are not available through the survey. *Legitimacy*, which refers to whether organizations (usually, political) duly represent their constituents, is inherently a group attribute, although a broader meaning of legitimacy touches on the basic political right of citizenship and the attendant right to vote (or to select one's representative), which is an individual-level attribute; however, information on voting behaviour was not collected by the survey.

The indicators of *inclusion*, *participation*, and *belonging* are used as dependent variables in a binary logistic regression model that incorporates the major life course stages with a set of individual, family, and community-level variables.[1]

Individual, Family, and Community Characteristics

Our aim is to explore the influences of individual, family, and community characteristics on the three dimensions of integration with the variables described below. Providing theoretical explanations for the influences of various factors on social integration is made difficult by the multidimensionality of the concept, with each characteristic possibly having an impact on each aspect of integration in different ways. For example, the effect of individual education, an indicator of human capital, is expected to be positive on both economic inclusion and political participation. Its effect on belonging, however, is not clear a priori. In addition, theories that seek to explain effects of family and community characteristics have been formulated mainly in relation to their impact on children and youth. The investment (or lack thereof) of family social capital, for example, seems to be a valid explanation for childhood or youth outcome (Coleman 1990; McLanahan and Sandefur 1994). Likewise, effects of community characteristics have been examined mainly for children and youth (Brooks-Gunn et al. 1993; Kohen et al., 1998; Aber et al. 1997). Whether they have a similar impact on integration of adults needs more investigation. In spite of these issues, some tentative explanations are offered below, which we hope will help formulate coherent theories that could relate these characteristics to various dimensions of social integration.

The individual and family characteristics used in this study to examine the differentials in social integration are as follows:

- Demographic variables – *Age group* is expected to capture variation brought about both by life course stage and by cohort membership; and *gender* the differences in men and women's integration.
- Family and living arrangements – Family characteristics such as *marital status* and presence of children indicated here by *living arrangements* can have an influence on integration, particularly for women who take on greater responsibilities for caring (Beaujot 2000). The presence of children could be a hindrance to economic inclusion but it could also encourage volunteering (Devlin 2001; Jones 2001; Ravanera, Beaujot, and Rajulton 2002).
- Human capital and health – *Education* as indicator of skills and knowledge is expected to positively affect integration, particularly through economic inclusion and participation in organizations (Ravanera, Beaujot, and Rajulton 2002; Ravanera, Rajulton, and Turcotte 2003). Healthy individuals (as indicated by self-rated *health status* and self-reported *activity limitation*) are also more able to be economically included and to actively participate in organizations (Kawachi, Wilkinson, and Kennedy 1999; Kawachi and Berkman 2000.).
- Culture and social network – Diverse cultures promote social integration differentially, especially through participation in organizations and community involvement. A broad indicator of culture is *first language* learned at home. Social networks also facilitate economic inclusion, promote political participation, and engender a strong sense of belonging to communities. *Immigration status* and *attendance at religious functions* are included to capture differences not only in culture and values but also the extent of social networks.

For community-level characteristics, we have included the following variables derived for enumeration areas from the 1996 census that were appended to the survey data.

- Age structure – Communities are characterized by age structure of the resident population, for example, retirement communities where elderly persons predominate or university communities populated mainly by young individuals. To capture the influence on patterns of integration or the predominance of a certain age group in a community, we include two variables: *proportion of population under 29 years of age and proportion of population age 60 and older.*
- Opportunity structures – Opportunities for economic inclusion or political participation may be closely linked to the *location and size of the communities. Proportion below the low-income cut-off* and *proportion with post-secondary education* are also used as indicators of availability of human or material resources in the community.
- Predominance and homogeneity of values – Predominance and homogeneity of values in communities may explain differentials in social integration, particularly regarding the sense of belonging. The *proportion of immigrants* is used as an indicator of homogeneity of values in communities, that is, the lower the proportion of immigrants, the more homogeneous the values in the community. And, as an indicator of predominance of traditional family values in the community, we use the low *proportion of separated/divorced.*

The discussion below starts with age differentials in integration that generally depict life course and birth cohort effects. This is followed by a discussion of the impact of family changes, human capital and health, culture and social networks, and community characteristics. The final section discusses the implications of the findings for policies.

Age Differentials in Integration: Life Course and Cohort Effects

To get a definitive contour of integration over the life course, we need longitudinal data for a number of cohorts. As our data are cross-sectional, the best that we could do is to assume that the experiences of the respondents at various ages are similar to what would be experienced by a synthetic cohort as its members move from one life stage to another. The differences in integration by age could then be interpreted as *life course effects.* An alternative interpretation of age differentials could be *cohort effects,* that is, the process of social integration is unique to members of that cohort and would not necessarily be experienced by succeeding cohorts.

TABLE 11.1 Proportions (%) Who Are Canadians Aged 15 and Older, Employed and/or Students, Who Volunteer, and Who Have a Strong Sense of Belonging, by Age Group and Sex, 1998

Age group	Employed and/or students		Volunteer		Sense of belonging	
	Male	Female	Male	Female	Male	Female
15–19	89.3	84.4	38.0	46.0	70.5	60.4
20–24	84.5	72.7	24.6	35.1	44.9	57.5
25–29	89.9	64.1	29.5	32.6	54.9	52.5
30–34	91.1	60.6	27.3	33.0	54.2	59.5
35–39	89.6	59.0	38.4	42.1	59.9	64.1
40–44	88.8	61.1	36.3	39.9	65.1	67.1
45–49	85.3	64.3	39.2	40.6	65.1	71.7
50–54	83.9	51.6	35.4	33.1	68.9	67.4
55–59	62.3	36.5	31.1	33.9	67.3	68.5
60–64	34.9	15.9	32.3	28.6	75.8	70.8
65–69	14.4	2.8	25.8	30.7	77.9	71.5
70–74	6.4	0.0	35.4	31.6	80.0	74.1
≥75	1.6	0.0	22.8	15.1	72.9	70.4

Source: GSS 1998.

Table 11.1 shows by age groups the percentages of men and women who are economically included, politically participating through volunteering, and who have a strong sense of belonging to communities. For a life course interpretation, these percentages or proportions could also be broadly taken as an individual's chances of being included, participating, or belonging. Integration through economic inclusion for both men and women is high at younger ages and starts to decline at around age 50. As seen in Figure 11.1, however, the level of economic inclusion differs between men and women. Men's economic inclusion is high from the start through involvement in both education and work, dips slightly as transition to work occurs, and remains high at mid-life before starting to decline as retirement age approaches. Women's level of inclusion is similar to men's at youngest ages (15–19) when inclusion is mainly through education. The divergence in inclusion by gender starts at about the time of family formation with the gap widening at mid-life but narrowing towards later life as both men and women retire from work.

Participation through volunteering is high when men and women are in their teens but decreases at about the time of transition to adult-hood (table 11.1 and figure 11.2). Between the ages of 20 and 35, young adults complete schooling, enter the workforce, form families, and make changes in residence, all of which reduce time and motivation for volunteering. At mid-life, volunteering is at its highest, most likely influenced by presence of children but also by other factors such as higher income and education (Ravanera, Beaujot, and Rajulton 2002). At later life, the proportion volunteering gradually decreases with higher levels at ages 70 to 74 but substantial decline by age 75, possibly because of age-related changes in health status. Women are only slightly more likely to volunteer than men in both early and mid-life stages, which implies that their lower economic inclusion is not fully compensated for by integration through participation.

A high proportion of the young feel a strong sense of belonging to communities (table 11.1 and figure 11.3), which is most likely brought about by being part of families embedded in communities as well as by volunteering programs that are available in educational institutions and in communities. The proportion declines in the twenties during the transition to adulthood but starts to increase from age 30 onward. Unlike the trend in volunteering, the sense of belonging does not peak at mid-life but continues to increase with age such that the highest pro-portion with a sense of belonging is at age 70-74 for both men and women. This may be due to factors positively correlated with age such as length of stay in communities and possibly accumulated effects of informal integration through socializing, as well as greater and more frequent contacts with families, neighbours, and friends.

Thus far, we have interpreted the age patterns of inclusion, participa-tion, and belonging in terms of life course effects, as they seem to fit well the broad patterns of school, work, and retirement (mainly for *inclusion*) and the general family life course (for *participation*). However, given the cross-sectional nature of the data used here, we cannot rule out cohort effects, not only for *belonging* but also for *inclusion* and *participation*. The increased sense of belonging over age, for example, could signify that older cohorts have strong attachments to communities that may not necessarily be felt by succeeding cohorts as they age. This is because individual, family and community factors that affect the process of inte-gration vary by cohorts. Cohabitation and divorce, for example, are more prevalent among the younger cohorts; employment over the life course is more likely among younger cohorts of women; and over their life time, a greater proportion of younger cohorts would have lived in

Figure 11.1 Economic inclusion (employed or students), by age and sex (%).

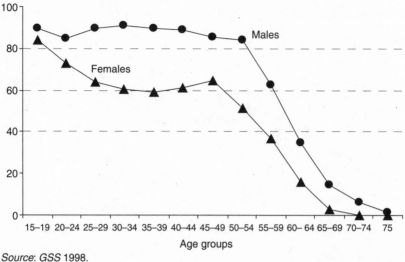

Source: *GSS* 1998.

Figure 11.2 Volunteering, by age and sex.

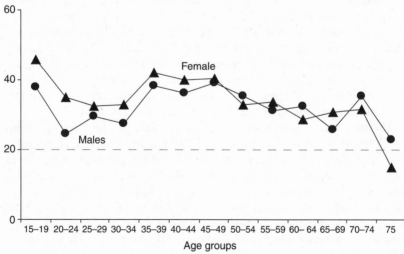

Source: *GSS* 1998.

Figure 11.3 Sense of belonging, by age and sex.

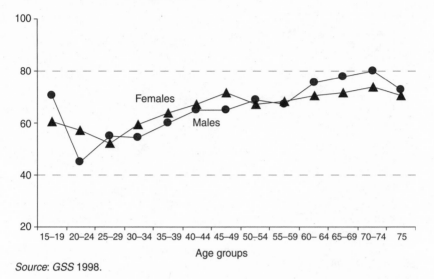

Source: GSS 1998.

urban rather than rural areas – all of which will definitely change the channels and levels of social integration in the future.

In the following sections, we discuss the influences of various factors on integration based on a multivariate logistic regression analysis of each dimension at different stages of the life course, conveniently classified into early life, mid-life, and later life. The results from the multivariate analysis are shown in table 11.2. The exponentials of the binary logistic regression coefficients given in this table indicate that compared with the reference category (with an exponential of 1), those belonging to other categories have higher (greater than 1) or lower (less than 1) likelihood of inclusion, participation, or belonging.

The first two demographic variables (age and gender) show patterns of effects that are similar to those presented in table 11.1 and figures 11.1, 11.2, and 11.3. This implies that controlling for other variables in the multivariate model does not alter the effects of age and of gender. For example, women are less likely to be included at all three stages of the life course. As for participation, the differences between men and women are not statistically significant except at early life when young women also have higher participation. And, at later life, men are more likely to feel a strong sense of belonging.

Impact of Family Transformation and Living Arrangements on Integration

We expect that integration into society would be influenced by family transformations during the past few decades that have brought about conspicuous changes in fertility, divorce, cohabitation, and lone parenthood (see Introduction). Some of these changes can be captured by marital status and living arrangement variables whose categories are tailored to the type of analysis done here. In table 11.2, for example, the living arrangements for young persons are categorized according to whether or not they are living with one or both parents to capture the effect of family structures. For those at mid-life, living arrangements are categorized by the presence of children at various ages. For those in later life, categorization by ages of children is not useful as most of their children would be adults themselves. Similarly, for marital status, 'common law' is a separate category for young persons and for those at mid-life, whereas for elderly persons such a separate category is not warranted as very few of them are cohabiting.

Parental Involvement Matters for Social Integration of Young Persons

Among young persons, the contrast is between those living with one parent and those living with both parents.[2] Table 11.2 shows that compared with young persons living with both parents, those living with lone parents are significantly less likely to be included through schooling or work, and less likely to be volunteering. These negative outcomes could be the result of such factors as inadequacy in parenting and poverty among lone-parent families; in other words, there is less investment of financial and social capital in children in lone-parent families compared with children of intact families. One positive note, however, is that living with a lone parent does not seem to have an adverse effect on the young person's sense of belonging to the community as indicated by the non-significant effect of the living arrangements variable.

Compared with those who are single, young persons who are or were in a relationship (common law, married, or separated/divorced) are less likely to be included, possibly because family formation at an early age could shorten the years spent in schooling and thus curtail accumulation of human capital. Another possible explanation along the lines of social capital is that marital union at a young age could place restrictions on social contacts. While a union could strengthen bonding with partners and families, it may weaken bridging towards a wider network that enhances the chances of inclusion.

Being Married or Living in a Common Law Union Makes a Difference at Mid-life

Table 11.2 shows that among those at mid-life, the married, especially those with children, are less likely to be economically included but more likely to be volunteering when compared with those in common-law relationships. The presence of children, particularly those aged 5 to 12, enhances both volunteering and the sense of belonging. Interpreting the relationship between social integration and types of union (being married or living common law) is best done when we consider women at mid-life. The lifestyle of this group of women, mainly baby boomers, started to diverge from that of the older cohorts but not uniformly. The innovators among them had radically different values and characteristics as demonstrated by their experience of common law unions[3] and by their involvement in the labour force (Ravanera, Rajulton, and Burch 1998; Ravanera, and Rajulton 2003). The difference in social integration by type of union points to a distinction between 'traditional' and 'emergent' types of integration, particularly for women. The 'traditional' channels of integration exemplified by married women give importance to volunteering in organizations and engender a strong sense of belonging to community through activities that are mostly children-related. The 'emergent' channels of integration, however, place more weight on economic inclusion, typified by women in a common law relationship.

Widowhood and Living with Children at Later Life

Table 11.2 shows that among those at later life, the formerly married (widowed, divorced, or separated) are significantly less likely than the married to be economically included. These are predominantly older *widowed* women because (1) women live longer than men, (2) not many elderly persons experienced divorce or separation, and (3) men are more likely to be married or to remarry (Legare *et al.*, 1998). Their living arrangements seem to make a difference. Compared with those who live alone, elderly persons who live with their children only (not with spouse and children) are more likely to be economically included and to feel a strong sense of belonging but they are less likely to be participating. That elderly persons living with their children are more

TABLE 11.2 Exponentials of Coefficients of Binary Logistic Regression of Dimensions of Integration, by Major Age Groups, Individual and Community Characteristics

	Inclusion			Participation			Belonging		
	Youth	Mid-life	Later life	Youth	Mid-life	Later life	Youth	Mid-life	Later life
Individual characteristics									
Demographic characteristics									
Age groups (by years of age)									
Youth / Mid-life / Later									
15–17[a] / 30–34[a] / 55–59[a]	1.00	1.00	1.00	1.00	1.00	1.00	1.00	1.00	1.00
18–19 / 35–39 / 60–64	0.34***	0.95	0.31***	0.59***	1.42***	0.88	0.79	1.07	1.14
20–24 / 40–44 / 65–69	0.21***	1.09	0.08***	0.32***	1.38***	0.83	0.56***	1.35***	1.16
25–29 / 45–49 / 70–74	0.22***	1.02	0.03***	0.33***	1.53***	1.09	0.67**	1.53***	1.46**
50–54 / 75–79		0.67***	0.02***		1.17	0.46***		1.48***	1.05
≥80			0.00			0.45***			0.99
Sex									
Female[a]	1.00	1.00	1.00	1.00	1.00	1.00	1.00	1.00	1.00
Male	2.59***	5.36***	3.24***	0.72***	0.94	1.03	0.99	0.92	1.21*
Family and living arrangements									
Marital status									
Common law[a]	1.00	1.00		1.00	1.00		1.00	1.00	
Married	0.81	0.61***		1.68***	1.41***		1.27	1.15	
Widowed/separated/divorced	1.09	1.09		1.66	0.99		1.23	0.80	
Single	1.60**	0.81		1.49**	1.10		1.20	0.75	
Married or common law[a]			1.00			1.00			1.00
Widowed/separated/divorced			0.40*			0.84			0.81
Single			1.22			0.92			0.88

TABLE 11.2 (Continued)

	Inclusion			Participation			Belonging		
	Youth	Mid-life	Later life	Youth	Mid-life	Later life	Youth	Mid-life	Later life
Living arrangement									
With both parents[a]	1.00			1.00			1.00		
With lone parent	0.61**			0.65***			1.11		
Not with parents	1.29			0.90			1.06		
Alone[a]		1.00	1.00		1.00	1.00		1.00	1.00
With spouse only		1.20	1.08		0.82	0.86		0.81	1.19
With children <5		0.82			1.00			1.09	
With children 5–12		1.04			1.56***			1.59***	
With children ≥13		1.09			1.23			1.24	
Other		1.07	1.99*		0.83	0.73			1.39
With spouse and child(ren)			1.16			0.77			0.88
With child(ren) only			2.50***			0.22***			1.67**
Human capital									
Education									
Some high school or lower[a]	1.00	1.00		1.00	1.00		1.00	1.00	
High school graduate	1.12	1.62***		1.02	1.61***		0.94	1.11	
Some college	2.05***	1.37***		2.44***	2.01***		0.97	0.96	
College/university graduate	2.28***	2.07***		2.34***	2.59***		0.91	0.98	
Elementary[a]			1.00			1.00			1.00
High school			1.16			1.77***			1.09
College			1.51*			3.23***			0.97
Health status									
Poor or fair[a]	1.00	1.00	1.00	1.00	1.00	1.00	1.00	1.00	1.00
Good	1.25	1.58***	1.75***	1.20	0.99	1.62***	1.48**	1.47***	1.70***

TABLE 11.2 (Continued)

	Inclusion			Participation			Belonging		
	Youth	Mid-life	Later life	Youth	Mid-life	Later life	Youth	Mid-life	Later life
Very good or excellent	1.46**	1.46***	1.86***	1.26	1.21*	2.03***	2.18***	2.34***	2.17***
Activity limitation									
No limitation[a]	1.00	1.00	1.00	1.00	1.00	1.00	1.00	1.00	1.00
Some limitation	0.66**	0.34***	0.24***	1.49**	1.00	1.32**	1.47**	1.17	1.02
Culture and social network									
First language									
English[a]	1.00	1.00	1.00	1.00	1.00	1.00	1.00	1.00	1.00
French	0.83	0.71***	1.16	0.90	0.69***	1.06	0.94	0.71***	0.76**
Other	1.53	0.84	1.16	1.12	0.61***	0.49***	1.55**	0.97	0.99
Immigration status (see note b)									
Born in Canada[a]	1.00	1.00	1.00	1.00	1.00	1.00	1.00	1.00	1.00
Long-time immigrants	0.66	1.54***	1.68***	1.48	0.70***	1.13	0.74	0.78**	0.68***
Recent immigrants	1.26	0.62***	1.57	0.50***	0.41***	0.79	0.65**	0.50***	0.62**
Religious attendance									
At least once a week[a]	1.00	1.00	1.00	1.00	1.00	1.00	1.00	1.00	1.00
Sometimes	2.01***	1.34***	1.55***	0.67***	0.53***	0.39***	0.50***	0.76***	0.55***
Never	1.65***	1.49***	0.89	0.45***	0.37***	0.25***	0.44***	0.49***	0.34***
No religion	1.34	1.24*	1.28	0.48***	0.53***	0.39***	0.41***	0.45***	0.39***

TABLE 11.2 (Continued)

	Inclusion			Participation			Belonging		
	Youth	Mid-life	Later life	Youth	Mid-life	Later life	Youth	Mid-life	Later life
Community characteristics									
Population structure									
Aged ≤29 years (%)									
0–30%[a]	1.00	1.00	1.00	1.00	1.00	1.00	1.00	1.00	1.00
31–40%	0.75	0.83	1.33	1.15	1.20	0.75	1.11	1.04	0.72*
41–45%	0.58*	0.85	1.25	1.16	1.09	0.94	1.29	1.03	0.72
≥46%	0.65	0.83	1.25	1.24	1.19	0.79	0.91	1.32	0.63*
Aged ≥60									
0–9%[a]	1.00	1.00	1.00	1.00	1.00	1.00	1.00	1.00	1.00
10–19%	1.29	1.08	0.77	1.38**	1.13	1.17	0.93	1.36***	1.26
20–29%	1.45	0.80	0.52***	1.34	0.89	1.20	1.14	1.54***	1.36
≥30%	0.96	1.23	1.11	2.19***	1.51**	1.04	1.29	1.68***	1.21
Opportunity structure									
Location and size of population									
Rural[a]	1.00	1.00	1.00	1.00	1.00	1.00	1.00	1.00	1.00
Urban <1,000–99,999	1.13	1.19	0.95	0.78	0.86	0.90	0.79	0.98	0.83
Urban ≥100,000	0.95	1.25*	1.09	0.82	0.73***	0.63***	0.71**	0.71***	0.62***
Low income (%)									
0–9%[a]	1.00	1.00	1.00	1.00	1.00	1.00	1.00	1.00	1.00
10–19%	0.91	1.20*	1.04	1.17	1.17*	1.02	1.28*	1.01	1.05
≥20%	0.82	1.24*	0.83	1.20	1.03	0.88	1.36**	1.12	1.34**
With post-secondary education									
0–40%[a]	1.00	1.00	1.00	1.00	1.00	1.00	1.00	1.00	1.00

TABLE 11.2 (Concluded)

	Inclusion			Participation			Belonging		
	Youth	Mid-life	Later life	Youth	Mid-life	Later life	Youth	Mid-life	Later life
41–60%	1.35*	1.16	1.00	0.82	1.01	0.85	0.92	1.32***	1.13
≥61%	1.36	1.36**	0.82	1.36*	1.30**	1.29	0.99	1.25**	1.41**
Predominant culture and values									
Immigrants (%)									
0%[a]	1.00	1.00	1.00	1.00	1.00	1.00	1.00	1.00	1.00
1–5%	1.67**	0.82	1.40	0.76	1.03	1.30	0.96	0.83	0.61**
6–14%	1.59*	1.08	2.26***	0.94	1.07	1.77***	0.95	0.84	0.67*
≥15%	2.06***	0.95	2.20**	0.85	0.83	1.58**	0.71	0.86	0.73
Separated/divorced (%)									
0–3%[a]	1.00	1.00	1.00	1.00	1.00	1.00	1.00	1.00	1.00
4–8%	0.93	0.86	1.00	0.95	0.93	1.07	0.78*	0.95	0.82
≥9%	0.88	0.76**	1.02	0.87	0.83	1.04	0.50***	0.77**	0.59***
Constant	1.42	0.86	0.13***	0.70	0.35***	0.27***	2.80***	1.06	4.80***
Weighted cases (n)	2,188	4,683	2,593	2,206	4,786	2,636	2,169	4,719	2,538
R^2	16.1%	26.0%	50.2%	12.1%	15.1%	19.9%	11.0%	11.8%	12.7%

Source: GSS 1998.
[a] Reference variable, group, or value.
[b] Recent immigrants for the youth and mid-life groups are those who came to Canada between 1985 and 1998; because of the small sample size, recent immigrants for the group in the later life stage are those who came to Canada between 1970 and 1998.
$*p < .10; **p < .05; ***p < .01$.

likely to be employed could be a positive point; however, this may camouflage their vulnerable conditions. It may be a matter of necessity rather than choice that they work, that is, they work to support themselves and their children (Legare *et al.*, 1998).

The results in table 11.2 also point to the more vulnerable conditions of elderly women living *alone* in comparison with those who are married. However, compared with those in institutions (who were excluded in the survey), these women may be in a better position – they may be healthier and have non-employment income, for example, pension and government transfers, that allows them to live independently.

Differential Effects of Education and Health on Dimensions of Integration

As the results in table 11.2 show, human capital, generally indicated by level of education, has a significant impact on social integration but mainly on economic and political dimensions. The young and those at mid-life who have had college and university education are more likely to be included and to be volunteering. As for elderly persons, the differential impact of education is greater for volunteering than for inclusion, as many of them would have retired and those with higher education are more likely to shift to volunteering from an active work life. A remarkable finding is that education does not at all have an effect on belonging at each major stage of the life course, which could be a positive point indicating society's inclusiveness regardless of levels of human capital.

Compared with those in poor health, those in good or excellent health are more likely to be economically included and feel a strong sense of belonging at all stages of the life course. Health status affects participation as well but its effect is highly significant only among elderly persons. Health status influences integration through *selection*, that is, those who are healthy select themselves into favourable economic and social positions. However, the causation could also be the other way, that is, integration through inclusion, belonging, or volunteering may contribute to good health.

Activity limitation significantly decreases the likelihood of inclusion, indicating that the market is not welcoming of those with disabilities. A positive point though is that young persons with activity limitations but who are otherwise healthy are more likely to volunteer and more likely to feel a strong sense of belonging. Elderly persons with activity limitation are also more likely to volunteer, and like those at mid-life, having activity limitation does not affect their sense of belonging.

Influence of Culture and Social Networks on Integration

Among young persons, culture as measured by mother tongue, has no effect on inclusion or participation. The finding that young persons whose first language is neither French nor English are more likely to feel a strong sense of belonging to community may be an indication that young persons are more tolerant of diversity. In contrast, culture seems to matter for those at mid- and later life in that French and 'other' mother tongue are associated with lower likelihood of integration in at least one of the three channels of integration. However, these findings need to be examined further. The difference in sense of belonging to community among the French and English, for example, might simply be due to difference in concepts of 'belonging' or of 'community' between the two language groups. In addition, because of small sample size, the 'other' language category lumps together several different cultures.

An indicator of the extent of social networks and of culture is immigration status. For inclusion, the effects are mainly seen among those at mid- and later life.[4] Compared with those born in Canada, long-term immigrants[5] are more likely to be economically included whereas more recent immigrants, particularly those at mid-life, are less likely to be economically included. Long-term immigrants have higher levels of education compared to those born in Canada and are more likely to have come from traditional sources of immigration, mainly, Europe and the United States. As for recent immigrants at mid-life, a possible reason for the lower level of economic inclusion, particularly among visible minorities and women, is the unequal opportunities that they encounter (Li 2003: 88-91). Several studies have pointed to structural barriers to economic equality such as non-recognition or devaluation of credentials obtained outside North America and the requirement for Canadian work experience (Basavarajappa and Verma 1985; Rajagopal 1990; McDade 1988).

The advantage that long-term immigrants have for economic inclusion does not seem to hold for participation and belonging. Immigrants, whether recent or long term, are less likely to feel a strong sense of belonging to community. Recent immigrants, in particular, are also less likely to participate through volunteering. A possible reason is a less dense social network, that is, they probably lack information and contacts that facilitate involvement. It is also possible that there are differences in values that hinder a feeling of identity and belonging to their community. This is speculative and needs to be checked with data on values and attitudes, which are, however, not available through the time-use surveys.

An indicator of both social network and values is religious attendance. Those who frequently attend religious functions are more likely to feel a strong sense of belonging and to participate through volunteering, which is not surprising given that religious functions bring together individuals of similar values and religious organizations provide the means and facilities for formal volunteering. However, there seems to be a downside in that those who attend religious functions weekly are less likely to be economically included, which seems to hold particularly for young persons and those at mid-life. One possible explanation could be that religious persons value market attachment less. Involvement with religion may be linked to traditional family values that, for example, lead particularly women to be stay-at-home moms or to work only on a part-time basis while raising children. Another possible explanation is that this may reflect the distinction between 'bonding' and 'bridging' social capital (Gittell and Vidal 1998; Woolcock 2001; Granovetter 1995); that is, while belonging to a closely knit religious group creates a strong bond with members, this may impede a bridge to the wider outside group, a link that facilitates economic inclusion.

Impact of Community Characteristics on Integration

We have categorized the community variables included in the analysis into indicators of population structure, opportunity structure, and predominance and homogeneity of values in order to facilitate the discussion of their effects (shown also in Table 11.2). As noted above, however, the explanations are tentative, and there is a need for further theorizing particularly as to the processes through which the effects are mediated.

Population Structure: Predominance of Elderly Population Promotes Sense of Belonging

Population structure influences the sense of belonging, depending on the individual's life course stage. The higher the percentage of persons age 60 and older, the greater the sense of belonging *among those at mid-*

life. This is also true for elderly persons although the coefficients are not significant. This could be a 'contagion' effect, that is, as elderly persons are more likely to feel a strong sense of belonging (age effect), it is possible that their sense of belonging is passed on through their interaction or socializing with not only persons of similar age but also with those younger than themselves. In contrast to this contagion effect, we also note that the higher the proportion of the young people in a community, the lower the sense of belonging among those at later life.

Communities with the highest percentage of elderly population seem to be conducive to volunteering among young persons and those at mid-life. There may be a greater need for volunteers in these communities, and young persons and those at mid life respond to such needs.

Opportunity Structures: Does Community Affluence Affect Integration?

While we have assumed that opportunity structures, indicated by size and location of communities that vary in physical or financial resources, the results show that this variable captures other aspects of communities as well. At each age group, those in large urban areas are less likely to feel a strong sense of belonging and those at mid-life and later life are less likely to participate. These effects are highly significant and validate the commonplace knowledge that people are more closely knit in rural communities than in big cities. In terms of social capital, networking in rural communities may be more intensive, and the norms governing relationships may be different from those in urban areas.

In contrast, size and location has positive though weak effects on economic inclusion. The lower likelihood of economic inclusion in rural areas is mainly seen for those at mid-life, most likely because young persons in search of higher education and work would have already left for bigger urban areas and most elderly persons would have already retired. (See discussion below of effects of proportion of immigrants.) Residents of urban areas are more dependent on the market for integration, whereas residents of rural areas give greater importance to participation in organization and belonging – an urban-rural divide in modes of integration.

The presence of people with post-secondary education in communities has positive though only moderately significant effects on the three channels of integration. Among the young and those at mid-life, persons living in communities that have the highest percentage of population with post-secondary education are more likely to be economically included and to participate through volunteering. They are also more likely to feel a strong sense of belonging, though this is true mainly among those at mid-life and at later life. It could be that a high proportion of highly educated individuals in communities attracts financial investment or generates it from within the community itself. As for volunteering, a 'bandwagon' effect may be operating, that is, since those with high education have a greater propensity for volunteering, their presence encourages more volunteers. In addition, a more highly educated population is possibly more tolerant, which helps in promoting a strong sense of belonging.

The sense of belonging among young and elderly persons is stronger in communities with greater proportions of low-income earners, though this effect is only moderately significant. This seems counterintuitive in a society that values material affluence. Nevertheless, it is possible that a certain level of neediness or shared feelings of vulnerability and insecurity bring people closer together.

Do Community Values Affect Integration?

We assumed that a low proportion of immigrants is an indication of homogeneity of population and hence, of values. Thus, we expected that this variable would have a significant effect mainly on the sense of belonging. While the direction of effect is as expected – that is, the lower the proportion of immigrants, the greater the sense of belonging for all age groups, it is statistically significant only for those in later life.[6] In contrast, economic inclusion is highest for young and elderly persons in places with high proportions of immigrants. Since immigrants generally gravitate to big cities, this variable captures opportunities in big urban areas where these opportunities are possibly linked to a climate of tolerance for diversity and the dynamism that immigrants bring.

The predominance of traditional family values as measured by the low percentage separated or divorced in the community is associated with a stronger sense of belonging for all three age groups. An explanation in terms of social capital – that is, availability of more adults (most likely, women) devoting time to children and youth – could be invoked for this effect on young persons. As the effect holds for those at mid-life and later life as well, this requires an explanation in line with values related to families. However, as with other community-level variables, the mechanism by which predominant community values affect integration needs further study.

Discussion and Conclusion

The age patterns suggest a general contour of integration over the life course. Youth seems to be an enviable stage, with young persons formally included and participating through their schools and feeling a strong sense of belonging to their communities, though the mainly positive response to the question on sense of belonging could be simply reflective of young people's optimism and their desire to fit in. Transition to adulthood brings changes in channels of integration, when the young move on to get work and find neither motivation nor time for volunteering and feel no strong attachment to their communities. But gradually conditions change yet again so that by mid-life economic inclusion and political participation are at their highest. At later life, people disengage from work, shift to volunteering in organizations, and reap the benefits of lifelong socialization and interaction in terms of a strong sense of belonging to their community.

There are deviations from this general pattern as integration is influenced by individual and family characteristics and by the characteristics of communities in which individuals reside. Men, the highly educated, and the healthy are more integrated through economic inclusion. People with children, those born in Canada and residents of rural areas feel a stronger sense of belonging than others do. Moreover, this broad picture of integration over the life course is drawn from analysis of cross-sectional data and the analysis of variations indicates that the pattern of integration may be modified as younger cohorts go through their own life course.

The life courses of the baby boomers (those at mid-life in our analysis) have deviated from those of older cohorts in a number of ways (Péron et al., 1999; Beaujot 2000; Ravanera, Rajulton, and Burch 1998; Ravanera et al., 2002). They have, for example, changed the norm on family formation through popularization of cohabitation; they have had fewer children, and many have gone through divorce and separation. In particular, women have higher rates of participation in the labour force. It would not be surprising, therefore, if their integration at later life would be different from those of older cohorts. The deviation could come in later disengagement from the labour force but also in different means of economic inclusion such as through after-retirement careers, return to colleges and universities, part-time work, or other novel work arrangements. They may also engage in different ways of participation, as those in full-time employment have less time to volunteer but have more opportunities to join associations and clubs and more resources to donate to organizations (Ravanera, Beaujot, and Rajulton 2002).

Succeeding cohorts have continued the family and life course trends set by the boomers, and have even greater rates of cohabitation and fewer children, and for women, greater involvement in paid employment, which, as shown above, are factors that impact inclusion, participation, and belonging. As young women's integration deviates from that of older cohorts of women, it tends to become similar to that of men's. However, while gains are being made towards gender equality, the traditional gender division of labour persists. From young adulthood, women are still more likely to take on greater responsibilities for the home (and for children, if any) and thus still less likely than men to be economically included (Ravanera, Rajulton, and Turcotte 2003). With high rates of family dissolution, lower levels of economic inclusion could have adverse consequences not only for the women themselves but also for their children, which could come in later life (Beaujot and Ravanera, 2001, and citations therein). In Canada, as in other western countries, men have increased their share in domestic and volunteering work but not enough to substantially reduce the caring responsibilities of women. This is understandable since the family as a whole will lose if men, who are generally paid higher, reduce paid work for domestic work (Esping-Andersen 1999: 58–9). Further improvement in women's economic inclusion will, therefore, greatly depend on the assumption of responsibilities for caring (particularly for children and elderly persons) by the state and the market.

Education and health are strong determinants of economic inclusion and participation. Elderly persons in future will be more highly educated and in better health and will live longer than the current elderly persons. However, while high education and good health are necessary, they are not sufficient conditions for extending economic inclusion to later life. Other conditions such as labour shortages and the changing nature of work together with education and health could help bring about an increase in the inclusion of elderly persons (Foot and Gibson 1994; McDonald and Chen 1994). Even with these conditions, the increased economic inclusion of elderly persons will not come about automatically. Employers and governments will need to exert effort and offer incentives to make a longer stay in the labour force worthwhile for elderly persons.

In a similar way, participation through volunteering can also be made more attractive. Contrary to the concept of social economy, which proposes that economic inclusion brings about political participation and belonging (Jenson 1998, citing Paquette 1995, and Bouchard, Labrie, and Noël 1996), our analysis of interrelation among the three dimensions show that political participation is significantly associated with belonging but economic inclusion is not.[7] Moreover, our analysis using the 2000 National Survey of Giving, Participating and Volunteering reveals that for men and women, full-time employment is negatively related to volunteering and that for women, it is positively associated with giving and association membership (Ravanera, Beaujot, and Rajulton 2002). It would seem, then, that efforts of both private and government sectors to increase participation, separate from those directed towards economic inclusion, could contribute towards greater social integration, not only in the political dimension of participation but also in the social dimension of belonging. (See Brock (2001) for a discussion of the role of the state in promoting voluntary action and civil society.)

Compared with economic *inclusion* and political *participation*, sense of *belonging* seems to be less influenced by individual characteristics. Those with low education, for example, feel as strong a sense of belonging as those who are highly educated, implying that individuals are integrated regardless of their knowledge, skills, or abilities, which is a positive point for an inclusive society. However, there are segments of the population that are less likely to feel a strong sense of belonging. Immigrants, for example, improve integration through economic inclusion as they stay longer in the country but a longer stay may not be sufficient to bring their participation and belonging up to par with the Canadian-born. Thus, efforts in the voluntary sector of encouraging participation might be helpful for all immigrants.

One of the values of children that is not often recognized is their role in encouraging parents' participation through volunteering and enhancing parents' sense of belonging. This is one more reason for concern over the currently low levels of fertility. While direct policies that encourage fertility would probably not be effective, those that could facilitate caring for children (e.g., childcare facilities, early childhood programs, parenting education) might help convey the message that children are important for social integration as well.

The types of communities wherein individuals reside influence the process of integration. Rural and large urban areas offer different opportunity structures that result in varying means of integration. Urban areas are somewhat better for economic inclusion while rural areas are significantly more conducive to participation and belonging. The distinction may be inherent to rural and urban areas and may not be amenable to interventions. For example, urban residents may be selected for their preference for less than tight-knit relationships within their communities, that is, privacy may be a greater value among the urbanites. Another distinction between the rural and urban residents may be a differential concept of community. The 'community' tapped by the survey may be one that is bounded by geographic space and thus possibly more relevant to those in the rural areas. Among those in the urban areas, 'community' may be a social construct unbounded by geography; that is, their 'community' could include persons related through work, leisure, common causes or interests, and these persons may not necessarily live in the neighbourhood. In spite of these differences, however, attempts could be undertaken to make urban areas more rural-like in participation and belonging, and rural areas more urban-like in economic inclusion though how is beyond the scope of this study.

Including community characteristics in this study has led to findings that require theoretical explanations for the mechanisms through which their effects operate. For example, communities rich in human resources (i.e., places with high proportions of highly educated individuals) enhance social integration through economic inclusion, participation, and belonging. Our results also show that communities with high proportions of immigrants are conducive to economic inclusion (or, as mentioned above, immigrants gravitate to places that have more economic opportunities). Moreover, communities with high proportions of separated and divorced people seem to be detrimental to integration. All this points to the need to investigate further the links between community characteristics and social integration.

This study has dealt with three dimensions of integration but still falls short of providing a full picture of integration. First, it does not include the economic dimension of *equality*, which possibly taps economic integration better than does *inclusion*. In other words, one can be employed (or included) and yet be so poor as to feel excluded. As seen above, elderly women living with children and lone parents, for example, may be more included as they work out of necessity to support themselves but they may, in fact, be poorer than women who are unemployed but living with their spouses. Second, the sociocultural dimension of integration is indicated only by sense of *belonging* to community, which is a big concept that is measured here by a fairly general question. *Recognition*, measured by values and attitudes, particularly trust and tolerance of diversity, might be as important as or more important than belonging. An individual could feel a strong sense of belonging to his or her community and yet be intolerant of those who do not belong to the same community or those different from themselves. Third, as for political dimension, while volunteering may be a good measure of *participation*, other means such as donations and association memberships might be as important as volunteering, particularly for those who are unable to find time to volunteer but are keen on being politically involved. Moreover, the study does not include an analysis of voting behaviour, which could be an individual-level measure of how well political institutions are representative of the constituents and thus tap on *legitimacy* of political institutions. Should measures for all the dimensions become available, an important area of research would be to examine the relative importance of each dimension and the relationships among them.

NOTES

1 The use of community-level, together with individual-level variables suggests multi-level analysis. However, the available data (survey data merged with variables derived from the census for enumeration area) do not allow the use of multi-level techniques as, in most instances, there is only one respondent for each enumeration area.

2 Those who are no longer living with parents are a select group in that they have become independent at a younger age.

3 In the sample of women at mid-life, 9% are in common-law relationship; 13% are separated, divorced, or widowed; and 68% are married. Some of the married, separated, or divorced women may have previously cohabited. A rough estimate of the 'innovators' or those who would have differed in values, attitudes, and behaviour is about 10% to 25%. A more accurate proportion cannot be determined, as the survey did not gather information on marital histories.

4 In an earlier study (Ravanera, Rajulton, and Turcotte 2003), young recent immigrants were found to be significantly more likely to be included in the economy, and we explained this mainly as the effect of greater human capital or higher education. This study shows that the likelihood of being included is still higher for recent immigrants, but the effect is no longer significant possibly because the level of education (not controlled for in the earlier study) captures some of the effect of immigration status.

5 Because of the small number of respondents, recent immigrants among elderly persons include those who came to Canada between 1970 and 1998, and
  thus, many of them are in fact long-term immigrants. That there is similarity
  between immigrants classified here as 'long-term' and 'recent' is reflected in
  the exponentials that are largely similar for both groups of immigrants (see
  table 11.2).
6 There are two more community-level variables included in this study that
  were not included in an earlier study on youth integration (Ravanera, Rajulton, and Turcotte 2003): proportion of the population that is aged 60 and
  over and proportion with low income. This could be a reason for the non-
  significance (though in the same direction) of the effect of the proportion of
  immigrants, which was statistically significant in the earlier study.
7 A binary regression of belonging with inclusion and participation as explanatory variables, controlling for other individual and family variables, shows
  the following exponentials of coefficients:

	Youth	Mid-life	Later life
Volunteer	1.37***	1.94***	1.88***
Employed	1.15	0.93	0.90

***$p < .01$.

REFERENCES

Aber, J.L., M.A. Gephart, J. Brooks-Gunn, and J.P. Connell. 1997. 'Development
    in Context: Implications for Studying Neighborhood Effect.' In J. Brooks-
    Gunn, G.J. Duncan, and J.L. Aber (eds.), *Neighborhood Poverty: Context and
    Consequences for Children* 44–61. New York: Russell Sage Foundation.
Basavarajappa, K.G., and R.B.P. Verma. 1985. 'Asian Immigrants in Canada:
    Some Findings from the 1981 Census.' *International Migration* 23(1): 97–121.
Beaujot. R. 2000. *Earning and Caring in Canadian Families*. Peterborough: Broad-
    view Press.
Beaujot, R. and Z.R. Ravanera. 2001. *An Interpretation of Family Change with
    Implications for Social Cohesion*. Discussion Paper No. 01-1. London, Ont.:
    Population Studies Centre, University of Western Ontario.
Berger, P. (Ed.). 1998. *The Limits of Social Cohesion: Conflict and Mediation in Plu-
    ralist Societies*. A Report of the Bertelsmann Foundation to the Club of Rome.
    Boulder, CO: Westview.

Bernard, P. 1999. *Social Cohesion: A Critique*. Discussion Paper No. F-09. Ottawa: Canadian Policy Research Network.

Bouchard, C., V. Labrie, and A. Noël. 1996. *Chacun sa part*. Rapport des trios members du Comité externe de réforme de la sécurité du revenu. Montreal.

Brock, K.L. 2001. 'Promoting Voluntary Action and Civil Society through the State.' *Isuma* 2(3): 53–61.

Brooks-Gunn, J., G.J. Duncan, P.K. Klebanov, and N. Sealand. 1993. 'Do Neighborhoods Influence Child and Adolescent Development? *American Journal of Sociology* 99(2): 353–95.

Coleman, J.S. 1990. *Foundations of Social Theory*. Cambridge, MA: Belknap.

Devlin, R.A. 2001. 'Volunteers and the Paid Labour Market.' *Isuma* 2(3): 62–8.

Esping-Andersen, G. 1999. *Social Foundations of Postindustrial Economies*. Oxford: Oxford University Press.

Foot, D.K., and K.J. Gibson. 1994. 'Population Aging in the Canadian Labour Force: Changes and Challenges.' In V. Marshall and B. McPherson (eds.), *Aging: Canadian Perspectives*, 97–112. Peterborough: Broadview Press.

Gittel, R., and A. Vidal. 1998. *Community Organizing: Building Social Capital as a Development Strategy*. Newbury Park, CA: Sage.

Granovetter, M.S. 1995. 'The Economic Sociology of Firms and Entrepreneurs.' In A. Portes (ed.), *The Economic Sociology of Immigration*, 128–65. New York: Russell Sage Foundation.

Jenson, J. 1998. *Mapping Social Cohesion: The State of Canadian Research*. Study No. F-03. Ottawa: Canadian Policy Research Network.

Jones, F. 2001. 'Volunteering Parents: Who Volunteers and How Are Their Lives Affected?' *Isuma* 2(3): 69–74.

Kawachi, I., and L. Berkman. 2000. 'Social Cohesion, Social Capital, and Health.' In L. Berkman and I. Kawachi (eds.), *Social Epidemiology*, 174–90. Oxford: Oxford University Press.

Kawachi, I., R.G. Wilkinson, and B.P. Kennedy. (Eds.). 1999. 'Introduction.' In *The Society and Population Health Reader: Income Inequality and Health*, xi-xxxiv. New York: New Press.

Kohen, D.E., C. Hertzman, C. and J. Brooks-Gunn. 1998. *Neighbourhood Influences on Children's School Readiness*. Working Paper Series of the Applied Research Branch of the Human Resources Development Canada. First Internet Edition. http://www11.sde.gc.ca/en/cs/sp/sde/pkrf/publications/rresearch/1998-000171/SP-361-02-01E.pdf

Légaré, J., L. Martel, L.O. Stone, H. Denis. 1998. *Living Arrangements of Older Persons in Canada: Effect on their Socio-economic Conditions*. Geneva: U.N. Publications.

Li, P. 2003. *Destination Canada: Immigration Debates and Issues*. Oxford: Oxford University Press.

McDonald, L., and M.Y.T. Chen. 1994. 'The Youth Freeze and the Retirement Bulge: Older Workers and the Impending Labour Shortage.' In V. Marshall and B. McPherson (eds.), *Aging: Canadian Perspectives*, 113–39. Peterborough: Broadview Press.

McDade, K. 1988. *Barriers to Recognition of the Credentials of Immigrants in Canada*. Ottawa: Institute for Research on Public Policy.

McLanahan, S., and G. Sandefur. 1994. *Growing Up with a Single Parent: What Hurts. What Helps*. Cambridge, MA: Harvard University Press.

Paquette, P. 1995. 'L'économie sociale, autre chose qu'un gadget.' *Nouvelles Pratiques Sociales* 9(1): 15–32.

Péron, Y., H. Desrosiers, H. Juby, E. Lapierre-Adamcyk, C. Le Bourdais, N. Marcil-Gratton, and J. Mongeau. 1999. *Canadian Families at the Approach of the Year 2000*. Ottawa: Statistics Canada, cat. no. 96-321.

Rajagopal, I. 1990. 'The Glass Ceiling in the Vertical Mosaic: Indian Immigrants to Canada. *Canadian Ethnic Studies* 22(1): 96–105.

Ravanera, Z.R., R. Beaujot, and F. Rajulton. 2002. 'The Family and Political Dimension of Social Cohesion: Analyzing the Link Using the 2000 National Survey on Giving, Volunteering and Participating.' Paper presented at the annual meeting of the Canadian Population Society,. Toronto. (University of Western Ontario, 26 May–1 June. Population Studies Centre Discussion Paper 02-07.)

Ravanera, Z.R., and F. Rajulton. 2003. 'Integration at Mid-Life: Analysis of General Social Surveys on Time Use.' Paper presented at the annual meeting of the Canadian Population Society, (University of Western Ontario, Halifax, 28 May–4 June. Population Studies Centre Discussion Paper 03-09.)

Ravanera, Z.R., F. Rajulton, and T.K. Burch. 1998. 'Early Life Transitions of Canadian Women: A Cohort Analysis of Timing, Sequences, and Variations.' *European Journal of Population* 14(2): 179–204.

Ravanera, Z.R., F. Rajulton, T.K. Burch, and C. Le Bourdais. 2002. 'The Early Life Courses of Canadian Men: Analysis of Timing and Sequences of Events.' *Canadian Studies in Population* 29(2): 293–312.

Ravanera, Z.R., F. Rajulton, and P. Turcotte. 2003. 'Youth Integration and Social Capital: An Analysis of the General Social Surveys on Time Use.' *Youth and Society* 35(2): 158–82.

Statistics Canada. 1999. General Social Survey, Cycle 12, Time Use Survey, 1998: User's Guide. Ottawa. Statistics Canada. Cat. No. 12 M0012 GPE.

Woolcock, M. (2001). 'The Place of Social Capital in Understanding Social and Economic Outcomes.' *Isuma* 2(1): 11–17.

12 Conclusion: Family Change and the Challenge for Social Policy

KEVIN MCQUILLAN

A Canadian who had been absent from the country since the early 1960s could be forgiven for reacting with astonishment to the changes that have taken place in family life in Canada. Looking back, we can see that the early years of the 1960s marked the beginning of the end for a model of family life that was relatively short-lived but had a profound influence on our social institutions and on popular perceptions of the contours of family living. The buoyant prosperity of the 1950s allowed the realization of a model of family life built on early and near universal marriage and a rising fertility rate. Low rates of divorce and declining mortality rates meant that the proportion of lone-parent families touched a historic low. Although more women were moving into the labour force, the great majority of children were being raised in families where the father was employed while the mother remained at home with the children. Yet no sooner had this model of the family reached its apogee that it began to come apart. Table 12.1 presents several indicators related to family life in 1961, just before the end of the period we now refer to as the baby boom, and 2001. The differences are dramatic, though by now well known. Age at marriage has risen, and far fewer women are married even when in their early thirties. Cohabitation has emerged as an alternative to legal marriage, but even when we include such unions, we find a larger share of women in their childbearing years are not living in any form of union. Partly as a result, the fertility rate has declined dramatically, while the proportion of children born to unmarried parents has increased. Of themselves, these changes need not imply greater instability in family life, but growing rates of divorce combined with the fact that cohabiting relationships have proven to be more prone to dissolution than legal marriages has

TABLE 12.1 Selected Indicators of Family Living in Canada, 1961 and 2001

Indicator	1961	2001
Median age at first marriage for women (years)	21.1	26.0
Women 30–34 who are married (%)	88.0	71.7[a]
Total fertility rate (children per woman)	3.8	1.5
Births to unmarried mothers (%)	4.5	31.3
Lone-parent families as % of all families with children	11.4	23.2[b]

Sources: 1961 and 2001 censuses of Canada; vital statistics, various years.
[a] Includes both legally married and cohabiting couples. Only 54.9% of women aged 30–34 in 2001 were recorded as legally married.
[b] Use pre-2001 definition of family.

meant that both adults and children experience greater instability in their family lives. Perhaps the most important result of this has been the large increase in the proportion of young children who live with only one parent.

The greater stability of family life prior to the 1960s should not be taken as evidence that all was well with Canadian families in those times. Greater stability did not automatically imply that Canadians were happier or more satisfied with their family life. For women, in particular, early marriage and life at home with three or four children may have been the fulfillment of a dream that was far less satisfying in reality than they had imagined. The extraordinary reception that greeted the publication of Betty Friedan's The Feminine Mystique (1963), a penetrating analysis of women and family life in the baby boom era, suggests that many women and, perhaps, men too were coming to question the model of family life that reached its apex during the baby boom. Still, it is impossible not to be struck by the rapidity and breadth of change that has occurred in an institution like the family that is so often thought of as the bedrock of social life.

In contrasting the situation in Canada today with what prevailed in the 1950s, it is important to emphasize that family life in the baby boom era did not constitute a 'natural' or timeless model for family living. Popular discussions of family change sometimes make the assumption that the family of the 1950s can be taken to represent families living in earlier generations. Many assume that for decades or even centuries, western societies were marked by the predominance of the breadwinner family, early and near universal marriage for men and women, and the near absence of divorce and single-parent families. The voluminous research by family historians has thoroughly demolished such assumptions. We now know that the breadwinner model of the family largely emerged with industrialization. Historical demographers have shown conclusively that from at least the eighteenth century through to the early twentieth century, men and women in Europe and North America married relatively late, usually in their mid to late twenties, and significant proportions of men and women never married at all. The higher rates of mortality that prevailed into the twentieth century meant that lone-parent families, formed through widowhood, were common. Thus, in reflecting on the changes that have occurred among Canadian families, we need to recognize the historical distinctiveness of many aspects of family life during the baby boom era. Nevertheless, there are, I would suggest, two good reasons for comparing the situation of families today with that which prevailed in the first decades following the Second World War. First, most assessments of the state of the family today, whether positive or negative, contrast the current situation with that which prevailed during the baby boom. Second, and perhaps most important, many significant social policies that affect families were developed in this era and assumed both a steadily growing population and the predominance of the two-parent, one-earner family that was common in those years. The high fertility of the baby boom years guaranteed a relatively youthful age structure with a healthy proportion of working-age contributors to the revenue stream needed to finance social programs. In addition, as Esping-Andersen (e.g., 2001) has argued, many of the social policies that were developed in modern welfare states in the postwar period implicitly assumed that stable, intact families with a regularly employed breadwinner would guarantee the basic security of the great majority of the population. Thus, the primary role for social policy was to provide support to the relatively small number of persons who did not live in such families or those who, as a result of unforeseen circumstances such as illness, death of a family member, or temporary unemployment fell upon hard times. The development of unemployment insurance, for example, was designed to provide short-term assistance to families when the primary breadwinner was laid off or between jobs. On the whole, this system worked well so long as most people lived in intact families with a reliable breadwinner. But, he argues, a new set of risks emerged in the later part of the twentieth century and the established policies of modern welfare states are not

well suited to respond. In part, these new risks are related to developments in the labour markets of advanced industrial societies. Higher
rates of unemployment, an increase in the importance of part-time and
contractual employment, and growing income inequality have undermined the financial position of many families. At the same time, the
changes in family life that have been the primary focus of this book
have also served to create new risks, especially for women and children. In this final chapter, I would like to focus on three of the most
important developments in family life that have far-reaching implications for social policy: the impact of low fertility, the precarious situation of many young children in our society, and the increasingly
difficult fit between the demands of work and family life. The brief discussion that follows will consider the significance of these changes for
families and society and discuss the challenges they present for the
evolution of social policy in Canada.

Low Fertility in Canadian Society

Canada's total fertility rate (TFR) first dipped below the level needed
to ensure the replacement of the population (approximately 2.1 children per woman) in 1972 and has never exceeded that level since.
Indeed, as Beaujot and Muhammad report in chapter 2 of this volume,
fertility has been quite stable for a long time now, with the TFR oscillat-
ing between 1.5 and 1.7 since the early 1980s. For the most part, social
scientists in Canada have studiously avoided discussion of this issue.
There are two important reasons for this, I would suggest. One is the
recognition that promoting higher fertility might well entail greater
costs to women than men. As a result, many fear that an argument for
higher fertility will be interpreted as an effort to take back gains that
women have made in other spheres of social life. A second factor that I
would suggest has limited discussion of the consequences of low fertility is a presumed trade-off between fertility and immigration. An argument in favour of higher fertility may be seen as an argument for
reduced immigration.

   While the reluctance of social scientists and policymakers to address
the issue of low fertility is understandable, the consequences of persistent below-replacement fertility are too great to avoid. Canadian society
is, one could argue, in the honeymoon phase of fertility decline. Our
past history of higher fertility means that the population continues to
grow. Meanwhile, the very large baby-boom cohorts are now in their

peak income-earning (and tax-paying) years. While the proportion of elderly is growing, the full weight of population aging still lies some years ahead. Bongaarts (2004) has recently demonstrated the very significant challenges for the pension plans of the industrialized nations. While Canada does not face as steep an increase in the proportion of elderly as is expected in most European nations, he projects that the old age dependency ratio (the ratio of persons aged 65+ to the population aged 15 to 64) will rise from 0.18 in 2000 to 0.43 in 2050 with attendant pressures on public expenditures, especially in the areas of pensions and health. An increase in immigration levels can be a part of the response to the forecast demographic change, but, in itself, will not solve our problems. As numerous analyses have convincingly demonstrated, immigration can forestall population decline but it has little impact on population aging. This is so, in large measure, because immigrants come quite quickly to experience fertility rates very similar to native-born Canadians (Bélanger and Gilbert 2003). Moreover, it is questionable whether a significant increase in immigration is feasible in Canada. Unlike many European nations, Canada already has a high rate of immigration. Our lack of success in redirecting newcomers to destinations other than Toronto, Vancouver, and Montreal, and the greater difficulty recent cohorts of immigrants have experienced in integrating into the Canadian labour market cast doubt on the likelihood of any large jump in the numbers admitted.

Higher fertility would, in time, slow down the aging of our population and ease the pressure on some of our most valued social programs, but is there any prospect of fertility increasing? Are there acceptable policy initiatives that might promote higher fertility in the years ahead? Discussions of this topic often hinge on one important question – is fertility so low because Canadian women simply do not want any more children, or are there impediments that prevent women from achieving their desires with respect to childbearing? If the former is true, there is little scope for social policy. Any effort to press women to have children that they do not want would be seen as unacceptable. There is some evidence, however, that desired fertility exceeds actual fertility in many industrialized societies (Van de Kaa 2001: 318-22). It is tempting to conclude from such findings that the right mix of policies might allow women to fulfil their desires and, in doing so, benefit society as a whole.

What kinds of policies might make up this mix? Three types are often suggested. One involves greater financial help for young families. Recent cohorts have experienced significant difficulty in entering the labour market, and the real incomes of young workers have declined in recent years. Moreover, at least some of the costs associated with childrearing – most notably, post-secondary education – have been rising. Greater financial support for young families might help them to establish themselves more quickly and have more children. There is great controversy in the literature over the success of such financial incentives. Many claim they influence the timing of childbearing but have little effect on the number of children couples are willing to have. Even those most supportive of financial incentives concede that, to have a significant impact, payments must be large. Canada has certainly been niggardly in support of young families and, the question of increasing fertility aside, a strong case can be made for offering more help to young parents. Nevertheless, financial incentives alone are likely to have only a small effect on the fertility rate (Grant et al. 2004).

A second policy-related issue concerns childcare. The high rates of labour force participation among both women and men in their twenties and thirties create a dilemma with respect to childcare. The opportunity cost of leaving the labour force is high, and one-earner families are now at a considerable disadvantage in comparison with their two-earner counterparts. But the limited availability and high cost of childcare significantly reduce the benefits of working for parents of young children. Quebec's childcare system has been cited as a model in providing quality care at a price that virtually all families can afford. Its impact on fertility, however, has been limited. While Quebec's fertility rate is no longer the lowest in the country, it is close to the Canadian average, and thus still well below replacement level. High quality, accessible childcare may be associated with healthier child development and reduced strain on parents but it is no guarantee of higher fertility.

A third line of thought on the issue of low fertility stresses the importance of gender equity in the larger society and in the family. As married women's involvement in the labour force increased, a series of studies noted the continuing disparity within the household regarding time spent on domestic work. Goldscheider and Waite (1991) drew attention to this issue in their book entitled *New Families, No Families?* suggesting that women might well come to demand greater equity within the household as a prerequisite for marriage and childbearing. No longer reliant on a man for economic support, women might increasingly choose to leave a relationship or forego forming one unless their workload at home is reduced. More recently, McDonald (2000) has extended this line of thinking to the question of fertility. A combination of greater equality in the labour market and continued inequality at home is a recipe for very low fertility. McDonald points to countries such as Italy and Spain, which now have among the lowest fertility rates in the world, as examples of societies in which gender inequality at home has led to low rates of marriage and cohabitation and very low fertility.

Again, as desirable as a more equal sharing of family responsibilities might be, the evidence of a clear link between gender equity and higher fertility is limited. Sweden has sometimes been cited as a case in which greater equity between the sexes has led to higher fertility. Sweden has done much to promote gender equity in all areas of social life. And the Swedish fertility rate, which had fallen well below replacement level in the 1970s, did recover during the 1980s, reaching 2.1 in 1991. The increase in fertility was temporary, however, and the rate declined through the 1990s. The TFR now stands at 1.6, higher than in southern Europe, to be sure, but similar to the fertility rate in Canada and in a number of other societies not especially known for high levels of gender equity.

Recent American data cast further doubt on the gender equity hypothesis as well. The United States has been more resistant to policies designed to ease the conflict between work and childbearing, such as parental leaves, than most other industrialized countries. Yet the United States is now the only advanced industrial nation with a fertility rate near replacement level. Moreover, fertility rates are higher in the most conservative states; seventeen of the twenty states with the highest fertility rates supported U.S. President George W. Bush in the 2004 election (U.S. Centers for Disease Control 2004). Torr and Short's (2004) recent analysis, using individual-level data, provides another perspective on the link between gender relations and fertility. They found that couples with either very high or very low levels of gender equity are more likely to have a second birth than couples who fall in-between. They hypothesize that disagreement between partners on the sharing of domestic work leads to lower fertility. Couples who share a common perspective, regardless of whether that perspective entails equal sharing or specialization of gender roles, are more likely to have higher fertility.

While many issues related to family change have become topics of public discussion, low fertility has yet to receive much attention in Canada. This is unlikely to remain the case in the future. As deaths come to surpass births and Canada's population continues to age, greater attention to the social context of childbearing will almost certainly occur. This may be what is necessary for fertility rates to rise closer to replacement level. Of major European societies, France now has the highest fertility rate. It is true that France has some of the most generous social policies in support of fertility (Grant et al. 2004: 74-80), but it is also true that there is greater attention to the significance of the birth rate in France than in any other advanced industrial nation. French leaders have been consistently outspoken in promoting pronatalist policies and their concern is shared by much of the population. It may be that a cultural shift which raises the importance people attach to having children is essential before fertility rates return close to replacement levels.

Canada's Disadvantaged Children

As fertility rates have declined, more attention has been paid to the intellectual and emotional development of children. Economists such as Gary Becker (1981) suggest that parents have become more concerned with the quality than the quantity of their children. There is considerable evidence to suggest that parents are increasingly attentive to their children's development and are prepared to invest substantial time and money in helping their children to succeed. At the political level as well, there is a growing realization that generating the resources needed to support social programs for an aging population will require a high level of productivity from those in the labour force. If there are to be fewer workers supporting each pensioner, then each worker must produce more.

Although many studies and popular analyses focus on the problems of the young, the overall evidence on the achievements of young people in Canada is positive. Perhaps most importantly, participation and completion rates at various levels of education have been improving. And, despite recurrent fears of the declining quality of education, recent data from international tests show Canadian children to be doing well. Crime rates, too, have declined among the young. Still, there is reason to worry that a significant minority of children and youth are not doing so well. As Kerr demonstrates in chapter 6, poverty levels among Canadian children have remained stubbornly high. High school dropout rates are worrisome as well, especially for boys. And, while crime rates have declined overall, a minority are involved in serious violent crimes.

Among the most debated questions in this area is the contribution of family change to the problems of children and youth. Has the increasing instability in family life contributed to the disadvantages experienced by an important proportion of our young? In some ways, what we have seen is a replay of an old debate in social science, one that goes back at least to the 1950s that focused on the situation of children from 'broken homes.' Many participants in this debate have centred on the problems of children from lone-parent families. For some, it is the family structure itself that hinders children's development. The instability caused by family breakup, the absence of a father from the household, and the disruption children experience as they change schools and homes contribute to lower academic achievement and higher rates of such worrisome behaviours as delinquency, earlier home leaving, and premarital pregnancies. For others, the problem lies not with family structure but poverty. The transition from a two-parent to a one-parent family is most often marked by a significant decline in family income. This generates the other problems children in single-parent families often face, such as more frequent moves and the accompanying change of schools and networks of friends. Increased support for one-parent families through more generous social transfers and more vigorous enforcement of child-support orders would alleviate most of the problems experienced by children in these families.

Fortunately, recent social science research has helped us to move beyond this often sterile debate and produce a better understanding of how changes in both labour markets and families have contributed to the difficulties faced by a significant minority of Canada's children. Growing inequality in earnings has certainly affected the well-being of children in families headed by parents with low education and limited earnings. But it is also true that these adverse developments in the economy often interact with changes in family life. Sara McLanahan (2004) has recently advanced a useful analysis of these issues. In her view, the changes in family life associated with the second demographic transition have played out quite differently for women with different levels of education. As mentioned in several chapters in this volume, the term *second demographic transition* has been used to describe a complex of changes that have occurred in family life in many advanced industrial societies since the 1960s (Lesthaeghe 1995). These changes include higher levels of cohabitation and divorce, later ages at marriage and childbearing, and the shift to two-earner couples. While we commonly assume that more educated women have been the trailblazers in creating alternative forms of family living, McLanahan finds that this is not always the case. She notes that while more highly educated women have indeed delayed marriage and childbearing and have high rates of labour force participation, they are also more likely to marry and stay married than are women with lower levels of education, who are at greater risk of having their first child at an early age and outside of a stable relationship. One result of these trends is that children born to mothers with greater education enjoy more in the way of family resources than was true in the past. They are likely to have two employed parents living with them throughout their childhood years. Moreover, there is evidence that both mothers and fathers in these families spend more time with their children (Gauthier et al. 2004) and that such parents are more likely to make use of more effective parenting strategies. By contrast, a larger share of children born to mothers with low education face deficits in terms of financial and emotional resources. They are more likely to live with only one parent during significant portions of their childhood and, as a consequence, have access to fewer resources in terms of both income and time spent with their parents. And, of course, it is the parents in these families who have been most hurt by the slow growth in wages and the increasing instability of employment for less educated (and low-paid) workers.

For children of recent generations, then, there is good news and bad. The increasing success of many women in the labour force has paved the way for families that are better prepared than ever to provide a host of advantages to their children. The greater involvement of many mothers and fathers in the lives of their daughters and sons has been a real gain for children. But for an important number of children, changes in economic and social life have robbed them of the resources they need to develop. How should society respond? One way is to provide greater financial support to disadvantaged families through transfers and tax policies, and/or labour market policies that boost employment for and remuneration to low-wage workers. Besides delivering a much-needed boost to the economic well-being of such families, help for the poorly paid in our society may have other positive effects as well. There is now considerable evidence that low income and instability in employment discourage young adults from forming stable unions. Thus improving the situation of young workers at the bottom of the income distribution ladder might well be an incentive to marriage and greater family stability.

Children in disadvantaged families would also benefit most from accessible, high-quality childcare. Better and more affordable childcare would make it easier for their parents to succeed in the labour market and might also help compensate for the more limited ability of less educated parents to give children the skills they need to succeed at school. More effective enforcement of child-support commitments is also needed to deliver resources to lone parents and their children. In addition, more vigorous enforcement might also encourage non-custodial parents who are paying the support to take on a greater role in the lives of their children. Finally, social institutions, including government, need to consider strategies to discourage childbearing in situations that entail high risk for children. Recognition of the negative consequences for both mothers and children of early childbearing has led to a significant decline in fertility rates for teens, but there is more to be done. There has been much greater reluctance to address the issue of childbearing among older women who are not in stable relationships. In popular culture, it is often the successful professional woman with no need of a husband who is seen as most likely to have a child on her own. Yet the data suggest that this is not the typical case. More often than not, women who bear children while living alone or in a fragile partnership are not well prepared to meet the responsibilities of parenthood and receive little in the way of assistance from the child's father. It is worth asking whether this question should be added to Canada's public health agenda.

Work and Family Life in the 24/7 Economy

A third major theme that emerges from a number of chapters in this book is the growing conflict between the demands of work and family life. This is a complex and difficult issue, not given to easy solutions. High rates of labour force participation for mothers and fathers and the extensive demands that many parents face at work pose serious challenges for Canadian families. These are exacerbated by the movement to a '24/7' world of work, one that sees a significant proportion of couples with work schedules that have them away from home at different times of the day (Presser 2003). The most obvious conflict created by these developments involves the care and supervision of children. But it is also true, as several authors in this collection point out, that couples with conflicting work schedules face greater strains in their marriages. Apart from each other for longer periods of time than is true for couples with similar working hours, and often exhausted by their efforts to balance work and family commitments, families with split shifts are at higher risk of conflict and separation. The problems that individuals and families face affect employers as well. Absenteeism is a major concern for Canadian employers, and family problems are frequently the reason employees cite for their absence from work. Thus, addressing the problems created by the often conflicting demands of work and family is an important challenge for government and business as well as for families.

Policy discussions on the issue of work-family conflict often lead to a divide between those who would promote policies designed to make it easier for families to respond to the increased demands of the workplace and those who see the only solution to be limiting the demands of the workplace. It is, of course, not impossible that governments may seek to place limits on the demands employers can make of their workers, not only with respect to hours worked but concerning the scheduling of work as well. After all, at the height of the Industrial Revolution, several governments introduced 'protective legislation' that allowed women to refuse to work night shifts. Yet, a movement in this direction would seem to run against the grain of recent history. The increasingly globalized nature of many businesses forces employers to operate longer and non-standard hours. This, in turn, creates a greater need for round-the-clock services. Increasingly, European economies, which had long resisted the pressure to extend hours of work in the retail and service sectors, have relaxed restrictions on employers. Thus, the focus of policy discussion is more likely to be on programs to help families deal with the pressures of their sometimes competing obligations.

The issue that has received most attention is the provision of better childcare. The Government of Canada has indicated on many occasions its determination to put in place a national childcare policy. Some provinces, most notably Quebec, have already taken important steps in this direction. As important as these developments are, they address only part of the problem created by the emergence of a 24/7 economy. New childcare programs, especially if they are integrated into the public school system, are unlikely to provide the flexibility of care that some parents, especially many single parents, require. Moreover, the focus of childcare policy discussions is usually on the needs of children too young to enter the school system. Yet many parents face problems of providing care and supervision to older children who attend school during the day but are likely to be left alone or with minimal supervision during evenings and weekends when their parents are away at work.

A second set of initiatives addresses questions of parental leave. The focus is usually on the period surrounding the birth of a child, and significant improvements have been made by both governments and some private sector employers in providing greater relief to parents of newborn or adopted children. The demands of family life do not stop with the end of infancy, however, and many families struggle to balance their work obligations with their commitments to children and, increasingly, their elderly relatives. There can be no magic solution to this dilemma, and sweeping policy proposals in this area should be received with scepticism. As the results in chapters 3 and 4 make clear, Canadian families demonstrate great ingenuity in dealing with their complex lives, and we should be hesitant to support schemes that provide greater public support to only certain solutions to these challenges. Nevertheless, it is apparent that governments and employers must recognize that there is both a public and a private interest in supporting families in their efforts to attend to their responsibilities in the workplace and at home.

The family in Canada and in other advanced societies has undergone dramatic change over the past generation, and it is hardly surprising that cries of alarm have frequently been heard. While it is possible to read the sociological evidence in many ways, the research presented in this volume and elsewhere provides little support for the view that the family is in crisis. Nonetheless, some significant challenges lie ahead for Canadian families and the larger society. The real impact of low fertility has yet to be felt. The effects of the glaring gap in the quality of childhood as experienced by children raised in families evermore attentive to healthy child development and children who grow up suffering economic and social disadvantages will raise new challenges for social policy. More than ever, in the years ahead Canadians will need to evaluate our efforts to help all of our children to succeed, and to do so using the kind of 'evidence-based' research that this volume presents.

REFERENCES

Becker, Gary. 1981. *A Treatise on the Family*. Cambridge, MA: Harvard University Press.

Bélanger, Alain, and Stéphane Gilbert. 2003. 'The Fertility of Immigrant Women and Their Canadian-Born Daughters.' *Report on the Demographic Situation in Canada 2002*, 127–52. Ottawa: Statistics Canada.

Bongaarts, John. 2004. 'Population Aging and the Rising Cost of Public Pensions.' *Population and Development Review* 30(1): 1–23.

Esping-Adersen, G. 2001. *Social Foundations of Postindustrial Economics.* Oxford: Oxford University Press.

Friedan, Betty. 1963. *The Feminine Mystique.* New York: Norton.

Gauthier, Anne H., Timothy M. Smeedling, and Frank F. Furstenberg. 2004. 'Are Parents Investing Less Time in Children? Trends in Selected Industrialized Countries.' *Population and Development Review* 30(4): 647–71.

Goldscheider, Frances, and Linda J. Waite. 1991. *New Families, No Families?* Berkeley: University of California Press.

Grant, Jonathan, Stijn Hoorens, Suja Sivadasan, Mirjam van het Loo, Julie DaVanzo, Lauren Hale, Shawna Gibson, and William Butz. 2004. *Low Fertility and Population Ageing.* Brussels: RAND Europe.

Lesthaeghe, Ron. 1995. 'The Second Demographic Transition in Western Countries: An Interpretation.' In Karen Oppenheim Mason and An-Magritt Jensen, (eds.), *Gender and Family Change in Industrialized Countries*, 17–62. Oxford: Clarendon Press.

McDonald, Peter. 2000. 'Gender Equity in Theories of Fertility.' *Population and Development Review* 26(3): 427–39.

McLanahan, Sara. 2004. 'Diverging Destinies: How Children Are Faring under the Second Demographic Transition.' *Demography* 41(4): 607–28.

Presser, Harriet B. 2003. *Working in a 24/7 Economy.* New York: Sage.

Torr, Berna Miller, and Susan E. Short. 2004. 'Second Births and the Second Shift: A Research Note on Gender Equity and Fertility.' *Population and Development Review* 30(1): 109–30.

U.S. Centers for Disease Control. 2004. 'Births: Preliminary Data for 2003.' *National Vital Statistics Reports* 53-9. Washington, DC: author.

Van de Kaa, Dirk. 2001. 'Postmodern Fertility Preferences: From Changing Value Orientation to New Behavior.' Population and Development Review 27 (suppl.): 290–331.